ON TIPTOE WITH
LOVE

ON TIPTOE WITH LOVE

John T. Seamands

BAKER BOOK HOUSE
Grand Rapids, Michigan

ISBN: 0-8010-7991-8

Preface

"What the world needs now is love, sweet love," is the punch line of a popular song we have been hearing on the radio and television recently. The song is true. What the world needs is a giant dose of love.

A basic question is, "What kind of love does the world need?"

Much is said about love these days. Novel after novel has been written, song after song composed, movie after movie produced with love as the theme. And yet people know less about true love than ever before. Love has lost its character, its content. The very *word* "love" stands in need of redemption.

Another important question is, "Where will we find this love?"

Men are seeking everywhere for love. Some seek it in our universities, in our homes, in our churches. Others seek it in nightclubs, in love-ins, in and out of marriage. And yet we are finding less and less of true love than ever before. There is bitterness, hatred, abuse, rancor, and violence on every hand. Love itself has turned to lust.

The Bible has much to say about love. "God is love" . . . "Christ loved" . . . "The fruit of the Spirit is love" . . . "Love God with all your heart, mind, soul, and strength" . . . "Love your neighbor as yourself" . . . "Love your enemies." True love is Christlike. It is pure, unselfish, sacrificial. True love is God-given. It is poured into our hearts by the Holy Spirit, who is granted to us.

If we want to know the true meaning of love—if we want to find genuine, eternal love, we must get back to God. God is the Source of love. Christ is the supreme demonstration of love. The Holy Spirit enables us to love.

Jesus said to His disciples, "By this all men will know that you are my disciples, if you have love for one another." It was said of the early Christians, "Behold, how these people love one another!"

It is not enough to say to the world, "God is love." People must see this love. The disciples of Christ must show it to them. And the only way to demonstrate love is first to receive it from God through the indwelling presence of His Spirit. The Spirit-filled life is thus the secret of a genuine life of love, for love is the fruit of the Spirit. Therefore we do not seek love by itself, but we seek the Holy Spirit, who is the Source of love. Where the Spirit is, there is love.

JOHN T. SEAMANDS

Contents

1

Living Below Par

In Hollywood, Florida, an elderly woman suddenly passed away. Her husband had been a lawyer in one of the New England states and upon his death she had moved to Florida. She dressed shabbily and lived alone in an old, ramshackle house. In sympathy the neighbors often picked her up in their cars and took her to the supermarket or out for an evening drive. Once a week a maid came and helped her clean the house.

One day when the maid entered the house, she found the lady dead in her bed. The maid immediately informed the police, and while they were inspecting the house, they found approximately a million dollars in currency, stuffed away in old shoe boxes and cartons. Upon further investigation they discovered that she had a savings account in the bank with almost another million dollars.

Since the widow's death was sudden, an autopsy was ordered by the police. Imagine the surprise of all when the diagnosis was made known. Malnutrition!

The story is told of a young Irishman who, many years ago, decided to migrate to the New World to make his way in life. He worked hard in his homeland until he had just enough money to purchase his steamship ticket across the Atlantic. With a little bit of change that remained, he bought some biscuits and a can of cheese, which he intended to use for his meals on board ship. So for several days at sea, at mealtime the Irishman went down to his cabin and ate his cheese and biscuits. But soon the salt air made the biscuits soggy and the cheese hard, and the young man became tired of this meager fare.

One noon he was sitting in his cabin, hungry and feeling sorry for himself, when a steward passed by the open door carrying a tray with a delicious-looking meal. He beckoned the waiter and asked him, "Sir, tell me, where can I get a good meal like that?"

"How did you get on board ship?" asked the waiter. "Don't you have a ticket?"

"Certainly I have a ticket," replied the young passenger.

The waiter looked at the Irishman in astonishment. "Sir, don't you realize that your ticket entitles you to all your meals on board ship? You can go to the dining room, order anything you want on the menu, and eat as much as you like."

Here the young man was existing on biscuits and cheese, when he could have been feasting all along!

Many Christians are like the elderly lady in Florida and the young immigrant from Ireland. They are living far below their spiritual resources and privileges. They are without joy, when God offers them "joy unspeakable and full of glory." They are without peace, when God wants to give them "peace . . . which passes all understanding." They are defeated and discouraged, when God wants them to be "more than conquerors" through Christ, the all-victorious One. They are fruitless and ineffective, when the Heavenly Father wants to endue them with "power from on high," so that they may bear much fruit.

In Jesus' parable of the prodigal son, the elder brother was quite indignant when he heard the news from one of the servants that his brother had returned home from the far country and his father was providing a feast for him. He reacted in jealousy and self-pity and refused to enter the house. His father had to come out and entreat him to join the party. Note the force of the dialogue that followed:

The elder son said: "These many years I have served you, and I never disobeyed your command; yet you never gave me a kid, that I might make merry with my friends. But when this son of yours came, who has devoured your living with harlots, you killed for him the fatted calf!"

The father calmly replied: "Son, you are always with me, and all that is mine is yours."

The elder son could have had many a feast. But he didn't have, because he didn't ask. He never claimed his possessions.

The Heavenly Father is saying to us today, "All that I have is yours. All My resources are at your disposal." If we are not living the abundant life, it is simply because we have not claimed our full inheritance in Christ. Jesus said that the Heavenly Father will "give the Holy Spirit to those that ask Him" (Luke 11:13).

Jesus spoke of the Gift of the Holy Spirit as *the promise of the Father*. God had given many promises to His children. We have lifted them out of the Old and New Testaments and have put them into mottoes on our walls. We sing them in our hymns; we memorize them; we treasure them in our hearts. But Jesus picked out this promise and called it *"the* promise of the Father." Of all the promises the Father gave, this is *the* promise. Why? Because all the other promises He gave were usually about gifts—the gift of peace, of comfort, of guidance, of sustenance. But here was the promise of the Gift of the Giver. The Giver was giving Himself, and there was nothing higher that He could give.

In the giving of the Holy Spirit, the Father was giving just that—Himself. No wonder it was *the* promise. This focused all the scattered promises into one. The gifts became one—the Giver! It is like the lover who has given many gifts to his intended bride—candy, perfume, flowers. But now he comes to the sacred marriage day, when he gives the final gift—himself. It is *the* gift. Without that all the other gifts would be bare. The gift of himself consummates all the gifts. Likewise the Heavenly Father, having given many gifts to His children, comes now to the consummating moment, the moment of giving Himself to the receptive one. If we miss this, we miss God's greatest Gift.

The Apostle Paul describes the gift of the Holy Spirit as "the guarantee of our inheritance until we acquire possession of it" (Eph. 1:14). The Greek word for "guarantee" is *arrabōn,* which literally means "down payment." The *arrabōn* was a regular feature of the Greek business world. It was a part of the purchase price of anything paid in advance as a guarantee that the rest of the price would in due time be paid. If a person sold a cow, he received so many drachmas as *arrabōn,* that is, as surety that the full price would duly be paid. If someone hired a group of entertainers, he paid so much in advance as a guarantee that the remainder of the money would be paid and the contract be honored after the performance had been given.

When I went to India as a young missionary I soon learned the meaning of a "down payment" or "advance." Whenever I called a carpenter or mason or coolie to do some job around the house, first we bargained about the total cost of the materials and labor. When this was agreed upon, the laborer always asked for a "down payment." For example, if the estimate came to fifty rupees, the man would ask for about five or ten rupees as an advance. This sealed the bargain and made the contract valid. When the laborer completed the work, the balance of the amount was paid.

So what Paul was saying is that the experience of the Holy Spirit which we have in this world is a foretaste of the joys and blessedness of heaven; it is the guarantee that someday we will enter into the fullness of our inheritance in Christ.

Suppose a lawyer unexpectedly called on you and

said: "Sir, you have a rich uncle who died recently in South Africa and left his entire estate to you. I have been appointed as executor of the will. Your uncle was a very wealthy man and owned vast shares in a diamond mine, a gold mine, and a uranium mine. Now it will take several months to settle the whole estate, but in the meantime if you are in need of some money, I'll be glad to give you an advance [*arrabōn*] to help you out."

Immediately you say to yourself, This is great. I could use a few hundred dollars to buy the family some clothes or make some repairs on the house. You say to the lawyer, "Yes, sir, I'll be happy to receive a small down payment. How much can you give?"

The lawyer says, "How would it be if I gave you a check now for $500,000? Would that help out?"

You can hardly believe your ears. "Did you say five thousand or five *hundred* thousand?"

"I said $500,000," replies the lawyer. "I'm sorry it's such a small amount."

"Small amount! How much then is the whole estate worth?"

"Oh, sir, it's far more than I can describe. It's beyond one's imagination."

When Paul speaks of the Gift of the Holy Spirit as the *arrabōn,* the down payment of our final inheritance, he is emphasizing the profound truth that the greatest and most intimate experience of Christian peace and joy which is possible in this life is only a faint foretaste of the joy into which we shall one day enter. It is as if God said to us when He accepts us as His children, "Son, Daughter, I can't usher you into My presence just now, for I have a task for you to perform on earth. But I'll do the next best thing. I'll give you My presence in the person of the Holy Spirit, and He will abide with you day and night, in sickness and in health, in joy and in sorrow. I can't bring you up into heaven right away, but I'll put a little bit of heaven inside of you. This will be a foretaste of what is yet to come."

"Lord, it's so wonderful to have You living in our

hearts through the Holy Spirit and to know that You are with us at all times. It's so marvelous to experience Your joy and peace amidst all the trials and sorrows of life. If this is just a foretaste of heaven, what must the final inheritance be like?"

God offers the fullness of the Holy Spirit and the abundant life to all His children. Have we claimed our inheritance? Are we living up to our resources?

2

Where Was He Before?

The last words of our parting loved ones are the most treasured and most heeded.

For many years I have kept within the pages of my Bible a little scrap of paper on which my precious grandmother scribbled her parting message to me before her death in November 1943. Grandmother was very dear to my brother and me. She became a widow at the age of forty-seven, and then when she was fifty-five years of age she moved her residence to India in order to make a home for the two of us so we could attend school in the city while our parents were engaged in missionary work in the interior. Later she moved to Wilmore, Kentucky, to keep house for my brother and me as we attended Asbury Academy and Asbury College respectively. Grandmother financed all our musical training and presented each of us with a piano, a trombone, and an accordion. So she was very much like a second mother to us.

Grandmother had suffered a serious heart attack at her home in Kentucky and, realizing that death was near, she sent the following message to me as a young missionary in India:

My darling J. T. This is good-bye. I'm going to be with Jesus. Your little Sylvia [our year-old daughter] is so sweet. Preach the Word and stick to the old Book. Be a good boy and meet me in heaven.

Love, *Grandma*

This was Grandmother's last message to me, so I have guarded it carefully down through the years. I have earnestly sought to preach the Word. Someday I intend to meet her in heaven.

Now if we treasure and respect so highly the last words of our earthly loved ones, how much more should we give attention to the last words of our divine Saviour and Lord!

What were the last words of Jesus to His disciples before He ascended to the Father? He had said many deathless things to them—"Love your enemies . . . Be the servant of all . . . Lose your life in order to find it," etc. But what did He pick out as of the greatest importance? The last thing of which He would speak? Note these two passages penned by Luke, the early Christian historian.

> *Behold, I send the promise of my Father upon you; but stay in the city, until you are clothed with power from on high. Then he led them out as far as Bethany, and lifting up his hands he blessed them. While he blessed them, he parted from them* (Luke 24:49-50).
> *And while staying with them he charged them not to depart from Jerusalem, but to wait for the promise of the Father, which, he said, "you heard from me, for John baptized with water, but before many days you shall be baptized with the Holy Spirit." ". . . you shall receive power when the Holy Spirit has come upon you; and you shall be my witnesses. . . ." And when he said this, as they were looking on, he was lifted up, and a cloud took him out of their sight* (Acts 1:4-5, 8-9).

Thus the last words of Jesus to His disciples were

concerning the Holy Spirit. Jesus knew that if they missed this truth they would miss the whole point of redemption. For the Holy Spirit is Redemption—continuing Redemption within us. Apart from Him, redemption is outside of us—in history, in the historical Jesus. But through the Holy Spirit the historical becomes personal; through Him the divine incarnation becomes the divine inhabitation.

So Jesus commanded His disciples not to depart from Jerusalem, but to wait for the enduement of power from on high through the fullness of the Holy Spirit.

During His earthly ministry Jesus uttered three important words. At the beginning of His ministry He said, *"Come"*—"Come to me, all who labor and are heavy laden" (Matt. 11:28). After His resurrection He commanded His disciples to *"Go"*—"Go therefore and make disciples of all nations" (Matt. 28:19). And just before His ascension He commanded them to *"Tarry"*—Tarry "in the city, until you are clothed with power from on high" (Luke 24:49). It is the tarrying that makes the coming and going effectual.

As in each case, along with the command Jesus gave His disciples a promise. When He said, "Come," He promised, "I will give you rest." When He commanded them to "go," He promised, "Lo, I will be with you always." And when He commanded them to "tarry," He promised, "You shall be baptized with the Holy Spirit . . . you shall receive power."

What was the response of the disciples to Jesus' final command? In the first place, they responded with *obedience*. They immediately returned to Jerusalem and went to the upper room. They made no detours; they wasted no time. The Master had said, "Tarry," and, "Receive," so they were determined in their hearts to tarry until they received the Gift of the Holy Spirit. All other plans and duties were laid aside for the moment. There was only one item of business on the agenda. Christ's command took precedence over everything else.

If we Christians today are to be effective instruments of redemption and reconciliation in a world of turmoil and tension, we will have to take seriously the injunction of our Lord to tarry for the baptism with the Holy Spirit. We will have to be obedient to the exhortation. Peter made it clear that God gives the Holy Spirit "to them that obey him" (Acts 5:32). The command to tarry is just as much a command as the command to repent of our sins or to believe on the Lord Jesus Christ. This is not something we can take or leave as we like. This is a must! For without the *fullness* of the Holy Spirit there can be no *usefulness*.

What would happen if the Church of today would momentarily push aside its building plans, its suppers and bazaars, its business meetings and financial drives, and just take time off to obey the Lord's command? We thrill at the very thought of it! It would probably spark one of the greatest revivals in history. Suppose the early disciples had not tarried for the enduement with power from on high. Would there be a Church today? Suppose we fail to tarry in our day. Will there be a Church tomorrow?

The record in Acts tells us that the disciples "with one accord devoted themselves to prayer" (Acts 1:14). They were not just gathered together in one place. They were of one heart and one mind. There was complete unity of purpose and desire. And they continued in prayer and supplication for several days, seeking for just one thing—the baptism with the Holy Spirit. Their prayers were all focused on this one objective.

The disciples not only responded to Christ's exhortation with obedience. They also responded with *faith*. They remembered the words of Jesus during His earthly ministry when He said, "If you then, who are evil, know how to give good gifts to your children, how much more will the heavenly Father give the Holy Spirit to *those who ask Him!*" (Luke 11:13). Jesus had also said, "Ask, and it will be given you. . . . For every one who asks receives" (Luke 11:9-10). Then, again, He had promised them just before His ascension that they would receive the baptism with the Holy

Spirit in just a few days. So the disciples asked and in faith took Christ at His word that those who ask do receive. They let their whole weight down upon His promise. And the record tells us that on the Day of Pentecost "they were all filled with the Holy Spirit." The promise passed into fulfillment!

We must not make the mistake of thinking that the Holy Spirit first entered the world on the Day of Pentecost; that He was hiding behind the curtain all this time and then suddenly stepped onto the stage of human history. As God, He is coeternal with the Father and goes back to the beginning of time—yes, even before time. He has been at work in the world from the dawn of the universe.

In the Old Testament the Holy Spirit is referred to more than ninety times. He is most often designated as "the Spirit of the Lord" or "the Spirit of God." Many times He is simply referred to as "the Spirit." Three times He is called "the Holy Spirit." Occasionally He is referred to as the Spirit "of wisdom" or "of judgment" or "of grace."

The divine activity of the Holy Spirit is evident throughout the Old Testament. The Word reveals the fact that the Holy Spirit was an Agent in the creation of the universe. In Genesis 1:2 we read, "The earth was without form and void; and darkness was upon the face of the deep; and the Spirit of God was moving over the face of the waters." It was the Holy Spirit who brought order out of chaos. In another place we read that the Spirit "garnished the heavens" (Job 26:13, KJV).

The Holy Spirit was also active in the creation of man. Elihu, one of the main characters in the drama of Job, confessed this fact when he said, "The spirit of God hath made me, and the breath of the Almighty hath given me life" (Job 33:4, KJV). The Spirit also sustains all life upon this earth. Job said, "All the while my breath is in me, and the spirit of God is in my nostrils" (Job 27:3, KJV).

One of the major aspects of the Spirit's activity was His part in inspiring the writers who gave us the history, laws, promises, precepts, and prophecies of the Old Testament. The authors, who came from various walks of life, recognized themselves as instruments of the Divine Spirit.

In the Old Testament we read that the Holy Spirit came upon certain men in a peculiar way for some specific service which they were to render to God. They were especially equipped by the Spirit for the physical, mental, or spiritual activity committed to them by God. The Holy Spirit granted special wisdom to men like Moses and Joshua and David, to enable them to govern their people more righteously. At times He came upon the judges and leaders of Israel to equip them with unusual courage and physical strength for special emergencies or crises. By the Spirit, Gideon was prepared to do battle against the Midianites (Judg. 6:34) and Samson was enabled to slay a lion (Judg. 14:6). Then again, at the time of the building of the Tabernacle and the Temple as places for God's presence and man's worship, the Holy Spirit imparted special intellectual ability and artistic skills to men like Bezaleel and David, who were appointed to these tasks (see Exodus 31:1-5 and I Chronicles 28:11-12).

In the Old Testament there are also certain precious promises regarding the greater and more widespread ministry of the Holy Spirit that was yet to come. In Ezekiel there was the promise of the work of the Spirit in regeneration or the new birth:

> *A new heart also will I give you, and a new spirit will I put within you: and I will take away the stony heart out of your flesh. And I will put my spirit within you, and cause you to walk in my statutes, and ye shall keep my judgments, and do them* (Ezek. 36:26-27, KJV).

Then, through the prophet Joel, God gave the wonderful promise of the fullness of the Holy Spirit, which was fulfilled on the Day of Pentecost:

> *And it shall come to pass afterward, that I will pour out my spirit upon all flesh; and your sons and your daughters shall prophesy, your old men shall dream dreams, your young men shall see visions: and also upon the servants and upon the handmaids in those days will I pour out my spirit* (Joel 2:28-29, KJV).

The Gospels are largely transitional between the Old Testament dispensation and the New Testament era. They are on the other side of Pentecost. However, they provide us with a rich treasury concerning the Holy Spirit's activity, especially in the life and ministry of our Lord Jesus Christ.

The conception of Christ's human nature in the womb of Mary was due to the operation of the Holy Spirit (Matt. 1:20). At the very beginning of His earthly ministry Christ was baptized by the Spirit and anointed for service (John 1:33). He was "led by the Spirit" into the wilderness for His conflict with Satan and returned victorious "in the power of the Spirit" (Luke 4:1, 14). All His mighty works were accomplished in the Spirit's power (Luke 4:18-19). He was raised from the dead by the agency of the Spirit (Rom. 8:1).

During His public ministry Jesus made several references to the Holy Spirit. To the Pharisees, He gave a warning concerning the sin against the Holy Spirit (Matt. 12:22-32). This was the sin of asserting that Christ's miracles were performed through the agency of a demon or evil spirit rather than through the power of the Holy Spirit. To Nicodemus, a member of the Sanhedrin, Jesus spoke about the necessity of being "born of the Spirit" in order to enter the kingdom of heaven (John 3:1-7). In the synagogue at Capernaum, He declared that the Holy Spirit is the Source of spiritual life (John 6:63). To His disciples He said that the Heavenly Father gives "the Holy Spirit to those who ask him" (Luke 11:13). On the last day of the Feast of Tabernacles in Jerusalem, Jesus announced that, when the Holy Spirit came in His fullness, He would flow like rivers of living water out of the life of the believer (John 7:37-39).

Jesus had much to say about the person and ministry of the Holy Spirit when He met His disciples for the last time in the upper room. He said to them:

> It is to your advantage that I go away, for if I do not go away, the Counselor will not come to you; but if I go, I will send him to you. And when he comes, he will convince the world of sin and of righteousness and of judgment (John 16:7-8).

Jesus told His disciples that the Holy Spirit would teach them all things and bring to their remembrance all that He had said to them (John 14:26). The Spirit would guide them into all truth and show them things that were to come (John 16:13). The Spirit would dwell in them and abide with them forever (John 14:16-17). In addition, the Spirit would bear witness to Christ and glorify Him at all times (John 15:26; 16:14).

After the Resurrection, Jesus continued to speak to His disciples about the Holy Spirit. When He first appeared to them, He breathed on them and said: "Receive the Holy Spirit" (John 20:22). Later He commanded them to remain in Jerusalem until they were endued with the power of the Holy Spirit (Luke 24:49). He promised them that they would be baptized with the Holy Spirit within a few days and that they would receive power to become effective witnesses for Him throughout the world (Acts 1:5, 8).

When we come to The Acts of the Apostles we find ourselves on this side of Pentecost, in a new era. The Holy Spirit is everywhere in the foreground. He is the chief Personality in the Early Church. If the Father was the primary One of Old Testament revelation, and the Son was the primary One of the period covered by the Gospels, then certainly the Holy Spirit is the primary One since Pentecost. The Book of Acts is really the Acts of the Holy Spirit. He is the One who carries on the work of the Kingdom through the chosen instruments He calls and prepares for service. He is mentioned forty-nine times in the Book of Acts, all the way from the beginning (1:2) to the end (28:25).

On the Day of Pentecost the disciples were all "filled with the Holy Spirit" and from then on were called men and women "full of the Holy Spirit." Pentecost ushered in the dispensation of the Holy Spirit and began a new and more intimate relationship between the divine Spirit and the human personality. In the old dispensation, the Holy Spirit was granted to a *select few;* in the new dispensation He is available to *all*. In the old dispensation the Holy Spirit was given in a *limited way;* in the new, He is given *without measure*—in His fullness. Formerly the Spirit was imparted *periodically*, at certain times, for certain tasks; now He comes to abide *permanently* and empowers the believer for everyday living. Previously the emphasis was often on *physical prowess;* now the emphasis is on *inner purity* and *spiritual power*. Formerly the Holy Spirit came *upon* individuals; now He comes to dwell *in* us.

Why is it that the Holy Spirit could not be given in His fullness before the Day of Pentecost? The Apostle John gives us the answer to this question in his Gospel:

> *On the last day of the feast, the great day, Jesus stood up and proclaimed, "If any man thirst, let him come and drink. He who believes in me, as the scripture has said, 'Out of his heart shall flow rivers of living water.'" Now this he said about the Spirit, which those who believed in him were to receive, for as yet the Spirit had not been given, because Jesus was not yet glorified* (John 7:37-39).

Here is the answer. "As yet the Spirit had not been given, *because Jesus was not yet glorified*." The pattern of power had to be fixed before that power could be given. Jesus had to live, die, and rise again. Then the pattern was fixed. It is a Christlike power. God could now give with both hands.

In the Old Testament we read that the Spirit came upon Samson and he went out and slew a thousand Philistines (Judg. 15:14-17). In the New Testament we don't read that the Holy Spirit came upon the disciples in the upper room, after which they went out and slew a thousand who were responsible for the crucifixion of Jesus.

Jesus gives us the pattern of the Holy Spirit, both in power and in purity. He was infinite sanctity and infinite sanity. He put proper content into the concept of the Holy Spirit. Just as we cannot know what God is like apart from Jesus, so we cannot really understand what the Holy Spirit is like apart from Jesus. Now we know that the Holy Spirit is like Jesus. He too is infinite sanctity and infinite sanity. So we're no longer afraid of Him. To be filled with the Holy Spirit means that we become like Jesus.

The minister of a large church on the west coast said to Dr. E. Stanley Jones: "Every time you mention the Holy Spirit, cold chills go up and down my spine." When asked for the reason he explained, "I'm afraid of rampant emotionalism."

Dr. Jones replied: "My friend, you are patterning the Holy Spirit after certain people who have gone off into extremes. Christ is our Pattern. He was more filled with the Holy Spirit than anyone who ever walked the face of this earth. Are you afraid to be like Christ?"

"Ah, that makes a difference," exclaimed the preacher. "In that case there is no reason to be afraid." From resistance to receptivity within a few minutes! When he got his pattern straight, his attitude was correct.

It took the life, ministry, death, and resurrection of Jesus to give us the proper concept of the Holy Spirit.

In addition, it took the completed ministry of Christ to enable the Holy Spirit to minister to the needs of men in an unlimited manner. It is the special task of the Spirit to witness to the person of Christ, and He could not do this until that divine Person had stepped into the stream of human history and lived out a perfect and victorious life among men. It is the ministry of the Spirit to make redemption personal to the individual, and He could not do this without the actual death and resurrection of the Saviour. It is the supreme objective of the Holy Spirit to glorify Christ upon earth, but this was not possible until Jesus had ascended to the Father and been glorified in heaven. When the Holy Spirit came in power on the Day of Pentecost, it was a sign and seal that Jesus was now glorified and that He was the exalted Lord.

Pentecost, therefore, is significant from the standpoint of the acceptance of the completed work of Christ on the Cross. Salvation can now become the experience of all who accept the offer extended to them from the exalted Lord. The messengers of the Cross can proclaim freely the good news—even the forgiveness of sins and the gift of the Holy Spirit. Believers have in heaven their Saviour and His accepted work; while on earth, they have, even within themselves, the Holy Spirit, who applies the finished work of Christ and all its benefits to believers.

Pentecost was the beginning of a whole new era in the history of redemption and in God's dealings with man. And when Pentecost becomes personal to us, it can usher in a new day in our spiritual lives.

3

He Didn't Qualify

In the eighth chapter of the Book of Acts we read of a remarkable evangelistic movement that took place in the city of Samaria under the leadership of the lay evangelist, Philip. When Philip arrived in the city, he discovered that the residents were under the strange spell of a magician named Simon. The whole town was at his feet. He claimed to possess a certain supernatural power, which the people were led to believe was the power of God. Undoubtedly he was a clever charlatan who knew how to mislead the people by exploiting them for selfish ends, under the guise of religion.

Philip was a man filled with the Holy Spirit. Boldly he began to proclaim Jesus and the kingdom of God. Under the power of the Spirit he also performed many remarkable miracles. The Samaritans gave heed to Philip, listening to his message and observing his deeds, and before long they received the Christ whom he preached. They turned from the spurious to the real, from the magic of sorcery to the miracle of salvation. Their lives were transformed, their bodies healed. They were baptized in the name of Christ, and the city was filled with joy.

All this was disconcerting for Simon Magus. He lost his crowd and his money. He felt that Philip had taken away his following. Really, it was not Philip, but his Christ, who had won the hearts of the people. So, in keeping with the popular slogan, "If you can't lick 'em, join 'em," Simon decided to link up with Philip and thus reestablish himself in the favor of the people. He received baptism and posed as a believer.

When word reached the apostles in Jerusalem that Samaria had received the message of Christ, they sent Peter and John, who gave themselves especially to a ministry in behalf of the new converts. They emphasized the baptism with the Holy Spirit, and before long the people of Samaria received their personal Pentecost.

Simon Magus watched with keen interest. He had supposed that water baptism would initiate him. But no, now it seemed to be in the laying on of hands. He thought he too could obtain that powerful touch, so he sought after it. He brought money and offered it to the apostles, saying, "Give me also this power, that any one on whom I lay my hands may receive the Holy Spirit." With this world's goods he thought he could buy heaven's power.

Simon Peter was probably suspicious of Simon Magus all along, but now he could see through him clearly. What a withering rebuke Peter gave him! "You want this power?" he thundered. "You want to bribe me? Your money perish with you. Your heart is not right in the sight of God and you have no part in this matter of the Holy Spirit. Repent and ask God to forgive you."

Simon Magus is a warning to all of us. He is a striking example of spiritual shallowness right in the church. He had been baptized and had been given his place in the fellowship of the community. He even posed as a leader. Yet he remained absurdly ignorant of the most elementary matters of the Christian life.

Like many in our churches today, Simon Magus had a very superficial conception of the Holy Spirit. In the first place, he thought of the Spirit as an intangible something—an *it*. Perhaps an influence, like "the spirit of '76" or "the school spirit." Or merely a driving force, like gasoline in the tank or electricity in the dynamo. He failed to understand that the Holy Spirit is a Person—One with whom we can have an intimate relationship.

As a Person, the Holy Spirit possesses all the attributes of personality. He has a mind, will, and affections. He thinks, He wills, and He feels. He performs personal acts: He speaks, testifies, calls, searches, and commands. Personal offenses may be committed against Him. He may be resisted, grieved, or sinned against. Thus the Holy Spirit should always be referred to with the personal pronoun "He."

The Holy Spirit is a divine Person. He is a Member of the Holy Trinity. He is God. He possesses all the attributes of divinity. He is omnipotent, omniscient, omnipresent, sovereign, and holy. Divine works are ascribed to Him—creation, preservation, regeneration, sanctification, and resurrection. As God, the Holy Spirit is the object of our honor and worship.

The Holy Spirit is the divine Executive of the Godhead. He is the Father and the Son in the world of men, in the hearts of men. He operates in nature and in history to carry out the decrees and works of the Godhead.

In the second place, Simon Magus thought that men had the authority to grant the Holy Spirit. He watched Peter and John laying hands on people and the people receiving the Holy Spirit. So he asked for power to lay hands on people and dispense this divine power. But no man, however spiritual or important he may be, has authority to bestow the Spirit of God. Sometimes the preacher or evangelist may lay hands on a person symbolically to help quicken his faith, but he cannot transmit the Holy Spirit by himself. The testimony of John the Baptist makes it clear that only Christ Himself can baptize with the Holy Spirit (Matt. 3:11; Mark 1:8; Luke 3:16; John 1:33).

Bishop James Thoburn, one of the illustrious pioneer missionaries of the Methodist Church in India, was once preaching on the baptism of the Holy Spirit in a camp meeting. As he came to the close of his message, he stepped from behind the pulpit and in a quiet voice said to the congregation: "I must acknowledge that even I as a bishop cannot administer this baptism. But I had an understanding with a Friend of mine before this service began. He is the only One who can administer this baptism. He assured me that He would be present so that if anybody would say, 'I want this baptism,' He would be here to administer it, to receive a full consecration, and to honor a sincere faith." The good bishop was right. No man, only Christ can grant the Holy Spirit—and He is ever available to do so.

Simon Magus thought the Gift of the Holy Spirit could be bought for a price. He actually brought money and laid it at the apostles' feet. Men may traffic for gain in the institutional forms of religion, but they can never traffic in the Holy Spirit. The baptism of the Holy Spirit, like all the blessings of God, is a *gift*. It cannot be purchased, or acquired, or earned by merit. As a gift, it can only be received. God gives the Holy Spirit to them that *ask* Him. "Ask, and you will receive." Some people say, "I have been *seeking* the Holy Spirit for years." The truth is, they haven't been *seeking;* they have been *resisting*. One need not seek; just ask and receive.

Simon Magus thought of the baptism of the Holy Spirit as an end in itself. He thought of Pentecost in terms of power to do the showy, the spectacular thing. He wanted to get back his lost prestige and following. He wanted to make an impression on the people. He was more concerned about his *conquests* than his *character;* more concerned about what he was going to *do* than what he was going to *be*. He wanted the Holy Spirit so that he could use the Spirit, not so that the Spirit could use him. He wanted to glorify *self*, not the *Saviour*. But the Holy Spirit is the self-effacing Spirit. He does not talk about Himself; He talks only about Christ. He seeks only to glorify

Christ. And He will not allow us to talk about ourselves or to put ourselves on exhibition. To desire the Holy Spirit involves the willingness to die to self and the desire to glorify Christ in all things. We must be willing for Him to use us.

Simon Magus thought of the Holy Spirit only in terms of power. But the *power* of God is not given apart from *purity*. Sir Galahad, in Tennyson's great poem, is quoted as saying, "My strength is as the strength of ten because my heart is pure." Power is the result of holiness of heart and Christlikeness in disposition. Many people want power, but not purity. But God will not grant His power to an unsurrendered, self-centered person. He gives His power only to the one who is willing to be cleansed. The Spirit is first of all the *Holy* Spirit—the One who purifies. Then He is the Empowerer.

The fact of the matter is, Simon Magus was not only mistaken in his conception of the Holy Spirit, but he failed to qualify as a genuine candidate for the baptism with the Spirit. It is quite clear from Peter's rebuke that Simon was an unregenerated person, out of fellowship with the Heavenly Father. He had not genuinely repented of his sins and received God's gift of forgiveness. He had never truly been converted. And the baptism with the Holy Spirit is offered only to those who have been born of the Spirit.

But, someone argues, does not the record tell us that "even Simon himself believed" (Acts 8:13)? Yes, but we need to examine Simon's faith. A person can actually be a believer of a certain kind and yet not be saved.

John, in his Gospel, tells about many who "believed" in Christ during our Lord's public ministry:

> *Now when he was in Jerusalem at the Passover feast, many believed in his name when they saw the signs which he did; but Jesus did not trust himself to them, because he knew all men and needed no one to bear witness of man; for*

31

he himself knew what was in man (John 2:23-25).

It is clear from this statement that there are some who are genuine believers and some who are not. There are some who have been attracted by certain things in the ministry of Christ and have yielded to Him a certain superficial allegiance. But the Master knows their inmost hearts and does not respond to them. Faith is more than giving mental assent to the truth. Genuine faith results in action. James writes in his Epistle: "Faith without works is dead . . . the devils also believe, and tremble" (2:20, 19, KJV).

Last year my wife and I made a trip through the islands of the South Pacific. Months ahead of time we made all the necessary arrangements and received complete information about the tour. We knew the number of each flight, the exact time of departure and arrival, the type of equipment, the cost of the ticket, the name of each airline, etc. We believed every word of the information and believed that the carriers would take us safely to our destination and back home again. But we could have believed all that and merely sat down and grown grey-headed, without ever crossing the Pacific. We had to act on our belief. We paid for our tickets and boarded the plane, bag and baggage. Up until the moment we walked up the steps, it was mere *belief*. The moment we stepped on board and fastened our seat belts, it became *trust*. We didn't actually say it in words, but in effect we said: "Captain, here we are for cloudy weather or for fair, for smooth flying or for rough. We commit ourselves to you and your crew, whose skill is a pledge that in five hours we shall be in Honolulu."

Or, to change the illustration, we may sincerely believe that if we write and mail a letter it will be delivered at its intended destination. But the belief does not become faith until we drop the letter into the mailbox and commit it to the postal authorities for their safe handling.

It is an absurd analogy, but we can believe every

word in the Bible and yet be eternally lost. We have to act out our belief. Faith is essentially an act of the will—entrusting ourselves to the person of Christ. We believe that the Bible is God's Word, that Jesus died to save sinners, that He can forgive sin—certainly. But there comes that moment when our faith looks up to Him and we say in our hearts: "Lord Jesus, I believe You died for *me*. I believe You forgive me *now*. And I entrust my whole life into Your keeping, in sickness and in health, in adversity and in prosperity, in sorrow and in joy. I believe You can take me safely through the voyage of life to the other shore." That is faith!

Simon Magus exhibited a type of mental belief, but he did not exercise saving faith. And because his faith was superficial, his "conversion" was superficial. He was baptized and joined the company of believers, but his heart was not right with God. Peter made that clear. Simon joined the church, but not Christ. He kept fellowship with Philip, the evangelist, but was not in fellowship with the Saviour whom Philip preached. He gave up his sorcery, but did not surrender himself. He was still self-centered. He was absolutely ignorant of the basic principles of the Christian life. As a result, there was no real change in his life. He was still the same old Simon Magus.

This is the test of conversion. Did something happen in your life? Oh, I don't mean a great burst of emotion, a flash of lightning, or a sudden vision. But was there a real change in your life? Were the springs of your character transformed? Did you come into touch with the living Christ?

The manager of a store saw a young lad pounding the candy-vending machine with his fists, big tears streaming down his face. "What's the trouble, son?" asked the manager. With choking voice the boy replied, "I put my money in the machine, but nothing happened!"

That's the trouble. A lot of people profess to believe, but nothing happens.

Conversion is not just an outer *change of label,* but

an inner *change of life*. It is not merely horizontal, a change of position along the same plane, a moving out of one camp into another. Conversion is basically *vertical,* a change from one level of living to another, a stepping out of self into Christ.

Some years ago a Catholic priest in India had a Muslim cook working in his home. One day, very unexpectedly, the cook said to his master, "Sir, I want to become a Christian. Please baptize me." Without inquiring into his motives, the priest baptized the cook and received him into the church. As he poured the water over his head, the priest declared: "You are no longer Abdul [a Muslim name]; from now on you are Da-ood [David]." When the baptismal ceremony was over, the priest said to the new convert, "There is just one stipulation I have to make. On Friday you should not eat mutton, but only fish." (Muslims are especially fond of mutton curry.)

For several weeks everything went well, until one Friday some very close friends of the cook appeared on the scene, and he felt he had to treat them with a feast of mutton curry. As he was preparing the meal, the aroma of the mutton came to the attention of the priest. He called the cook and said to him sternly, "Da-ood, I distinctly told you not to prepare mutton on Friday, only fish."

Da-ood replied, "Sir, this is not mutton; this is fish."

"You can't fool me," answered the priest. "I know you are preparing mutton."

And so they had an argument back and forth, the cook insisting the meat was fish, and the priest insisting it was mutton. Finally, in desperation, Da-ood said to his employer, "Sir, I'm just as clever as you are. You poured some water on my head and said, 'You are no longer Abdul; from now on you are Da-ood.' Well, I poured some water on this meat and said, 'You are no longer mutton; you are fish!' "

That is an example of a superficial type of conversion which ends in a mere change of label with no corresponding change of life. But in another city in India, a Hindu university student carefully studied the New Testament, came to the conclusion that Jesus is the Saviour of the world, and put his trust in Him. He was baptized and received into the church. Shortly afterward a Hindu friend of his stopped him on the street and said, "Prabhudas, I hear that you have changed your religion." Quick as a flash the new Christian answered, "No, you've got it all wrong. My religion has changed me!"

That is conversion. A genuine transformation of life!

What a difference there was between Simon, the magician, and Simon Peter, the apostle. Simon Magus "believed," but nothing happened; he was the same old person. Simon Peter also believed, but he was changed. When he first stood before Jesus, the Master looked at him and said: "You are Simon the son of John? You shall be called Cephas," or Peter, which means "rock" (John 1:42). When on one occasion Jesus said to His disciples, "Rejoice that your names are written in heaven," Peter's name was included in the list. Peter was also included in the final prayer of Jesus, when He said concerning His disciples, "Father . . . they have kept thy word . . . they have believed that thou didst send me . . . they are thine . . . I am glorified in them . . . they are not of the world, even as I am not of the world" (John 17:1-19).

Peter was a candidate for the baptism with the Holy Spirit on the Day of Pentecost because he was a converted man. It is true he denied his Lord on the night of the Crucifixion, but he immediately repented of his sin and returned to his Lord. As for Simon Magus, he was not a fit candidate for the fullness of the Spirit, for he had never truly been converted. He was not in relationship with the Heavenly Father. He lacked true repentance and faith.

Before a man can be baptized with the Spirit, he first must be born of the Spirit.

4

This Is Where We Start

A man named Nicodemus came to Jesus one night for a private interview. Many have speculated about why he came at night. Some have suggested that Jesus was a very busy Man and was constantly surrounded by crowds of people during the day. The only time He could be approached in private would be in the quiet of the late evening hours. Some have commented that Nicodemus himself, being a member of the Jewish Sanhedrin, had many responsibilities during the day and thus could find time to visit Jesus only after "office hours." Others suspect that Nicodemus was afraid of public opinion and so slipped in to see the Master under cover of darkness. Whatever the real reason may have been, the midnight setting became the occasion for discourse on a high-noon subject. You will find it recorded in John 3:1-15.

Nicodemus began the interview by paying Jesus a high compliment. "Rabbi," he said, "we know that you are a teacher come from God; for no one can do these things that you do, unless God is with him." He recognized that Jesus was not just a run-of-the-mill religious commentator like the rest of the scribes. He was Someone special who spoke and acted with authority.

The Master, however, sidestepped the compliment and spoke straight to the spiritual need of the visitor. Jesus looked beyond the man's flashy exterior and peered deep into his heart. He said to Nicodemus, "Truly, truly, I say to you, unless one is born of water and the Spirit, he cannot enter the kingdom of God. . . . 'You must be born anew.' "

THE NECESSITY OF THE NEW BIRTH

Here we are face-to-face with the dire necessity of the new birth. In the first place, it was Jesus Himself who spoke these words. Not some man—a bishop or professor of religion perhaps—but the Son of God, who knew the heart of man better than anyone else. Then again, He used the strongest language possible. He didn't say, "It would be a good thing for a man to be born of the Spirit," or, "I recommend that you be born again." He said, "You *must* be born anew. . . . Unless one is born anew, he cannot see the kingdom of God." "Must," "unless," "cannot"—these are compelling words. And almost every time, Jesus prefaced His statement with the phrase, "Truly, truly, I say to you." In the language of that day, this was equivalent to saying, "I am about to say something of prime importance. You had better sit up and take notice." Furthermore, Jesus emphasized the necessity of the new birth over and over again. In slightly different form He repeated the command three times (vv. 3, 5, 7). Could there be any doubt of the significance He placed upon the subject?

In the second place, we begin to understand the necessity of the new birth when we realize to whom Jesus spoke these words. Nicodemus wasn't an ordinary man—someone off the street. He was an important person in Jewish society. The Gospel writer tells us that he was a Pharisee, a member of one of the strictest religious groups of the day. The Pharisees prided themselves in their observance of the Law, right down to the last detail. They fasted regularly. They prayed often. They paid a tithe of their income. They followed the traditions of the elders. They built tombs for the prophets. They zealously sought to make proselytes (see Matthew 23).

Nicodemus was also a "ruler of the Jews," a member of the Sanhedrin. He was one of the seventy elders who governed the religious and social life of the people. This meant that he had authority and prestige. He was educated and, most likely, financially well-off. He was respected in the community. And yet to such a man of religion and rank Jesus said, "You must be born anew." This is what was so startling to him. To say this to the man possessed with an evil spirit wouldn't be surprising. If He had said this to the woman taken in adultery or to the thief on the cross, it would be expected. But Nicodemus was an outwardly moral, seemingly upright Pharisee. Wasn't Jesus going a little too far?

Not in the least. Jesus says to each and every one of us today, regardless of our religious background, our nationality, or moral achievements—"You must be born again. Unless you are born of water and the Spirit, you cannot enter the kingdom of God."

Jesus would say to the illiterate inhabitant of the remote jungle and to the sophisticated university professor, "You must be born again." He would say to the poor man in the ghetto and to the millionaire on Lakeshore Drive, "You must be born again." He would say to Asian, African, Mongolian, and European, "You must be born again." He would say to Buddhist, Muslim, Hindu, and nominal Christian, "You must be born again." He says the same thing to every man, everywhere. The new birth is a universal human necessity.

In India the rural preacher delights in telling the story of the rich merchant who was being rowed across the river by the village boatman. As they started across, the merchant began to relate how many schools he had attended and how many books he had read. "How far did you study in school?" he asked the boatman.

"Sir," answered the oarsman, "I've never been to school in my life. I can't even read or write."

"Too bad. You have lost one-fourth of your life," remarked the merchant. Then he began to relate how far he had traveled and all the great sights he had seen. "How much traveling have you done?" he asked the boatman.

"I have never set foot outside this county," came the embarrassed reply.

"You unfortunate man! You have missed half of your life," commented the merchant. Then he began to boast of his wealth—his fields and houses and bank account. "How much money have you put away in the bank during your lifetime?" he asked.

"Sir, I have no money in the bank. I live from hand to mouth."

"Poor man! You have lost three-fourths of your life," remarked the merchant.

Suddenly, in midstream, a strong gust of wind overturned the boat, throwing both men into the water. The boatman, with strong strokes, started swimming toward the shore.

"Help, help!" cried the merchant. "I'm drowning!"

"What?" called back the boatman. "With all your money and education and travel you never learned how to swim? I'm telling you straight. You are about to lose your *whole* life!"

The one thing the merchant needed at that moment —the ability to swim—he did not have. Everything else was of no avail. Likewise, the one basic spiritual requirement for all men is the new birth. If anyone misses this, he misses life itself. There is no substitute.

NATURE OF THE NEW BIRTH

When Jesus said to Nicodemus, "You must be born anew," Nicodemus completely misunderstood the import of these words. His mind drifted toward the scene of a midwife in a dimly lit room. He thought of the new birth purely in physical terms. He asked the Master, "How can a man be born when he is old? Can he enter a second time into his mother's womb and be born?"

Jesus replied, "Nicodemus, I'm talking about being born of the Spirit. 'That which is born of the flesh is flesh, and that which is born of the Spirit is spirit.' " He was emphasizing the basic biological principle that "like produces like." From the vegetable comes the vegetable. From the animal comes the animal. From man comes man. Likewise, from the Spirit comes the spiritual. Physical birth can produce only physical life. It takes a spiritual birth to initiate spiritual life. Man, therefore, requires two births. He has to be conceived by his parents in order to receive physical life and enter into this world. He must also be conceived by the Spirit of God to receive spiritual life and enter the kingdom of God. By being born of human parents he becomes their son. By being born of the Spirit he becomes a child of God.

Thus the birth that Jesus is talking about is not physical but spiritual. In essence Jesus was saying to Nicodemus, "You can be conceived in your mother's womb a hundred times—yes, a thousand times—but all you will have will be physical life. What you need is a spiritual birth wrought by the Spirit of God Himself."

Man is the only creature who is capable of living in two distinct worlds at the same time. As a physical being, created in the spiritual image of God, he can live in both the physical and the spiritual realms. He can be born a son of man and a child of God. It is possible, however, for a person to be very much alive physically and at the same time to be spiritually dead. He may be a "walking corpse," moving about in the flesh, but dead in the spirit. Paul, in his Epistles, often describes the sinner as being "dead in trespasses and and sins" (KJV; Eph. 2:1, 5; Col. 3:13). He declares solemnly that "the wages of sin is death" (Rom. 6:23).

Why is it that many people have no desire to read

God's Word or spend time in prayer? They're spiritually dead and do not know the One who inspired the Book. Why is it they have no love for the church and seem to get nothing out of the worship services? They're spiritually dead and are insensitive to the movements of the Spirit. Why is it they neither witness for Christ nor serve their fellowman? Because they're dead and insensitive to the spiritual needs of others.

I once heard of a black preacher who was pastor of a sophisticated urban congregation. He preached and labored faithfully, but the people did not seem to respond. So, in despair, one Sunday morning he declared that the church was dead and announced that he would conduct its funeral on the following Sunday. "There's only one thing to do with a corpse," he said, "and that is to bury it."

On the appointed day, motivated by sheer curiosity, the people crowded the church to participate in the "funeral." The ushers rolled in a casket, and the pastor preached the funeral sermon. At the close he announced that the casket would now be opened and anyone who so desired could come forward and review the remains of the dead church. When the first person leaned over and looked into the casket, he jumped back with a surprised look on his face. So did the next, and next. For on the bottom of the casket the preacher had placed a large mirror, so that everyone who peered in saw his own reflection!

It is a sad fact that many churches today are spiritually dead, and they're dead because the people who make up the congregation are dead. They have never been born of the Spirit and quickened with spiritual life. The tragedy is that often they do not realize they're dead, and they'll never know the truth about themselves until they gaze into the mirror of God's Word.

When a man is born of the Spirit, he suddenly comes alive. His conscience is alive to the promptings of the Spirit. His mind is alive to spiritual truth. Prayer takes on new meaning as dialogue with a Friend. God's Word becomes a personal love letter.

Witness and service become a spontaneous expression of love.

Furthermore, when a man is born of the Spirit, he receives a new nature. As a child of God, he partakes of the holiness of God. This results in a radical change of character and conduct. The Apostle Paul described it thus: "If any one is in Christ, he is a new creation; the old has passed away, behold, the new has come" (II Cor. 5:17). This is more than just patchwork or an outer reformation. It is an inner, moral transformation. Like the young man who testified at the close of a summer "ashram" (retreat): "I came here expecting the Lord to do some repair work, but instead He has given me a brand-new engine!"

A few years ago a Methodist minister in a midwestern city preached a sermon on the new birth at the regular Sunday morning service. He used the catchy title "New Tricks for Old Dogs." Several days later an attractive young lady called on him in the church office. "Do you remember the sermon you preached on the new birth?" she asked. "Well, that message really got through to me." Then she went on to relate how she had been having an affair with a well-to-do businessman in town. Whenever he made a business trip out of town, she accompanied him on the plane and stayed with him in his hotel room. The man's wife had become aware of the situation and was broken-hearted.

As a result of the minister's sermon, the young lady became convicted of her sin, went home from the service, prayed in desperation, and surrendered her life to Christ. When she arose from her knees, she immediately called the wife on the phone, asked for forgiveness, and assured her that she would break off the relationship with her husband. The next day she called on the businessman in his office. "It's all off," she said. "This is the last time you will see me."

"You will be short of cash, Honey," he said. "You won't be able to buy all those beautiful clothes anymore."

"That's alright," she replied. "I'll find a job and support myself."

"You'll miss all the travel and good times," he continued.

"I have found a new joy in life," she replied softly.

"What's wrong with you?" he asked angrily. "Have you fallen in love with someone else?"

For a moment the young lady was taken aback. Then she smiled and said, "Yes, that's it. I have fallen in love with Someone else."

He stood up, pale with rage. "Tell me his name and I'll kill him," he shouted, pounding his desk with his fist.

"I'm afraid you can't do that," came the quiet reply. "You see, I have just fallen in love with Jesus!"

As the young lady finished her story, she said to the minister, "You see, Pastor, something happened inside of me that Sunday morning. I'm not the same person. It's as if I had been born all over again."

THE MYSTERY OF THE NEW BIRTH

Seeing the puzzled look on the face of His visitor, Jesus went on to say, "[Nicodemus,] do not marvel that I said to you, 'You must be born anew.' The wind blows where it wills, and you hear the sound of it, but you do not know whence it comes or whither it goes; so it is with every one who is born of the Spirit" (vv. 7-8).

In other words, there is a mystery about the birth of the Spirit. The new birth is something difficult to explain or understand. But one does not need to stumble over the mystery. It is not necessary to understand all about the new birth before a person can experience its results in his life. It is like the wind, says Jesus. We don't know all about the wind, where it comes from and where it goes; but we see its effects everywhere. We feel its cool breeze on our faces. We see it scatter the leaves all over the yard. We watch it bend the limbs of the trees. So it is with the Spirit of God. We cannot see Him or understand all about Him.

But we know when He breathes new life into us. We joyfully respond as He witnesses to us that we are now the children of God. We see the change that He effects in our daily lives.

There are many mysteries in life. Electricity is one of them. How much does the average person really understand about electricity? But is it necessary for us to know all about electricity before we can enjoy its benefits? All we need to know is how to flip the switch, and immediately we can enjoy the light or turn on the motor.

The food we eat is a mystery. Do we fully understand how meat and vegetables and fruit turn into blood and bone, cell and tissue? But this doesn't keep us from going to the table three times a day. All we know is that when we eat we receive new life and energy. I don't understand how a brown cow eats green grass and gives white milk. But that doesn't stop me from drinking milk.

There are those who hesitate to accept the truth of the new birth because they find it difficult to understand or explain. But they do not need to fully understand all about it in order to experience it. In fact, after they have been born of the Spirit and the eyes of their understanding have been opened to spiritual things, they will understand far more about the new birth than they were able to do previously. A few months of walking in the Spirit will teach them more than a dozen courses on the subject.

The new birth is a mystery because it is a miracle—a miracle wrought by the Spirit of God Himself. It is, therefore, in the realm of the supernatural.

There are three stark miracles in the world. The first is the miracle of creation, when God said, "Let there be," and there was. This was the introduction of life into dead matter. The second was the miracle of the Incarnation, when God took on the form of man so that through Christ He might reconcile the world unto Himself. This was the invasion of the life of God into human history. The third is the miracle of the new creation, when a person is born of the Spirit. This is the introduction of God's life into the life of an individual. Something new is begun.

Many beautiful gospel songs have been written to describe the miracle of the new birth. Here are two by John W. Peterson:

> It took a miracle to put the stars in place;
> It took a miracle to hang the world in space;
> But when He saved my soul, cleansed and made
>   me whole,
> It took a miracle of love and grace!

> I believe in miracles;
>   I've seen a soul set free.
> Miraculous the change in one
>   Redeemed on Calvary.
> I've seen the lily lift its head
>   Up through the stubborn sod;
> I believe in miracles,
>   For I believe in God.

THE MEANS OF THE NEW BIRTH

After Jesus had emphasized the necessity of the new birth and had sought to describe its nature and results, Nicodemus turned to Jesus and asked pointedly, "How can this be?" In reply Jesus said, "No one has ascended into heaven but he who descended from heaven, the Son of man. And as Moses lifted up the serpent in the wilderness, so must the Son of man be lifted up, that whoever believes in him may have eternal life" (vv. 13-14).

Thus Jesus made it clear that the new birth is made possible by His vicarious death on the Cross. There was no other way. He gave His life that we might have life. He died that we might live. The Son of God became the Son of man, that the sons of men might become the sons of God.

The story is told of two brothers who lived in the

same town. The elder brother was the local judge and was an upright, good man, respected by all. The younger brother, however, was a wayward young man, always getting into trouble. He refused to accept the advice of his elder brother; and furthermore, since his brother was the judge in the city, he felt he would never be condemned for any crime he committed.

One day the younger brother became involved in a drinking brawl, struck another man, and killed him. He was arrested and brought to trial. His own brother was the judge. The jury rendered a verdict of "guilty of murder," and the judge decreed that the criminal should be hung. When the young man heard the decree, he rushed up to the front, fell at the feet of the judge, and cried out, "You are my brother! Have you no love for me? Are you condemning me to die?"

The judge replied solemnly, "It is true I am your brother, but this is a court of law and here I sit as your judge. You have committed murder. You must die for your crime."

The young man was escorted away and placed in solitary confinement. As the time for his execution drew near, he became more despondent and fearful. Just an hour or two before he was to be hung, the elder brother, dressed in his official robe, came to the prison and asked for the privilege of seeing the prisoner. When he stepped into the cell, he said, "There in the court of law, I was the judge and had to see that justice prevailed. But here I stand as your brother who loves you and wants to set you free. But there is only one way. Take off your prison clothes and put on my judge's robe, and walk out of here a free man. I will take your place."

The two men exchanged clothing, and the younger brother walked out into freedom. Not long after, the prison guards came, took the prisoner out, and hung him. Suddenly the younger brother came running from a distance, threw his arms around the lifeless form of his brother, and wept bitterly. "O my brother," he cried, "you died in my place!"

The guards were astonished when they realized what

had happened. But it was too late. A life had been given. The penalty was paid.

This is exactly what Christ has done for us. We all stood before the Judge of the universe, guilty and condemned. The verdict read, "The wages of sin is death." But because He loved us with an everlasting love, the Judge became our Elder Brother that He might become our Redeemer. "God was in Christ reconciling the world to himself." Christ took our sin upon Himself and died in our place. He took the initiative and did for us what we could not do by ourselves.

The important question now is, What are we going to do about what God has done for us? He has acted. How shall we react? Shall we respond in gratitude or ingratitude? In faith or disbelief?

Faith is the door into life. Jesus said, "Whoever believes . . . may have eternal life." John wrote, "To all who received him [Christ], who believed in his name, he gave power to become children of God." We must accept the truth that Christ died for our sins. We must receive the gift that He offers us in a nail-pierced hand. We must put our trust in Him and commit ourselves into His keeping.

When we respond in faith—which also is a gift from God—then the Holy Spirit becomes the Agent of regeneration in our lives. It is He who quickens us from death unto life. As the Divine Obstetrician, He "delivers" us into the new world of God's kingdom and breathes into us the very life of God. We are then "born of the Spirit" and become "children of God."

Jesus says to every man, "You must be born anew. Unless a man is born of water and of the Spirit, he cannot enter into the kingdom of God." This is the *sine qua non*, the indispensable requisite for spiritual life. The Christian walk begins with the birth of the Spirit.

The new birth is the prerequisite for the baptism with the Spirit. The gift of the fullness of the Spirit is offered, not to sinners, but to the children of God. It was to His immediate disciples—men who had forsaken all to follow Him, men who had been converted

and whose names were written in the book of life—
that Jesus promised they would be baptized with the
Spirit "before many days."

But once a man is born of the Spirit, he is a
candidate for the baptism with the Spirit. This is God's
intention and will. This is Christ's provision and
promise. No child of God should be satisfied until he
has claimed his full inheritance in Christ and experienced a personal Pentecost in his own life. To fail to
do so is to fall short of God's highest will and to miss
His finest gift.

5

What Happened Upstairs?

Many things took place on that eventful day in an upper room in Jerusalem. But the danger for us is to see only the outward physical manifestations and miss the real inward transformation that resulted. There was the sound like a rushing mighty wind that filled the whole house where the disciples were assembled. There were cloven tongues like fire that rested upon each of them. The disciples all spoke in other languages so that people of all nations gathered in Jerusalem could understand in their own native tongues what was being said.

But is this what we should expect from Pentecost today—wind, fire, other languages? Or is there something deeper involved?

We must distinguish between the *passing* and the *permanent* aspects of Pentecost; between the *temporary* and the *timeless*; between the *incidental* and the *fundamental*; between the *historical framework* and the *personal fact*.

The Temporary Framework	The Permanent Fact
1. The Day of Pentecost, a Jewish agricultural festi-	1. Any day that we are willing to meet the con-

val commemorating the firstfruits of the harvest	ditions; a spiritual festival representing the fruit of the Spirit
2. One hundred twenty disciples in an upper room in Jerusalem	2. Any number of disciples anywhere, united, yielded, and praying for the outpouring of the Spirit
3. Cloven tongues like fire	3. The refining fire of the Holy Spirit, sanctifying the individual and empowering him for service
4. Extraordinary speaking in different languages	4. The demonstration that in the Church of the living Christ there is neither Jew nor Gentile, bond nor free, and that the gift of the Holy Spirit is for *all*
5. Outer signs and wonders	5. Inner strength and well-being of holiness. The greatest sign of all and the greatest wonder—adequate power for holy living and for fruitful service

Thus we must distinguish between the picture and the frame, between the gift and the wrappings. On the one hand, the *Day of Pentecost*, as a great historical drama in God's plan of salvation, is an event of the past and cannot be repeated. It was the beginning of a new era and the birthday of the Church, and in its historical significance can never be repeated any more than the Manger, or Calvary, or the Resurrection, or the Ascension can be repeated. On the other hand, the *experience of Pentecost* has been repeated over and over again down through the Christian centuries and can be repeated—anytime, anywhere a disciple or group of disciples is willing to meet the conditions of obedience, surrender, and faith.

Many times in the Book of Acts other people were filled with the Spirit. Thousands of Christians across the world can testify today to a personal experience of Pentecost. Paul, in his Epistles, plainly commands that all Christians be filled with the Spirit; and Peter, on the Day of Pentecost, explicitly stated that the gift of the Holy Spirit is for all. "The promise is unto you, and to your children, and to all that are afar off, even as many as the Lord our God shall call" (Acts 2:39, KJV).

A careful reading of the Acts of the Apostles reveals to us that the fundamental results of the experience of Pentecost are three: (1) The plentitude of the Spirit, (2) purity of heart, and (3) power for service.

THE PLENTITUDE OF THE SPIRIT

Luke, the historian, tells us that on the Day of Pentecost the 120 disciples were all *filled with the Holy Spirit*. This was basic to everything else that followed.

As has already been pointed out, it does not mean that this was the first time the Holy Spirit was operating in the lives of Christ's followers. The Holy Spirit was not a stranger to them. Jesus made this very clear in His last discourse in the upper room, when He met with His disciples for the celebration of the Passover. He said, "You know him [the Holy Spirit], for he dwells with you" (John 14:17). At the same time Jesus made it clear that the disciples would shortly enter into a more intimate relationship with the Holy Spirit. "He dwells with you, and *will be in you* . . . with you for ever. . . . Before many days you shall be baptized with the Holy Spirit" (John 14:17, 16; Acts 1:5). In other words, this was to be the *fullness* of the Spirit.

Here again we must be careful to understand what this means. We must not get the idea that the Holy Spirit is fragmented or disconnected, and that He comes only in parts or portions, so that when we are born of the Spirit we receive part of Him, and then when we are baptized with the Spirit we receive the rest of Him. The Holy Spirit is a Person, a perfect Personality. He cannot be split up into segments. He cannot be divided into "more" or "less" stages. It may be possible for us to be split personalities, to be double-minded, but not for Him. When we are converted, we *have* the Holy Spirit—*all* of the Holy Spirit that we will ever have. So to be baptized or filled with the Spirit certainly does *not* mean that we get *more* of the Spirit; rather, the Holy Spirit gets *more of us*. For though we have all of the Spirit, He does not have all of us. He must have uncontested control of our lives, so that He does not simply dwell in us, but dwells unhindered; that is, in all His fullness.

In a certain city the members of the ministerial association were making plans for a city-wide evangelistic campaign. Many persons were being suggested for the evangelist. When someone proposed that they invite Dwight L. Moody, one minister objected strongly. "We've had Moody before," he argued. "Why do you want to invite him again and again? Does Moody have a monopoly on the Holy Spirit?"

"No," replied another quietly, "but the Holy Spirit has a monopoly on Dwight L. Moody."

That's the secret of the Spirit-filled life. The Holy Spirit must have a monopoly on us.

But someone asks, "Cannot a person be regenerated and filled with the Spirit at the same time? Cannot a person make a complete consecration to Christ the first time he comes to Him? Cannot God perform both acts of regeneration and sanctification at one time?"

The answer is, theoretically, "Yes." There is no limitation on God's part. He will fulfill His promises the moment we meet the conditions. But from the practical standpoint, the records of the New Testament and the experiences of thousands of sincere Christians confirm the fact that, as a rule, one does not experience the birth of the Spirit and the baptism with the Spirit at one and the same time. The limitation is on our part.

Some time ago I read Lawson's little book, *Deeper*

Experiences of Famous Christians. I found the theology and nomenclature varied considerably. Each individual expressed his experience within the particular theological framework and terminology of his own denomination. But the common denominators in all the experiences were apparent. This "deeper experience" was always subsequent to the experience of conversion, and usually followed a period of great soul-searching and spiritual desperation. There was a new and deeper surrendering of the individual self to God. There was a greater sense of the presence and power of God in the person's life, as he began living on a permanently higher plane.

There seems, therefore, to be general agreement that the infilling of the Holy Spirit comes after the crisis of conversion. The individual makes an initial surrender to Christ when he receives Him as Saviour. But then as he walks day by day in the Christian life, he begins to discover that there are areas of his life that are not fully committed to the Master's will. Christ is not really Lord in every part of his being. He also discovers that within himself are attitudes, desires, and reactions that are unchristian and act as a drag on his spiritual life. He now makes a fuller surrender of himself, crowns Jesus as King in his life, and permits the Holy Spirit to sanctify his innermost being. To this experience countless sincere Christians could testify.

Suppose you turn on the ceiling light in the living room of your home. Immediately light floods the room and dispels the darkness. But still there may be a few areas in the room where partial darkness prevails. The couch, the chairs, the piano, and other pieces of furniture cast shadows across the room. Underneath the couch it may be quite dark. Then suppose you remove all furniture from the room. What happens? The light immediately permeates every part of the room, for now there are no longer any hindrances. The amount of light is the same, but the area of penetration is greater.

In the same way, the Holy Spirit may be residing in a believer and yet may not be able to penetrate every part of his being. There are too many hindrances. Resentments, uncontrolled temper, pride, doubt, and other unchristian attitudes are casting shadows in his heart. What the individual needs is not more of the Spirit, but to allow the Spirit to possess more, yes, *all* of him. Then he will be "filled with the Spirit."

PURITY OF THE HEART

The second basic result of Pentecost was heart purity. Peter made this clear when he addressed the first Christian council at Jerusalem: "And God who knows the heart bore witness to them, giving them the Holy Spirit just as he did to us; and he made no distinction between us and them, but *cleansed their hearts by faith*" (Acts 15:8-9, italics mine).

In essence, what Peter said was this: "Exactly the same thing that God did in our hearts on the Day of Pentecost, He has now performed in the hearts of the Gentiles." And what was it God did? He "cleansed their hearts by faith."

The word "heart" is used symbolically to denote the seat of our affections, emotions, desires, attitudes, and motives. Cleansing of the heart, therefore, refers to a radical inner cleansing of the center of our personalities.

Such cleansing was very evident in the lives of Christ's disciples. Before Pentecost, on many occasions they manifested un-Christlike attitudes and reactions. For example, they exhibited pride. They argued among themselves who was greatest in the kingdom of heaven (Luke 9:46). They manifested selfishness. They requested Jesus to grant them thrones on the right and on the left when He established His kingdom (Mark 10:35-40).

They also demonstrated narrow-mindedness. Once when they saw someone who was not of their group casting out demons, they sought to restrain him (Mark 9:38). The disciples at times reacted in anger. Once, while traveling through Samaria, when they were refused lodging and hospitality by the Samaritans, they wanted to call down fire upon these people (Luke 9:54-56). They exhibited carnal fear and cowardice. On the night of Christ's arrest and trial, they fled and hid themselves. Peter denied his Lord three times (Matt. 26:56, 69-75).

At Pentecost the Holy Spirit performed radical spiritual surgery in the disciples' hearts. Pride was replaced with humility, self-seeking with the spirit of service, narrow-mindedness with sympathy, anger with love, and carnal fear with holy boldness. Many present-day disciples of Christ need a similar divine operation in their lives.

The desire to be filled with the Spirit must be accompanied by the willingness to be made pure. The Spirit of God is fundamentally the *Holy* Spirit. It is a law in logic that when you affirm something you automatically deny the opposite. When you say of an object, "This is white," you are automatically saying, "It is not black." When you say, "This is a rectangle," you at the same time deny that it is a circle. When you declare, "This is wood," it means it is not metal. In the same way, the Holy Spirit is absolutely, irrevocably opposed to evil.

To affirm that I want to be filled with the Spirit is to declare that I am willing to be emptied of all my unholy attitudes and spirit. Many of us pray with our lips, "Lord, fill me," but inwardly we say, "Lord, don't expose my resentments; don't disturb my comforts." But God cannot compromise with sin. He puts His finger upon anything that gets between us and Him, and between us and our fellowmen. With the fire of the Holy Spirit, He wants to purify us in our innermost being.

An evangelist friend of mine was invited to conduct a preaching mission in a certain city and was entertained in the home of a middle-aged couple. When the hostess escorted the evangelist to the guest room, she said in a welcome voice, "Now, I want you to make yourself completely at home. Hang your suits up in the closet and put your other clothes in the drawers. This is your room." The visitor took the hostess at her word, removed everything from his suitcase, and spread it out on the bed. But when he went to the closet to hang up his clothes, he found it jammed full of suits, dresses, slacks, and topcoats, with no empty hanger. When he opened the top drawer of the dresser, it was full of old clothing and rags. He tried the next; it was full also. Likewise, the bottom drawer was crammed with old picture albums and family heirlooms. There was absolutely no room for his clothes, so he put them all back into his suitcase.

When we say to the Holy Spirit, "Make yourself at home," we can't expect to keep anything hidden in the secret closets and drawers of our hearts. We must be willing to be emptied of all that is contrary to His nature and will. He must be more than a guest; He must be Lord. This means He will do a thorough job of housecleaning and will rearrange the furniture to His own plan.

POWER FOR SERVICE

The third major result of Pentecost is power. Just before He ascended to the Father, Jesus said to His disciples, "You shall receive power when the Holy Spirit has come upon you; and you shall be my witnesses in Jerusalem and in all Judea and Samaria and to the end of the earth" (Acts 1:8). On previous occasions He had commanded them to tarry in Jerusalem until they were "clothed with power from on high" (Luke 24:49; Acts 1:4).

Here again we notice the difference in the lives and ministry of the disciples before and after Pentecost. Before the outpouring of the Holy Spirit in His fullness, the disciples often displayed moments of weakness. Sometimes there was vacillation, or doubt, or a carnal fear of men. This was especially true in the last days before Calvary. They forsook their Master and went into hiding. Peter shamefully denied his Lord. But after the experience of Pentecost, the disciples displayed a stronger faith, a new spirit of confidence and courage. They possessed power beyond themselves to withstand persecution and temptation, and to witness boldly to the resurrection of the Lord.

How the Church today needs this supernatural power—power to reach out beyond the confines of brick and mortar, and to carry the spiritual offensive into the strongholds of society! The Church needs power to break out of routine and formality, and to perform exploits in the Master's name; power to call people to repentance and true righteousness; power to transform individuals and change society!

The Church of our day has great buildings, but little boldness. It has numbers, but little nerve. It has comfort, but no courage. It has status, but lacks spirit. It has prestige, but no power.

I remember watching the TV program "Candid Camera" a few years ago. A woman coasted downhill in a car and rolled into a filling station. "Fill it up with regular," she said to the smiling attendant, "and check the oil, please."

Imagine the look of astonishment on the man's face when he lifted up the hood and found there was no engine! The Church in many places reminds me of a car that has lost its engine. It has lost its source of power.

One New Year's Day, in the Tournament of Roses parade at Pasadena, California, a beautiful float came along Colorado Avenue in the middle of the procession. Its collection and arrangement of flowers was breathtaking. Suddenly the truck which was powering the float sputtered and came to a standstill. It was out of gas. The whole parade was held up while someone went for a two-gallon can of gas. The crowd roared with laughter when somebody said, "That float represents the Standard Oil Company!" With all the resources of this great company at its disposal, its truck was out of gas!

The Church today need not go on in its powerless, ineffective condition. All the mighty resources of the Holy Spirit are at its disposal. The individual Christian need not remain spiritually weak and anemic. He can tarry in surrender and faith and be "clothed with power from on high." Just as atomic power represents the release of hidden forces in the physical world, so Pentecost represents the release of invisible forces in the realm of personality.

Again, let us understand clearly that power cannot be separated from purity. Power is not an entity in itself. It is basically the unhindered flow of the Spirit's energy in and through a life that is utterly yielded to Christ and has been subjected to radical surgery by His skillful hand. We cannot experience the power until we're willing to be made pure. Purity and power go hand in hand.

These then are the permanent and fundamental characteristics of Pentecost: (1) the fullness of the Holy Spirit; (2) purity of heart; and (3) power for witnessing and service. These are the results that took place in the lives of the apostles and early Christians in the first century, and these are the results that can take place in the lives of any and all of Christ's followers in the twentieth century.

Pentecost was not merely a historical event; it is a present possibility. It was not a fleeting incident, external to the real core and course of the life of the Church. It is a profoundly vital experience with abiding values and permanent principles. It was not only a particular day, but is an extended dispensation. The baptism of the Holy Spirit was not for the Apostolic Church only; it rests, as both obligation and opportunity, upon the Church of every generation.

Pentecost is age-long and planet-wide. Given a child of God utterly yielding, trustfully expecting, any room may become an upper room, any day a Day of Pentecost.

6

What Must I Do?

Now having established that the experience of Pentecost is the birthright of all God's children, and having examined closely the permanent results of Pentecost, we come to the all-important question, How do we receive the fullness of the Holy Spirit?

There are some who declare that we simply grow into the experience. They say, "Just give me time. Let me grow. After a while I will be more like a saint." All this sounds good, but it ignores the facts both of Scripture and of general Christian experience. It is a false and dangerous idea. As A. W. Tozer reminds us, time has no more power to sanctify a person than space has. After all, time is only a human fiction. It is only our way of experiencing reality. It is change, not time, that leads us into the deeper life—change wrought by the Holy Spirit Himself. The truth of the matter is, there are many who were much better Christians shortly after the time of their conversion than they are right now. Why? Because they have not sought to be filled with the Spirit, and as a result have settled down to a halfhearted, dilatory Christian life. They have been drifting—not growing.

Now there is a certain sense in which we do grow

toward the experience of the fullness of the Holy Spirit —that is, there is often a process or series of minor crises that leads to the final event of the infilling. Most of us have to *grow up* to a certain place in our Christian lives where we are able to see the need of a deeper work of cleansing and are able to make a more complete surrender of ourselves to Christ. Perhaps we ought to say *grow down* rather than *grow up* to this place of readiness. For the truth of the matter is that not many of us grow gradually and steadily. We are too stubborn and self-centered for that.

God has to bring us *down*, again and again, with crisis after crisis. He has to let us get knocked down, to let us try and fail perhaps several times, until we finally are so utterly desperate that we come to the absolute end of all our own resources and strength. We discover that we are not just sinners, but sin itself, that in us "dwelleth no good thing." We realize that all our working and striving are as filthy rags, tainted with the subtle evil called self-glorification. Then in sheer desperation we give up, and make the surrender, and cast ourselves upon the grace of God. If we think that comes about by pleasant and gradual growth, we are sadly mistaken. It is really a facing of a series of crises, a seeking that is progressively more desperate, until finally we receive the fullness of the Spirit.

SURRENDER YOUR SELF

The first step in the Spirit-filled life is self-surrender. It has already been pointed out that the reason why many Christians are not filled with the Spirit is because the Spirit does not have all of them. They have not fully surrendered themselves to the Saviour and crowned Him King in their lives.

Why does the Christian faith place so much emphasis on self-surrender? Simply because the unsurrendered self is the cause of all our spiritual problems. Just as the fingers are rooted in the hand, so our sins are rooted in the palm of the unsurrendered self. Why does a man steal? To gain something for the self.

Why does a man lie? To protect the self. Why does a man get angry? The self has been crossed. Why does a man get jealous? Something is getting ahead of the self. Why does a man think evil thoughts? To gain pleasure for the self.

Take the little word SIN. Right in the middle of the word is the letter *I*. It is the unsurrendered ego, the I, that is the root of our problems.

The unsurrendered self is manifested in many different forms. Sometimes it manifests itself in *self-seeking*. The individual, instead of seeking first the kingdom of God and His righteousness, seeks his own pleasure, position, plans, and prestige. Like the prodigal son who said to his father, "Give me—give me." He wanted to take his possessions and spend them on his own interests. And like the two disciples, James and John, who requested Jesus to permit them to sit on His right and left when He established His kingdom on earth. They were seeking for thrones and scepters to glorify themselves, while Jesus was on His way to the Cross to give Himself for the redemption of the world.

Sometimes the unsurrendered ego manifests itself in *self-love*. The individual, instead of loving God supremely and his neighbor as himself, is actually in love with himself. He thinks more highly of himself than he ought to think, and becomes proud and censorious. A university professor was so conceited and infatuated with himself that the students jokingly referred to him as "a self-made man who worshipped his creator."

The unsurrendered ego sometimes manifests itself in *self-assertion*. The individual likes to be the center of the group. He likes to dominate the conversation. He likes to talk about himself, where he has been, and what he has accomplished. He frequently makes use of the personal pronoun "I."

When my brother was working on his master's thesis at Hartford, Connecticut, some years ago, he rented a typewriter from a local agent. As the man was setting up the typewriter in the apartment, he made a few casual remarks about his business that proved most interesting. He said to my brother, "You know the letter on the keyboard that we have to replace more often than any other is the letter *I*. The reason for this," he went on to explain, "is not so much because people use this letter more than any other, but when they use it, they strike the key so hard!"

At times the unsurrendered self is manifested by *self-indulgence*. The individual is motivated, not by principle, but by desire. This may lead to excess, gluttony, enslaving habits, or even immorality.

Self-justification is another characteristic of the unsurrendered ego. The person finds it difficult to admit that he was mistaken. He is slow to apologize. He constantly seeks to justify his actions and to vindicate his position.

Then there is *self-sufficiency*. The individual, instead of relying wholly on the resources and grace of God, depends on his own wisdom, his own ability, his own efforts. Like Peter, if all the other disciples forsook the Master and fled, he alone would be faithful to the end, even unto death. But when the time of testing came, he miserably failed and denied his Lord three times. He thought he was strong enough on his own.

A little girl was singing to herself in the living room of the house one day, while her mother was working in the kitchen. It was an old, familiar song, but this must have been the revised version. The mother smiled as she overheard the daughter singing, "Count your blessings, name them one by one, and it will surprise the Lord what you have done." Self-sufficiency!

Then again, the unsurrendered self is manifested by *self-will*. Perhaps this is the crux of the matter. The individual, instead of seeking God's will in every decision and area of life, often desires to go his own way. In his wonderful book entitled *The Great Divorce,* C. S. Lewis suggests that in the last analysis there are only two groups of people in the world. The first group comprises those who say to God, "Not my will, but Thine, be done." Jesus was the great Example of this attitude in life, when He prayed this very prayer in the Garden of Gethsemane, just before His crucifixion. The second group of people are those to whom God eventually has to say, "Not My will, but thine be done. You wanted to have your way; alright, you can have it—forever." And Lewis suggests that when God eventually and decisively says this to any man, that is hell.

The self is usually the last thing we are willing to surrender. It's easy to *give to* Christ, to give *things;* it's hard to *give up* to Christ, to present *ourselves.* We usually are willing to give anything to Christ—money, possessions, even service—everything but our own selves. I remember a layman in India who confessed before the congregation, "All these years I have given my offerings faithfully to the Lord, but I have never really given myself." A young single missionary, who went out to India to pastor an English-speaking congregation in a large city, said in a retreat one day, "I had left my home and loved ones, a good job and a fine salary, to come to India to work for God, but until today I had not really surrendered myself." Simon Peter, acting as spokesman for the disciples, said to the Master on one occasion, "Lo, we have left everything and followed you. What then shall we have?" (Matt. 19:27). Note the last part of the statement. Peter had given up his home, his boats, and his fishing, but he hadn't given up Peter, and consequently he was constantly getting entangled in his unsurrendered self.

We must be careful to understand that self-surrender does not mean self-extinction. You can never get rid of the self. If you put it out through the door, it will come back through the window. The self is the eternal part of human personality. It is that which makes you a person, which gives you individuality. A selfless person would be a contradiction in terms. You can be unselfish, yes, but never selfless.

Self-surrender is a radical shift from self-centeredness to Christ-centeredness, so that life is no longer revolving around oneself, but around Christ. We must take that letter *I* and bend it around until it becomes a zero or an *O*. Then the word SIN will be changed to SON. When the unsurrendered I or ego bends itself to the Master's will, this leads to true sonship in Christ.

We pointed out previously that when the prodigal son left home the words on his lips were: "Give me—give me." We now observe that when he returned home, the words on his lips were these: "Make me—make me." The center had shifted from himself to his father.

When we study English grammar, we learn how to conjugate a verb thus: First person, *I;* second person, *you;* third person, *he.* I make; you make; he makes. But in self-surrender our spiritual grammar must be reversed. First person, *He;* second person, *you;* third person, *I.* God must be first in my life; He must have the preeminence. You, my neighbor, must be next.

There are basically two patterns of life: one revolving around as the center. The New Testament symbolically speaks of these patterns as "the old man" and "the new man." All of the events and stuff of which life is made fall into one or the other of these two patterns. Indeed, to some extent in unsurrendered hearts these patterns exist simultaneously, overlapping, so that when pictured geometrically there is an elipse where a circle ought to be.

In his book entitled *The Spirit of Holiness*, Dr. Everett Cattell illustrates this common spiritual condition by passing a horseshoe magnet under a sheet of paper on which have been sprinkled iron filings. Looking from above one cannot see the magnet, but one can tell the location of its poles by the behavior of the filings, which instantly arrange themselves around the poles and form two overlapping patterns. "In the lives of converted men," suggests Dr. Cattell, "there are still two great poles—self and God. All of the particles that go to make up life group themselves around these two poles in patterns of life which are partially self-centered and partially God-centered. It is conceivable that the particles where the patterns overlap have a hard time making up their minds as to which pole to obey."

We must be cleansed of self-centeredness. This

duality of pattern must go out of existence. The self as a pole apart from God must yield up its aloofness, its separateness, its enmity against God, its independent sovereignty, by an act of utter surrender. It must move over and become hid with Christ in God. The self then continues to live, but it lives in God. The poles are now—so to speak—identical, and the pattern of life is one—integrated.

This spiritual paradox is most concisely and intriguingly expressed by Paul in his oft-quoted words, "I have been crucified with Christ; [nevertheless I live;] it is no longer I who live, but Christ who lives in me; and the life I now live in the flesh I live by faith in the Son of God, who loved me and gave himself for me" (Gal. 2:20). This is an amazing verse. It emphasizes self-surrender, or self-crucifixion, and yet at the same time it speaks so much of the self. The personal pronouns are prominent. But we must follow Paul carefully in his line of reasoning.

It is evident he is speaking about three different egos, or more correctly, three facets of the one ego. "I have been crucified with Christ," he begins. This is the part of the ego that needs crucifixion. It is that proud, perverse, self-centered ego which always seeks to glorify itself. The only cure for this is crucifixion, a "death to self." Then Paul goes on, "Nevertheless I live" (a phrase occurring in the King James version). This is the part of the self which lives on after the crucifixion. It is our essential selfhood, the real self, imperishable, eternal. God Himself has created it and He will not destroy it. It will live on forever. "It is no longer I who live, but Christ who lives in me," Paul concludes. Herein lies the secret. When the carnal, self-centered ego is crucified, then there can be a true self filled and possessed by Christ. It becomes a Christ-centered ego. Thus Paul in one breath said, "I am dead," and in the next breath says, "I am alive." Then he qualifies that by saying, "It is really Christ who is living in me." It's a death that leads to life.

There is the story of a man who was glancing over the obituary section of the morning newspaper when, to his surprise, he found his own name in the list. He looked again. Sure enough, the initials, name, and address were all correct. He was reported as dead. At first he laughed over the matter, but soon the telephone began ringing, as many of his stunned friends sought to inquire about his sudden death. Finally, he became irritated and called up the newspaper editor. "Sir," he said, "you have reported my death in the morning paper, but I'm very much alive. It's causing a lot of confusion among my friends. I demand you set this right!"

The editor was at first nonplussed and apologetic, but then in a flash of inspiration he said, "Don't worry, sir. I'll make things right. Tomorrow I'll put your name in the birth column!"

This is a spiritual parable. If we die out to the old carnal self, then suddenly we will find ourselves alive in Christ—alive as never before. For after the crucifixion comes the resurrection. The old self dies and a new self arises. We put our names in the death column and immediately we find them placed in the birth column.

A note of warning needs to be sounded at this point. The crucifixion of the old self that we have been emphasizing cannot be brought about by the individual himself. That is, self cannot crucify itself. It is irrevocably opposed to its own crucifixion. The only thing the individual can do is to *become willing* for the self to be crucified by the Holy Spirit, who alone is the Executioner. As Paul clearly states, "No man can say 'Jesus is Lord' except by the Holy Spirit" (I Cor. 12:3). But when we are willing, then we find He is able.

RECEIVE THE FULLNESS OF THE SPIRIT

The full surrender of the self is not an end in itself. It is merely clearing the channel so that the Spirit may give Himself in His fullness. This must not, however, be interpreted as a form of celestial bargaining, whereby we give our all and in exchange He gives His all. By a full surrender we are not in any sense making ourselves worthy to receive the fullness of the Spirit. No one is worthy, but all Christians are eligible. This is God's gift, and it is for the asking. Jesus said, "If you then, who are evil, know how to give good gifts to your children, how much more will the heavenly Father give the Holy Spirit to those who ask him!" (Luke 11:13). All we need to do is to ask the Holy Spirit who lives in us to take full control and sanctify and fill.

In seeking the fullness of the Holy Spirit, our eyes must be upon the Giver Himself, and not upon one of the gifts. Paul makes it clear that the Holy Spirit distributes His gifts "to each one individually as he will" (I Cor. 12:11). All do not receive the same gift; neither does any person possess all of the gifts. We cannot dictate to the Holy Spirit what gift He shall give us. This is His prerogative. We can, however, all receive the gift of the fullness of the Holy Spirit Himself. The promise is unto all!

It was shortly after my wife and I arrived in India to begin our missionary career that the Japanese attacked Pearl Harbor and drew the United States into World War II. Within a few months, Japanese forces had advanced to the borders of India, and the U.S. ambassador was urging all American citizens to evacuate. My wife and six-month-old daughter returned by troop transport to the United States, but I remained behind on the field. It was two years and seven months before we were reunited.

During the long period of separation my wife and I suffered many hours of loneliness. My wife wrote to me regularly, but in those war years mail was slow and the censorship was strict. Often whole sections of a letter were cut out. At times she mailed me a parcel with some special gift as a token of her love. On one occasion while I was holding special revival meetings in Calcutta, a thief broke into the parsonage, and, among other household articles, stole my best suit and fountain pen. When my wife heard of the loss, with her meager savings she bought me a new suit and fountain pen, and mailed them out to me in India. I was, of course, delighted to receive the gift. But I wrote to her and said, "Dearest, I thank you for all your letters which assure me of your love and prayers. I thank you for all the parcels, and especially for this most recent one. But, Darling, I am getting to the place where I am not satisfied with just letters and parcels. I long for you and you alone. If I could just look into your face and hold you in my arms, that would be worth more than thousands of letters and parcels. The next time you send me a parcel, just wrap yourself up and come out!"

There came a time in my spiritual life when I had to say much the same thing to the Holy Spirit. I said in my heart, "Lord, I thank You for all your gifts—for forgiveness, for peace, for comfort and strength. But, Lord, I want more than just gifts. I want only You. I want You to permeate and fill every part of my being."

We must desire the Lord more than anything else in the whole world. We must want Him and Him alone.

Finally we must receive the Holy Spirit in His fullness *by faith*. Peter said before the council in Jerusalem, "And God who knows the heart bore witness to them, giving them the Holy Spirit just as he did to us; and he made no distinction between us and them, but cleansed their hearts *by faith*" (Acts 15:8-9, italics mine). All the gifts of God are received by faith.

Many Christians seem to surrender themselves, to die out to self, but it's all so morbid, so depressing. They're surrendered, but empty. They need to take the positive step of faith. Surrender says, "I am crucified with Christ." Faith says, "Christ lives in me." Surrender says, "Empty and cleansed." Faith says, "Filled and fitted for the Master's use." Surrender says, "I give my all." Faith says, "I receive Your all."

Faith is merely taking God at His word, letting my whole weight down on His promises. He assures us that the Gift of the Holy Spirit is for all; that He gives the Holy Spirit to those who ask Him; that if we shall ask anything in His name, He will grant it. So I say in my heart, "Lord, I know what You say is true. I now ask to be filled with the Spirit, and I believe that You fill me at this moment. Thank You, Lord."

Since this experience is entered into by faith, it can happen in our lives anytime, anywhere, when we ask and believe.

In a certain church I was giving a series of messages on the subject of the Holy Spirit. A young housewife, a sincere child of God, became hungry for the fullness of the Spirit. One morning, all alone in the house, she was working in the kitchen. In her mind, however, she was meditating and praying. Suddenly she lifted her eyes and said aloud, "Lord, the preacher said we can receive the baptism with the Holy Spirit by faith. This, I see, is in accordance with Your Word. So, Lord, right here and now I ask You to fill me with the Holy Spirit, and I believe You do." In the evening service she stood and testified that she had the inner assurance that the Holy Spirit had filled her. It happened while she was in the kitchen, washing the breakfast dishes!

A few years ago, at a quiet retreat for preachers and laymen in New York State, I delivered the same series of messages on the Holy Spirit. At the end of the first session, time was given for questions and discussion. The ministers became involved in the theological pros and cons of the subject. Suddenly a layman, whose first name was Sam, interrupted the discussion and called out. "I don't follow all this theological jargon. All I know is that I need the fullness of the Holy Spirit. Tell me how I can find it." So I briefly outlined the steps of self-surrender and faith.

When the evening session was over, the leader of the retreat explained that we would now begin a period of silence until the morning devotional period. He also informed us that on our way out we should pick up a card containing the name of one of the persons present at the retreat. We were to pray for that person in particular before retiring for the night. Immediately I said in my heart, "Lord, give me Sam as my prayer partner." When I picked up my card and looked at the name, it read "Sam ————." Coincidence, you say. But that would be difficult in a stack of approximately a hundred cards. I felt it was providence. I went to my room and prayed earnestly for Sam, that he might be filled with the Spirit.

In the morning we all gathered for corporate, silent devotions. At the end of the period, Sam jumped to his feet and said excitedly, "I could hardly wait for the silence to be broken. I am bursting to share the good news with you. Last night the Lord filled me with the Holy Spirit. I asked and believed, and the Lord answered my prayer." It happened while he was taking a shower!

Many years have passed since a tall, lanky, red-headed Kentuckian, a civil engineer student in the University of Cincinnati, was walking down the side-walk on Clifton Avenue near the university campus. It was a cold, dreary evening in January. The previous summer at Sychar Camp Meeting in Mount Vernon, Ohio, this young man had been converted and called to go to India as a missionary. Recently he had received instruction concerning the baptism with the Holy Spirit and was earnestly seeking the experience. Walking along the sidewalk, deep in thought, he said audibly, "Lord, I have placed my ambitions, my career, my marriage, my all on the altar. What more should I do to receive the Holy Spirit in His fullness? This is what I need and desire more than anything else." An inner voice said quietly, "Just ask and believe." So the young man—my father—lifted his eyes heavenward and said from the depths of his heart, "Lord, I do believe. Fill me now!"

Not long ago my father took me to Cincinnati and pointed out the spot where it happened. We stood there and shared in a time of thanksgiving and prayer.

I remember the time when I was a student at Asbury College in Wilmore, Kentucky, how I first received the fullness of the Spirit. I had been a Christian for about two years and had started out very zealously in my Christian life. But then I seemed to hit a plateau. I was making little progress spiritually. I was deeply distressed at the discovery of certain attitudes and desires in my heart that were clearly contrary to the spirit of Christ. I was a divided person; there was civil war within. The doctrine of the Holy Spirit and sanctification was not new to me. I had been reared in the Wesleyan tradition. All I needed was to appropriate the truth personally and turn doctrine into experience. Then one morning, sitting alone at the desk in my private devotions, I prayed silently within myself, "Lord, You said, 'Blessed are those who hunger and thirst for righteousness, for they shall be satisfied.' Well, I'm hungry now. I'm thirsty. I want to be cleansed and filled with the Spirit more than anything else. Lord, fulfill Your promise now. I believe." At that moment I felt as if I had had a good bath. I felt clean all over. And there was the assurance that the Holy Spirit had taken possession of my being. Sad to say, I haven't always been faithful to the Master. There was a time when I miserably failed my Lord and lost the assurance of His fullness. But the Spirit was faithful in His ministry of conviction and discipline and brought me back to the place of full surrender and faith. The assurance of His fullness is real today.

These then are the steps to the Spirit-filled life. Surrender yourself completely to His will and die to the old self. Receive Him in His fullness by faith. Realize that it is God's intention to fill you with His Spirit. Make it your intention to be filled. Then the promise will pass into fulfillment in your life, and Pentecost will be as real to you as it was to the disciples in the upper room at Jerusalem.

7

Love Is the Sign

The greatest statement in all human language is, "God is love." Not just, "God loves," but, "God *is* love." He is the personification of love. Love is the very fiber of His being.

All the acts of God spring from this basic fact. For example, love is the basis of His creative action. Why did God create? Because love involves relationship. It requires objects upon which it can lavish its affection. And so God created man in order that He might pour out His love upon him. Parents create for the same reason. They desire children whom they can call their very own, upon whom they can shower their love, and who in turn will respond in love.

Love is the basis of God's redemptive action. "For God so loved the world that he gave his only Son, that whoever believes in him should not perish but have eternal life" (John 3:16). "In this the love of God was made manifest among us, that God sent his only Son into the world, so that we might live through him" (I John 4:9). "By this we know love, that he laid down his life for us" (I John 3:16). It was a dangerous thing for God to create. His creatures might go wrong and break His heart. But God took this chance.

75

He knew He would have to lay His love alongside the sin of man. The Cross was, therefore, inherent in creation. Jesus was called the Lamb slain from the foundation of the world (Rev. 13:8). Not just two thousand years ago. The moment man disobeyed and became a sinner, a cross was formed in God's heart. This was inevitable. But how could we know that God cared, that He suffered on account of our sin? The only way was for Him to lift up a cross at some point in history for all men to see. Through the outer, wooden cross on Calvary, we see the inner, invisible cross in the heart of God. And so because God is love, He loved the world and gave His Son, and the Son gave His life.

Love is also the basis of our approach to God. Suppose I were a sinner in need of help and guidance, and came to you for advice. You might say to me, "God is *omnipotent*. Go to Him, and He will help you." But I dare not go to God on the basis of His omnipotence. I am frail and finite. He may crush me in His mighty hand. Again, you might say, "God is *omniscient*. Go to Him and He will help you." I dare not approach God on the basis of His omniscience, for He knows all about me—every act I have committed, every word I have spoken, even my innermost thoughts and desires.

Then suppose you say, "God is *holy*. Go to Him for help." But I dare not approach Him on the basis of His holiness. He is Absolute Perfection, while I am a miserable sinner. The closer I get to Him, the greater is my embarrassment. Again you say, "God is *just*. Go to Him for help." But I dare not approach Him on the basis of His justice. I have sinned against Him, and stand guilty in His presence. Justice demands that I be condemned for my sin.

Finally, you say to me, " 'God is *love*'; go to Him and He will have compassion on you." Then I forget my embarrassment, my unworthiness, and I rush into His outstretched arms, pleading His mercy. And because He loves me, He will welcome, pardon, cleanse, and receive me. Love is the only basis upon which I can approach Him.

Since love is one of the basic characteristics of God,

it is, therefore, one of the basic characteristics of the Spirit-filled life. This is the truth that Paul emphasizes in his First Epistle to the Corinthian church. Having discussed the various gifts of the Spirit in chapter 12, he concludes by saying, "I will show you a still more excellent way." Then in chapter 13 he gives us his great tribute to love, some of the most magnificent words in Scripture and in all literature.

> If I speak in the tongues of men and of angels, but have not love, I am a noisy gong or a clanging cymbal. And if I have prophetic powers, and understand all mysteries and all knowledge, and if I have all faith so as to remove mountains, but have not love, I am nothing. If I give away all I have, and if I deliver my body to be burned, but have not love, I gain nothing (I Cor. 13:1-3).

In essence Paul is saying: We may proclaim the most wonderful words; we may possess the most marvelous gifts; we may perform the most noble deeds. But if we do not possess and practice love, we are nothing. All is in vain.

This is the reason why Jesus, when questioned, declared that the greatest commandment of all is to love—to love God supremely and to love our neighbors sincerely.

> "The first [commandment] is, 'Hear, O Israel: The Lord our God, the Lord is one; and you shall love the Lord your God with all your heart, and with all your soul, and with all your mind, and with all your strength.' The second is this, 'You shall love your neighbor as yourself.' There is no other commandment greater than these" (Mark 12:29-31).

Since God is love and man is made in the image of God, it follows that man is created with the capacity to love. Previously psychologists used to say that there were three basic urges in man—self, sex, and the herd: the desire for self-preservation, the desire for self-propagation, and the desire to be in the company of others. But in recent years psychologists have been insisting that there is really only one basic human urge, and that is the desire to love and to be loved. Man must love something. If he doesn't love God and his neighbor, he will at least love art, music, literature, sports, his country, or a good cause. This is why we commonly remark, "Love makes the world go round."

The opposite of that adage is also true: "The lack of love makes the world go wrong." The basic cause for many broken homes and for much of our juvenile delinquency today is right at this point. Many husbands and wives have lost their first love. Many sons and daughters have not experienced true love (which includes discipline) in the home. Many young people who run off and get married at an early age are really seeking for love which they did not receive from their parents.

I remember reading in an Illinois newspaper a few years ago about the abduction of a three-week-old baby in Metropolis, in the southern part of the state. A woman in her late thirties called on the parents of the child and identified herself as the representative of the Massac Memorial Hospital. She claimed the baby had been selected as "baby of the month," and said she wanted to take it to the hospital for a photograph. When she hadn't returned after several hours, the frantic mother phoned the hospital, then the police. The abductor was discovered with the baby in Chicago a few days later. When the authorities asked her why she stole the baby, she replied tearfully, "I just wanted something to love." Then it was discovered that within the past month both her husband and father had died, and she herself had suffered a miscarriage, and now she was left with no children of her own. So in desperation she stole the baby in order to have "something to love."

So religion and psychology both say, "You shall love." This is basic in the Christian life. But someone asks, How can you command love? Love is not really genuine unless it is spontaneous—from the heart. The answer is, when God *commands* love, human nature *commends* it. If we violate the law of love, we violate the law of our being. If we don't love God and our neighbor, we can't really love ourselves. Suppose I am addressing a group of people, and at noon I say to them, "Go to lunch now." That would be in the nature of a command, but there would be something within each person that would respond to the order. In like manner, when Christ requires us to love, our inner nature responds to the demand, for we were endowed with the capacity to love.

Then Jesus goes on to say, "You shall love the Lord your God." God is to be the Object of our love—a Person, not merely a doctrine, or an idea, or just a cause. This is to be a personal relationship.

God is the *perfect Object* of our love. He is absolutely good and holy, with no faults or defects. He is completely dependable and will never let us down. Sometimes my wife says to me, "Honey, I love you in spite of all your faults." And I can say the same to her. As human beings we all have our faults. We have to love one another in spite of our weaknesses and shortcomings. But we can't look into the face of God and say, "Lord, I love You in spite of Your faults." He has none. He is the one Person in all the universe who is absolutely perfect and dependable.

God is also the *eternal Object* of our love. This is a loving relationship that has no end. In the world of human relationships, there comes a time when we lay husband, wife, child, or friend in the grave, and the former intimate relationship of love is broken. But when we fall in love with Christ, this is the beginning of an eternal romance. For neither height nor depth, principalities nor powers, not even death itself can separate us from the love of Christ (Rom. 8:38-39).

A small boy had a pet rabbit which his father gave him for a birthday gift. He dearly loved the rabbit and carried it around with him wherever he went. But one day a couple of stray dogs pounced on the pet and tore it into shreds. The boy's heart was broken and he wept for days. Then his father presented him with a beautiful puppy, and soon the lad forgot all about the rabbit. He cuddled his dog and played with it for hours at a time. It followed at his heels wherever he went. But one day while playing, the puppy ran across the street after a ball, and was killed instantly by a swiftly passing car. Again the boy's heart was broken and he wept profusely over the loss of his second pet. He climbed up on his father's lap and through his tears cried out, "Daddy, my rabbit is gone and my puppy is gone. Can't you get me something to love which won't ever die?"

There is something in the heart of man that cries out in similar vein: Isn't there something or someone in the universe that I can love, who will never die? Yes, there is Someone. The Lord Jesus Christ. When we fall in love with Him, we fall in love forever. This is an eternal romance.

Then Jesus goes on to say, "You shall love the Lord your God with all your heart, and with all your soul, and with all your mind, and with all your strength." He emphasizes the word "all." Our love for God is to be *complete*. He desires *all* our devotion. Isn't this true of us also? The wife wants all of her husband's love; the husband wants all of his wife's love. We are not satisfied until we have all. Can God be satisfied with anything less?

Our love for God is to be a *well-balanced love*, expressing every aspect of our personality. We are to love Him with all our *heart*, with all *the sincerity of our emotional nature*. We are to love Him with all our *mind*, with all *the sanity of our intellectual nature*. We are to love Him with all our *soul*, with all *the intensity of our volitional nature*. We are to love Him with all our *strength*, with all *the vitality of our physical nature*. The whole of man is to be brought under the sway of God. This makes for unified personality, for fixation of purpose.

Many are loving God in an unbalanced and, therefore, weak way. There are those who love Him with the strength of the feelings and weakness of the mind. This makes the *emotionalist* in religion. Some love with the strength of the emotions and weakness of the will. This makes the *sentimentalist* in religion. Others love Him with the strength of the mind and weakness of the emotions. This makes the *intellectualist* in religion. Still others love Him with the strength of the will and weakness of the emotions. This produces the *legalist* in religion, the man of iron—very moral, but unloving and unlovable. The really strong Christian is the one who loves with the strength of the mind, the strength of the whole personality. The entire being is caught up in a passion of love and self-surrender to Christ.

Jesus follows the first great commandment—love God with your whole being—with a second commandment: "Love your neighbor as yourself." The two cannot be separated. They are like the two rails of the railroad track or like the two wings of a bird. To talk of loving God without loving our fellowman is a farce. It would be comparable to putting our arms around a person and then kicking him in the shins. Spell Christian love with a capital *L*. The vertical stroke, representing our relationship to God, is immediately followed by a horizontal stroke, which represents our relationship to our fellowmen. If we love God, we will love people.

My father spent his adolescent years in Tucson, Arizona. While he was a student in high school, one summer vacation he worked on the levee near the Mexican border. It was there that for the first time he saw Indians from southern Asia. Several men had come over to Mexico at the invitation of the government to work as day laborers on certain public projects. When my father saw these Hindu "coolies" with their caste-marks and strange customs, and heard their weird music around the campfire at night, he said to himself, These people are the offscouring of the earth. They are the most loathsome people I have ever seen. Little did he realize that within a few years he would receive a call from God to serve as a missionary in India! But before this latter event he was converted at Camp Sychar in Ohio and then later filled with the

Holy Spirit. He received such a baptism of love in his heart that his attitude toward the Indians was completely transformed. India became his beloved country; the people of India became his own. It can truthfully be said that no one loved India, nor was anyone loved by the Indians, more than my father.

A few years ago I conducted a one-day ashram in an Episcopalian church in Baltimore, Maryland. An attractive university coed came to the retreat, but when she saw a good number of Negroes present, she became resentful and almost decided to go back home. However, she exercised self-restraint and remained. She listened attentively to the messages on the Holy Spirit, and when the invitation was given to come forward and pray at the altar, she readily responded to the call. In the closing session she stood before the group, confessed her resentment, and asked the Negroes present to forgive her. Then with a note of excitement in her voice, she said, "You know, I asked God to fill me with the Holy Spirit, and He answered my prayer. Now I suddenly find that my attitude of race prejudice is gone, and for the first time I am able to love everybody, even my black brothers and sisters." From rejection to acceptance within the period of six hours! It was truly a miracle of God's grace.

I am writing this chapter in the heart of the Congo in Africa, where I am attending the annual conference of the Methodist Church. There is a young missionary here, Paul Law, and his lovely wife, who recently graduated from Asbury College. They have come to minister to the Congolese people. Six years ago Paul's father, Burleigh Law, missionary-pilot of the Methodist Church, was shot and killed by rebels during the civil war that took place. He is buried on the mission station at Wembo Nyama. Today his son, Paul, is back at the same station, preaching Christ to the people of the area. Humanly speaking, one would expect Paul Law to feel ill will toward the people of Congo for murdering his father. One would think that he would never want to see Congo again. But here he is, back at the scene of his father's martyrdom, loving and serving in the name of Christ. Nothing but the love of Christ could help a man to do that.

In his letter to the church at Rome, Paul states that "God's love has been poured into our hearts through the Holy Spirit which has been given to us" (Rom. 5:5). Then in the Galatian Epistle he writes that "the fruit of the Spirit is love, joy, peace, patience, kindness, goodness, faithfulness, gentleness, self-control" (Gal. 5:22-23). Thus love with all its various manifestations is the supreme evidence of the indwelling presence of the Holy Spirit. And when we are completely yielded to Christ and filled with the Spirit, His love is evident in our lives in even greater measure.

The gifts of the Spirit are important and should be used for the edification of the Church and for the glory of God. But the Holy Spirit distributes the various gifts according to His own will. To one He gives the gift of prophecy (or proclamation), to another the gift of discernment, to another the gift of tongues, and so on (see I Cor. 12:4-11, 27-31). No one person possesses all nine gifts; neither do we all have identically the same gift. Therefore we cannot claim that any one particular gift is the evidence of the baptism with the Spirit. However, every Spirit-filled person possesses *all* the *fruit* of the Spirit. The Holy Spirit doesn't give one person love, another person patience, another person peace, and so on. Each one of us needs all these Christian graces. We all need "love, joy, peace, patience, kindness, goodness, faithfulness, gentleness, self-control."

The fruit of the Spirit is the supreme evidence of the Spirit's indwelling presence. It is significant that the fullness of the Spirit was first granted on the Day of Pentecost, which was a Jewish agricultural festival commemorating the first-fruits of the harvest. The baptism with the Holy Spirit is a spiritual festival, producing the fruit of the Spirit in our lives. And love is the chief characteristic of the fruit, for all other graces are merely manifestations of love. Joy is the emotional expression of love. Peace is love in repose. Patience and gentleness are love in behavior. Goodness and meekness are the disposition of love. Faith is the quiet confidence of love. Temperance is love in control.

One of the greatest needs of the Church today is a new baptism of love. It is only when God's divine love is "poured into our hearts" (Rom. 5:5) that we will be able to see every man as a person for whom Christ died and as a potential child of God. Then only will we be able to "love one another earnestly from the heart" (I Peter 1:22), and will men know that we are truly Christ's disciples.

When Jesus appeared before His disciples for the third time after the Resurrection, He prepared a fire on the shore of the Tiberias Sea and served them bread and fish for supper. After the meal He spoke personally to Peter. This was the Master's final examination of this rugged fisherman, who had been a student in His walking Seminary for the previous three years. There were three questions on the exam and all three were essentially the same. "Simon, son of John, do you love me?" And the record tells us that Peter was grieved when the Lord repeated the question for the third time. For he suddenly remembered a similar scene just a few weeks previously when, warming himself at a fire, he had denied his Lord three times. He had miserably failed to take his stand for Christ, for his love was vacillating and weakened by fear of men. Now his Lord was demanding a love that was constant and complete. But there came a time in Peter's life, on the Day of Pentecost, when his love for Christ was strengthened with a moral fiber that sent him out ready to face a hostile world and willing to lay down his life in the Master's service.

Notice that every time Peter answered the Lord's question, the Lord immediately told him to take care of His lambs and sheep. In other words, our love for Christ must be expressed in service to our fellowman. Love is not a passive emotion that folds its hands and sits in quiet contemplation. Love is aggressive action, ready to roll up its sleeves and dirty its hands in ministering to needy people.

In elaborating upon His command to love our

"neighbors," Jesus gave the story of the good Samaritan. He emphasized that love does not sit on the sidelines as a spectator, wagging its head in a mild form of pity. Love is willing to get down off its position of comfort and privilege and become involved in the sufferings and struggles of needy people. The Samaritan traveler not only had compassion on the man lying in the ditch, but he got off his horse, went to the man, bound up his wounds, took him to the nearest inn, and even paid the bill! Love always expresses itself in action and in self-giving.

The Master today is giving each of us the same examination and exhortation: "Do you love me more than these? . . . [Then] Feed my sheep." He is commanding each one of us: Love God supremely and love your neighbor sincerely. But this is possible only when we have experienced a personal Pentecost in our lives and the marvelous love of God is poured into our hearts by the Holy Spirit.

We need to pray in the words of the hymn writer:

> *Teach me to love Thee as Thine angels love,*
> *One holy passion filling all my frame;*
> *The kindling of the heaven-descended Dove,*
> *My heart an altar, and Thy love the flame.*

8

Keep Walking

There are two major fallacies concerning sanctification or the Spirit-filled life. One is the idea that the fullness of the Spirit is the result of spiritual growth and therefore, a gradual process. We have already pointed out that, though there may be certain steps preparing us for the baptism with the Holy Spirit, we can never really grow or slide into the experience. There comes a time in our Christian lives when we realize our inner need for a deeper work of the Spirit, we make a full surrender of ourselves, and trust God to fill us with the Holy Spirit. This is as definite a crisis as conversion or the new birth.

However, it is just as fallacious to look upon the fullness of the Spirit as *only* a crisis, resulting in a fixed or final condition of existence, beyond which there is no room for growth. The Spirit-filled life is both a crisis and a process. After we have been sanctified by the Spirit, we still must grow in grace until we reach spiritual maturity and the full stature of Christ. Like Paul, we must constantly press on to perfection (Phil. 3:12).

The Christian life is not fixed or static. It is dynamic and progressive. What the Holy Spirit fills, He expands. He is the divine "wind," the "breath of God," filling us, and thus expanding us. We maintain the fullness by never settling down in a static level of holiness, but by continuously receiving His infilling. In the nineteenth chapter of Acts we read how Paul challenged the Ephesian disciples to receive the baptism with the Holy Spirit and how they entered into a great crisis experience (Acts 19:1-7). But later, in his Epistle to the Ephesians, he exhorts them to be continuously filled with the Spirit (Eph. 5:18). This is the force of the Greek tense he uses—the present imperative— which literally may be translated, *"Be being filled* with the Spirit." The Spirit-filled life is not like a vessel filled to the brim with water and left standing somewhere. We are to be channels of spiritual blessing to a needy world. We are as a vessel placed under a running faucet, so that the water is constantly flowing in and flowing out, while the vessel remains full at all times.

The Spirit-filled life is primarily a relationship to the Holy Spirit. As long as we maintain this intimate relationship, He will keep on cleansing and empowering us from day to day, and the fruit of the Spirit will be evident in our lives. The moment we mar this relationship, the Spirit is hindered from perfecting His work in us, and we are in spiritual danger.

How is the Spirit-filled life to be maintained? In exactly the same way that the fullness of the Spirit is received for the first time—by self-surrender and faith. The initial act must now become a perennial attitude. The crisis must become a daily walk.

ATTITUDE OF SURRENDER

Like sanctification, self-surrender is both a crisis and a process. There comes a moment when we surrender completely for the first time in our lives, but then that act of surrender must be followed by a day-by-day attitude of surrender and obedience. It's like the marriage relationship. At the altar we say one big "Yes" which determines the direction of our whole lives. "Forsaking all others, I take this woman [this man] as my wedded wife [husband], in sickness or in health, for better or for worse, till death do us part." But then, those of us who are married know that there are a lot of little yeses to say down through the years, as husband and wife relate to one another in all types of situations and trials.

There is a sense in which we have to make a new surrender from time to time. Just because we are fully surrendered to God at this moment does not mean that we will never discover new areas for surrender down the line. The light which the Holy Spirit shines into our hearts is not so much like a searchlight, suddenly turned on full power, revealing every single item in our lives that is contrary to His will. That would probably overpower and frighten us to death. The Spirit works more like a rheostat, turning up the light gradually. As it becomes brighter and brighter it exposes new areas that need to be adjusted to His will. Since we have already said the big "Yes" at the altar of surrender, we now immediately and willingly follow with another "Yes, Lord, I surrender this too." In gratitude we say, "Lord, I didn't realize this defect in my life. Thank You for showing it to me. I am ready to obey."

In India there was a village Christian who was respected for his piety and exemplary life. He was poor and illiterate, and wore only a *dhoti* (cotton wraparound), and a blanket thrown over his shoulder. But he was truly a converted man and filled with the Spirit. One year at the annual camp meeting he gave his testimony. He told how just recently he had been resting in the shade of a mango tree, meditating and praying, when an inner voice said to him, "Jettiyappa, I have something against you."

"What is it, Lord?" he asked.

"Jettiyappa, you smoke," the inner voice continued. "I could use you more effectively if you would be willing to give up this habit."

Immediately Jettiyappa responded, "Lord, I didn't realize I was displeasing You by this habit. Thank You for revealing this to me." And so saying, he threw away his bundle of country-made cigarettes and never smoked again.

In like manner, from time to time the Holy Spirit will speak to us and lead us on to new depths of surrender. If we are sincerely walking in the light, we will be sensitive to His prompting and respond quickly in obedience.

Dr. H. C. Morrison, for many years president of Asbury College, used to say that consecration is always in two bundles—the bundle of the *known* and the bundle of the *unknown*. We have to place both bundles on the altar. We surrender all that we are aware of at the present and all that is to come in the future. Thus, consecration is not like writing on a sheet of paper a list of all the things that we are turning over to God and then signing our names at the bottom. It is like signing our names at the bottom of a blank sheet, handing it over to the Lord, and saying, "Here, Lord, You fill it in. It may take You five years or fifty years, but I am ready to accept Your will at all times."

When we talk about self-surrender, we really mean a commitment of our wills to Jesus Christ. We put our willingness into His hands. But we are not actually surrendering anything concrete until we face the particular issue at hand. Psychologically speaking, it is impossible to surrender anything of which we are not aware. At the moment we can only affirm our willingness to decide in God's favor whenever we become aware of some specific issues before us. We say to God, "Lord, I renounce the right to make my choices on the basis of my own plans and desires. In every event I will always seek to know and to do Your will." But the content of that will and the practical outworking of that willingness in the daily arena of life are things we will be dealing with the rest of our lives. As each new crisis arises we will have to reaffirm our initial surrender by saying, "Lord, I choose Your will now in this particular situation."

It is right at this point that we sometimes have problems, however. As we face each specific situation, there can still be a struggle between our emotions and our wills. Feelings and desires can give us a rough time. Sometimes the battle may be severe. We may be tempted to feel that we never really made a full surrender in the first place. But the best thing to do in such circumstances is to face our feelings with complete honesty and tell God what these feelings are. Then by the help of the Holy Spirit we surrender to His will in the particular situation. We ratify, as it were, our original treaty with Him. Victory continues to be ours.

Perhaps the finest Biblical illustration of this truth is found in the life of Jesus Himself. Few, if any, of us could ever fully grasp the tremendous struggle that took place in His heart and mind as He prayed in the Garden of Gethsemane on the night of His arrest. Three times Jesus threw Himself on the ground, we are told, and prayed in desperate agony. "His sweat became like great drops of blood falling down upon the ground" (Luke 22:44). Remember that just a short while before He had said to His disciples, "Let not your hearts be troubled." And now the Gospel writer tells us that he "began to be greatly distressed and troubled" (Mark 14:33). Jesus Himself said to His disciples, "My soul is very sorrowful, even to death" (v. 34).

Why all the struggle? Hadn't Jesus from the very beginning of His life and ministry made a total surrender of Himself into the hands of the Father? Didn't He affirm over and over again, "My will is to do the will of My Father"? Is there any question about the reality and depth of His surrender? Absolutely not. But there was a terrific struggle between the emotion of the moment and His will. There was the natural human aversion to death. There was the natural shrinking from the excruciating pain and shame of the Cross. There was the horrifying realization that He was about to bear the sin of the world.

It is interesting to note that Jesus accepted His own emotions and struggles without any embarrassment. Even the Gospel writers made no attempt to hide them. But Jesus won the victory when He finally prayed, "Not my will, but thine, be done." At that moment He reconfirmed the attitude of obedience and surrender that He had maintained from the very beginning. So He "in every respect has been tempted as we are, yet without sinning" (Heb. 4:15).

Who is there among you, even the most mature child of God, that has not gone through a similar experience? We all need to be as honest about our own inner struggles as the New Testament is concerning the struggles of Jesus. Young Christians must not get the false impression that surrender is something that we do once and for all and that's the end of the matter. We can make a lifelong commitment. We can say, "I surrender all," and mean every word of it. But to put this commitment into practice, to actualize it, to make it real in concrete situations is a continuous, lifetime affair. Again and again, in each new crisis, we have to say, "Not my will, but thine, be done." But this is where the growing process takes place. We become stronger in our commitment, we become more sensitive to His leadings, as we become more mature in our spiritual lives.

In Arabia, certain horses are trained especially for the service of the king. The primary lesson is that of obedience. For example, whenever the trainer blows his whistle a certain way, the horse must learn to run toward him. The training goes on for months, and then a very interesting test is given. For several days the horses are deprived of water, until they become frantic with thirst and pace excitedly around the fenced-in area. Then suddenly the gate leading to the pond is opened, and the horses rush toward the water to quench their thirst. But just as they are about to drink, the trainer blows his whistle. The horses instinctively stop where they are. A tremendous struggle goes on within them. There is the maddening desire to stoop and drink, but their wills have been trained to obey the sound of the whistle. Those horses which turn away from the water at this critical moment and run back to the trainer are the only ones considered fit for the service of the king. In like manner, those children of God who have learned to be sensitive to the leadings of the Spirit and to obey the will of the Father at all times are the only ones fit for the service of the King of kings.

ATTITUDE OF FAITH

We receive the fullness of the Holy Spirit by faith. We realize it is God's desire to fill us with the Spirit, so we take Him at His word and let our whole weight down upon His promises. We reach out the hand of faith and accept the gift. This is a definite act of the will, resulting in a crisis experience. But from then on we must maintain this attitude of faith from day to day. So faith, like surrender, is a process as well as a crisis. It is a constant attitude as well as a definite act. It is a disposition of the mind as well as a decision of the will.

The temptation will arise to doubt the validity of our experience. This is especially true if we permit our faith to be influenced by our emotions. Our feelings often fluctuate. They vary according to daily circumstances, our temperaments and moods, and even the weather. They are, consequently, a very shaky foundation for our faith.

Suppose one day the weather is bad, everything seems to go wrong, and, on top of it all, I am afflicted with a severe migraine headache. I say to myself, I don't feel very good today. I don't think I'm married anymore. Ridiculous, you say. You're right. What has the fact of my married status to do with the way I feel at any given moment? But is this any more foolish than saying to myself on a cold, rainy day, when everything seems to be adverse, "I don't think I'm filled with the Spirit today"?

Rev. John Thomas, the Welsh evangelist, delighted in telling this quaint, homespun parable. Three men were sitting on a wall—Fact, Faith, and Feeling. Feeling slipped and fell and pulled Faith down with him. But Fact remained steadfast; nothing could shake him.

In time he reached down and pulled up Faith, who in turn helped Feeling to climb back up.

The interpretation of the parable is this. If we allow our faith to depend on our feelings, then as our feelings go down, faith will also be dragged down. But if we make our faith depend upon fact, upon the truth of God's Word, then nothing can shake it. In fact, the tendency is to help stabilize our feelings as well. The promises of God are the only safe foundation for our faith.

There will also be the temptation to allow our faith to depend on outer manifestations and signs. We may be led to believe that because we do not possess a particular gift of the Spirit therefore we do not possess the Holy Spirit Himself. But as we have already pointed out, there are various spiritual gifts and the Holy Spirit reserves the right to distribute them according to His will. Each one of us does not receive all the gifts, nor do we all receive the same gift. We cannot dictate to the Holy Spirit how He will manifest Himself in our lives. That is His prerogative. We should each one receive in gratitude the gift that He offers us, and then unitedly use all these gifts for the edification of the Church and the salvation of sinners.

When I was pastor of an urban, English-speaking church in south India, there were several elderly shut-ins who were members of the congregation. It was my custom to visit them in their homes, read a portion of Scripture, and pray. Many times I took my accordion along and sang one of the old familiar hymns of the Church. But there were times when it was inconvenient to take my accordion, so I didn't play and sing. Now it would have been ridiculous for one of the shut-ins to say, "Mr. Seamands didn't come to my home today, because he didn't bring his accordion and sing." The important thing was my presence in the home, not that I played an instrument and sang a hymn. In the same way, the manner in which the Holy Spirit manifests Himself is not as important as the basic fact of the reality of His presence in our lives.

Sometimes Christians are prone to doubt simply because they feel the tug of temptation in their lives. They fail to distinguish between temptation and sin, and think that, because they are tempted, therefore they have sinned. But temptation itself is not sin. It is only yielding to temptation that produces sin. If temptation itself were sin, then we would be forced to acknowledge that Jesus Himself sinned, for He was often sorely tempted. But the Word tells us that He was in every respect tempted as we are, yet *He did not sin* (Heb. 4:15). We will never reach the stage in this life where we will be immune from temptation. As long as we are in this world we shall be tempted and tried. Even the greatest of saints have their temptations.

The important question is, How do we face temptation? What do we do, for example, when feelings of jealousy or resentment begin to arise? Do we harbor them in our hearts and allow them to develop, or do we immediately plead for cleansing and find victory over them? What do we do when lustful thoughts creep into our minds through the eye-gate, as we suddenly view a sensual billboard along the highway, or a sexy advertisement on television? Do we allow them to lodge in our minds and begin to meditate and enlarge upon them? Or by the aid of the Holy Spirit do we immediately cast these thoughts out of our minds? We are not responsible for such thoughts entering our minds from the outside, but we are responsible for receiving them and making them our own. As Martin Luther used to say, "We cannot prevent the birds from flying overhead, but we can certainly prevent them from building a nest in our hair."

There may be an occasion when some temptation catches us off guard and gets the best of us. Does this mean that we have completely lost our relationship to Christ or the presence of the Holy Spirit? Should we give up our faith and deny our whole Christian experience? No. The Holy Spirit is not like a policeman peeking around the corner to catch us in some violation of divine law. He doesn't walk off and leave us at the least deviation from His will. Jesus said that the Holy Spirit comes to abide forever (John 14:16). He comes, not as a transient guest, but as a permanent Resident.

It is the Spirit's intention to stay. Whenever we slip from the path or grieve Him in any way, He instantly checks us and convicts us of our sin. Our immediate response should be that of penitence and obedience. If we have wronged someone, we ought to seek reconciliation and restore the relationship as quickly as possible. If we have been unwittingly caught in a transgression, we should confess our sin immediately and ask His forgiveness. Then we shall find Him "faithful and just to forgive us our sins, and to cleanse us from all unrighteousness" (I John 1:9, KJV). Our relationship to God will remain intact.

However, if our sin is a calculated, premeditated one, we grieve the Spirit out of our lives. If we neglect the repeated promptings of the Spirit and allow some barrier to persist between us and our fellowmen or between us and God, then in time we will crowd out the Spirit. His presence will not longer be ours.

The sanctified life is not a state of sinless perfection. We never arrive at a stage where it is impossible to sin. In his magnificent First Epistle, the Apostle John, after declaring unequivocally that "the blood of Jesus his Son cleanses us from all sin," and after clearly exhorting us to refrain from sin, then goes on to say, "But if any one does sin, we have an advocate with the Father, Jesus Christ the righteous" (I John 1:5—2:2). In other words, John implies that even after sanctification it is possible to sin. In such cases, he assures us, Jesus stands ever ready as our Advocate to plead our cause.

However, we must never use this provision as an easy excuse for sin, or for rationalizing questionable conduct. This is an emergency arrangement, not a license for promiscuous living. We don't keep a spare tire in the trunk of the car just so that we may have a puncture. We keep it there just in case we do have a puncture or blowout. We hope we will never need the spare tire, but we feel safe with it on hand. Likewise, God has provided a way of escape for His children who go astray. This is our constant comfort and assurance. But His intention is for us to remain always in the way. The norm is victory, not defeat.

Thus by maintaining an attitude of surrender and obedience, and by keeping our faith grounded on God's Word, we can walk constantly in the Spirit and know the joy and power of His presence. Each day becomes more glorious and meaningful as we continue our earthly pilgrimage with Him.

9

Is This the Answer?

Is Pentecost restricted to dark cloisters and ivory towers or is it related to the marketplace, the campus, the home, the major issues of life? Is it real? Is it relevant? Is it revolutionary?

We need not theorize about the matter. God Himself has given us the answer to these questions in the manifestations of His presence and power on numerous occasions of revival and spiritual renewal. The most recent of such outpourings was the visitation of the Spirit upon the campus of Asbury College, which subsequently spread to hundreds of college campuses and churches across the nation. God spoke clearly and decisively.

I shall long remember that eventful day of February 3, 1970, when God manifested himself in great power. My wife and I were having lunch when suddenly our daughter, Sandy, burst into the room. "You simply wouldn't *believe* what's happening at the college," she exclaimed excitedly, as she flung her coat on a chair. "I want to eat lunch in a hurry and go back. I can't stay away!"

"What is happening?" we asked. "You're half an hour late."

My wife and I listened eagerly as Sandy, a sophomore in the college, told the story. That morning the student body had filed into Hughes Auditorium for the regular 10 a.m. chapel service. Instead of the usual song, prayer, and sermon, the period was given over to voluntary testimonies. Anyone who so desired could stand and relate to his college mates what God was doing in his life. As several students witnessed to fresh, personal encounters with Jesus Christ, others began to recognize the spiritual needs in their own lives. An unusual awareness of the Spirit's presence prevailed throughout the entire auditorium.

It soon became evident that the service was an extraordinary one. Fifteen minutes before the end of the chapel period, one of the professors walked up onto the platform and expressed a feeling that opportunity should be given for prayer at the altar. Immediately a number of students responded; soon others followed. By now the atmosphere was electrified. There was a spirit of expectancy in the air.

As the students found spiritual victory at the altar, many of them went up to the pulpit and used the microphone to express their praise to God for His forgiveness and grace. Some made open confession of their sin and hypocrisy; others confessed hidden feelings of resentment and hostility; still others expressed their new-felt joy through song. Here and there throughout the auditorium there were tender scenes of reconciliation as old enmities were melted away by the fervent love of God.

What began as a routine chapel service on that February morning turned out to be the longest and perhaps the most significant chapel service in the eighty-year history of Asbury College. It ended exactly one week later. Meanwhile all classes were cancelled, and Hughes Auditorium continued to be the center of activity. By the second morning the revival had crossed the street to its sister institution, Asbury Theological Seminary. Townspeople from Wilmore were starting to attend, and visitors from other states were beginning to arrive. During the hours of daylight as many as twelve hundred persons gathered in the auditorium; during the night hours there were never less, than fifty to seventy-five people present. On Sunday the attendance grew to fifteen hundred. All during these days there was no preaching—only praying at the altar, singing, and witnessing.

Soon news of the "marathon revival" began to spread throughout Kentucky and across the nation. The *Lexington Leader* and *Louisville Times* both carried front-page reports with pictures. Station WLEX of Lexington ran a three-minute film clip on the revival during its evening telecast. Newsman Bill Thompson introduced the report by commenting that nothing in his thirty-four years of newscasting had impressed him as much as the Asbury story. Later on, leading newspapers like the *Indianapolis Star, Chicago Tribune,* and *St. Louis Post-Dispatch* also carried editorials and reports on the movement.

As a result of all this publicity, hundreds of pastors and numerous college officials began to phone in requesting student-teams to come and share the story with their congregations and student bodies. Every Saturday for the next several weeks, a large procession of cars left Wilmore, headed for all points of the compass. Many students traveled by air to distant assignments. By the end of May, approximately fifteen hundred witness teams had gone out on missions from Asbury College alone, not to mention numerous teams from Asbury Theological Seminary. They ministered on almost 140 college campuses and held services in several thousand churches in practically every state of the Union and even in Canada. Two seminary couples traveled to Colombia, South America, during the spring vacation, and witnessed to missionaries and national church leaders in twenty-five different gatherings.

In a few instances, the students' testimonies sparked an unusual, spontaneous revival that lasted for days and influenced the entire community. In the Meridian Street Church of God at Anderson, Indiana, revival services continued every night for fifty days. People from all over the city filled the sanctuary nightly. In South Pittsburg, Tennessee, revival broke out among the students of the local high school. It was estimated that perhaps five hundred out of the entire student body of seven hundred made commitments to Jesus Christ.

As one looks back over the events which followed that initial outpouring at Asbury, one thing stands out clearly. That is the "given-ness" of revival movement. Though there are evidences of certain human factors that prepared the soil for revival, namely, the spirit of prayer and expectant faith in the hearts of a concerned nucleus of Christian young people, this revival was definitely not the result of human manipulation. It was a "divine happening." God acted sovereignly and graciously. Most of us were taken by surprise. Even outside visitors and secular newsmen who came to observe the event said in awe, "This is God's doing!"

What was God's purpose in all this? Was He trying to say something to us as a people?

I believe there is something significant about the timing of this revival. The decade of the sixties was an explosive decade. It was a period of violence, with strikes, demonstrations, riots, burnings, and assassinations. It was a sordid decade, obsessed with the bizarre and unseemly, when "situation ethics" and free love held sway. It was a period of racial animosity, characterized by white prejudice and black power. The close of the decade left us exhausted, frustrated, and despondent. Was there any hope for the future?

Then suddenly, at the dawning of the seventies, God stepped into the picture. He visited His people. He demonstrated His power. He poured out His love. True, He manifested Himself only to isolated portions of the country, but is not God trying to press home a point to the entire nation? Is He not trying to tell us that we have tried every way but the right way—that He has a way to lead us out of our mess? I have a strange feeling that He is.

It is breathtaking to analyze the characteristics of this God-given movement.

A YOUTH REVIVAL

Many of the young people of our land are in trouble. They have given themselves to demonstrations and violence, to booze and pot, to crime and sex. For them life has no meaning, the future no hope. Then suddenly God became real to a group of college young people. They found a new purpose in life, a new joy in living. Fired with enthusiasm, they committed themselves to a cause far beyond their own resources.

I heard a student in Indiana say to a large congregation, "It's really groovy to be high on the Lord, to be tanked up with the Holy Spirit. It's great, man, it's great!"

Several young people who had become enslaved by drugs and pills found glorious deliverance through the power of the Holy Spirit. One twenty-year-old student from Miami, Florida, said to a news reporter of the *Louisville Courier-Journal,* "I had taken trips on everything before coming here; drugs, sex, booze, gambling—everything. I was smoking joints [marijuana] like they were going out of style. Now I don't need to get 'high' on drugs or booze. With drugs you get 'high' and then come down hard. With Christ, I'm going to try to stay on an even keel and try to get all my friends to do the same."

A high school senior in Tennessee said to the entire student body gathered in their assembly: "I've finally found what I've been looking for all this time; not in all this other stuff—sex and booze and drugs—but in Christ."

Through the revival was not God trying to teach us that in the power of His Spirit He has the answer to youth's problems of today?

AN ETHICAL REVIVAL

During the past decade we witnessed an appalling

moral sag in our nation, a decline in basic integrity and in common decency. We heard much about the "credibility gap" and "situation ethics." The double standard was in vogue; divorce reached an all-time mark.

The recent revival produced a renewal of Christian ethics. Students confessed to turning in false reading reports. Some husbands confessed to cheating on their wives. Several employees made restitution for stolen articles. I heard one young man say as he arose from the altar, "This commitment is going to cost me several hundred dollars. I must set things right." The editor of a newspaper in an Indiana city told the congregation that he would no longer accept advertisements for X-rated movies. A man who was running a liquor store in Tennessee quit the business. A couple who had operated a strip-tease nightclub in San Antonio, Texas, for seventeen years closed down the "joint" and placed over the front door this sign: "Closed forever. We have decided to follow Jesus. See you in church Sunday."

A certain congregation will probably never forget the confession of a man in his mid-fifties who stood before the microphone and said, "I have been an active church member for years. I have directed many summer youth camps but I've been a phony." Then he went on to relate how in the new reorganization of schools in the city he had been so hostile to certain members of the school board that out of spite he had placed dead skunks in their mailboxes and smeared red paint on their driveways. When the Holy Spirit convicted him of his meanness, he went to each one of the homes and confessed that he was the culprit. In the first home the elderly couple broke down and wept. In the second home the husband said angrily, "I threatened to shoot the man if I ever found him out. I feel like shooting you now." Later he mellowed and expressed admiration for the man's courage in confessing.

The answer to our moral problem is found in the

holiness of God and the transforming power of Jesus Christ.

A Revival of the Church

The Church has been the target of much criticism in recent years. It has been called "irrelevant," "out-of-date," "out of touch," "a dead organization," "a social club with an ivory-tower mentality," and so on. Much of the criticism is justified. The Church, in many places, is indeed lifeless and impotent.

But as hundreds of young people from many college campuses went out to share their faith with the people, dozens of churches across the country suddenly became alive. These students were talking about a personal encounter with God, how God had delivered them from their "hang-ups" and "turned them on." Their witness had the ring of reality.

Pastors and people responded. The sermon and order of service were pushed aside for the moment. Many church members, tired of pretending for so long, took off their masks and exposed their hypocrisy and phoniness. Broken in spirit, they confessed, prayed, and shared together. Church altars which for years had been nothing more than pieces of furniture now became hallowed places where men met God and brother was reconciled to brother. The usual stiffness and formality gave way to a new freedom in the Spirit. People forgot about the clock and food. They sat for hours in the sanctuary, basking in the presence of God.

An elderly lady in a large church in Atlanta stood, and lifting her hands in the air, prayed, "Lord, thank You for saving us from the sin of sophistication." The pastor of a leading church of another denomination in the same city cried out in prayer, "O God, You have done more in one moment than we have done in five years." A businessman, on seeing the Spirit at work and sensing the new feeling of Christian fellowship, said excitedly, "This is the New Testament Church!"

Talk about an ecumenical movement! This was it!

The revival cut across all denominational barriers. It spread to "old line" churches steeped in formalism, to evangelical churches whose altars had grown cold. Witnessing knew no bounds of creed. Denominational labels were incidental. The pastor of a church in Robinson, Illinois, testified that he saw Presbyterians, Episcopalians, and United Methodists all kneeling together at the altar. Businessmen of several denominations met together each noon for a time of prayer and sharing in the city hall during the revival movement in Anderson, Indiana. Everywhere the revival reached, there was a marvelous sense of unity in the Spirit.

Is not God demonstrating to us these days that the Church is still the body of Christ, that it can be gloriously renewed by His Spirit, and that it can once again be an instrument of redemption and reconciliation in the world? Is He not trying to teach us that, without the vitality and purity of the Church, organic unity by itself is inadequate?

A REVIVAL OF MISSION

In recent years there has been a perceptible sag in the missionary outreach of the American church. Many theologians are questioning our right to evangelize and convert the followers of other religions. Many congregations are wondering if the day of foreign missions is past. Fewer young people are offering themselves for service abroad.

The Asbury revival was a remarkable demonstration of the words of Jesus, "You shall receive power when the Holy Spirit has come upon you; and you shall be my witness. . . ." As students received a new touch of the Spirit, they felt impelled to share their newfound joy with others. They began phoning their families, friends, and pastors to tell them the "good news."

A call went out to Newsman Paul Harvey, Senator Mark Hatfield, and a close aide of President Nixon. One girl phoned Madalyn Murray O'Hair, perhaps the nation's best-known atheist, and witnessed to her about God's love and power.

The Holy Spirit could not be contained within the city limits of tiny Wilmore. Soon students and faculty members were fanning out across many states to carry the torch of revival. Many who were previously shy and self-conscious, afraid to speak in public, broke through to new confidence and freedom in the Spirit, and boldly testified to the redemptive power of the risen Lord. One college student flew to Azusa College in California, another to Seattle Pacific College in Washington State. A team went to Oral Roberts University in Tulsa, Oklahoma. Others went to college campuses, home churches, and gatherings in many of the eastern states. One group crossed over into Canada.

In each place they witnessed there was the same response—confession, prayer, testimony, singing, reconciliation. Then, in turn, these groups started going out to surrounding cities to share their newfound victory and joy. Meridian Street Church in Anderson, Indiana, alone sent out witness teams to thirty-one states and to Canada. As a result, thousands upon thousands of people made new commitments to Jesus Christ.

A student from Azusa College in California called on the Sirhan home in the Los Angeles area and for an hour and a half shared with the mother and brother of Robert Kennedy's assassin his witness of the love of Christ.

An Asbury Seminary student went to the Fulton County jail in Atlanta and preached to the prisoners. Out of the ninety-seven men who voluntarily gathered in the chapel, eighty responded to the challenge to accept Christ as personal Savior.

When two student pastors related the story of the revival in a large church in Atlanta, there was a great response from the congregation and many came to the altar for prayer. Three young men received a call to missionary service. When one of the men went home and told his wife about the call, she was quite upset. She said, "Honey, this is one time you'll have to go it alone. I'm not one of God's children and don't intend to be a minister's wife." However, she accompanied her husband to the evening service, and when the invitation was given, she went forward and surrendered herself to Christ. She then went to the microphone, confessed what she had said to her husband in the morning, and went on to say, "Now I am a child of God and I'm on the team with my husband."

I was present at the chapel service in Asbury College on the morning of March 7. The missionary dimension of the revival was much in evidence. President Kinlaw told of receiving a letter from Colombia, South America, asking for some college students to come down during the summer and hold meetings among the youth. "I don't know where the money will come from," he remarked, "but it will have to come from this side."

A seminary professor called from the balcony, "I would like the privilege of giving the first $100." Then a professor from the college made a pledge of $250. A student walked to the platform and told how his witness team had received an offering of $200 the previous weekend. "Our group would like the amount to go to this missionary project," he said. An attractive coed stood up and said, "Here's a $10.00 bill I was planning to spend on a new skirt this afternoon." Then someone suggested an offering basket be placed on the platform. Before the chapel service ended, over $1,000 had been collected for the mission. Later the total increased to over $2,000. As a result, a group of college students went down to Colombia that summer, ministering in the name of Christ.

God's cure for the missionary slump in American churches is a fresh outpouring of the Holy Spirit upon the people of God. He alone is the Originator and Promoter of Christian missions.

A REVIVAL OF LOVE

How much bitterness, hatred, and violence we witnessed in the decade of the sixties, between "doves" and "hawks," blacks and whites, student body and administration, labor and management! It was the decade of the clenched fist and sharp tongue.

The secular newspaper spoke of the Asbury revival as a great "love-in." They were right. God gave His people a new baptism of love. Resentments were exposed, jealousies cleansed; hostilities melted away. As people were reconciled to God, they were reconciled to their fellowman. It was a common sight to see someone stand in the congregation, call out the name of a person seated there, ask forgiveness, and then to see the two meet in the aisle and embrace. Often husbands and wives, holding hands, walked down the aisle and knelt together at the altar, or stood behind the pulpit, with arms around each other, and spoke of their newfound love for God and for one another. I saw a most beautiful sight when I peeked into the seminary chapel late one afternoon. The pews were empty, but the altar was filled with young married couples kneeling together in prayer and jointly making new commitments to God.

This was no sentimental emotion or momentary effervesence. This was the love of God "poured into our hearts through the Holy Spirit." In church after church the atmosphere was charged with love.

When an African student who is studying at Asbury College went to a church in Ohio to tell the story of the revival and give his personal testimony, spontaneously several members of the congregation stepped forward and put their arms around him as an expression of their love. Kneeling beside a businessman in an Indiana church, I heard him pray through tears, "Lord, I thank You for making it possible for me to love the colored folk and many people who were so obnoxious to me before. Now I feel I can love everybody."

When revival broke out in South Pittsburg, Tennessee, the small sanctuary of the church where the meetings were being held soon became inadequate for the overflow crowds. Someone suggested they move the services to a a large church which was located in the same block. But this posed a problem. Many Negro students were attending the services each evening, and so far the congregation of this big church had not opened its doors to the blacks. But God's Spirit broke down all barriers. The minister very graciously offered his church for the rest of the week and announced over the radio that there would be perfect freedom for all to attend. He even contacted three of the leading Negro citizens in town and made it clear that the blacks were welcome.

It was this atmosphere of love that helped to bridge the "generation gap" also. New lines of communication were opened up between parent and child, between adult and teen-ager. The revival started with the youth and then spread to the adults. Both age-groups listened to and got through to each other. Teen-agers felt they could trust those over thirty; the elderly felt they could learn something from the adolescent. Age no longer seemed a barrier. People forgot who was old and who was young. One moment a youth in his twenties would be sharing his testimony at the microphone; the next, a gray-haired old man; followed by a schoolgirl in her early teens. In a large rally in Anderson, Indiana, where two thousand people were present, a hippie with full beard and shoulder-length hair received Christ as his Saviour and gave a witness before the whole congregation. An eighty-year-old grandmother, with snow-white hair done up in a bun, went forward and hugged him!

God is trying to teach us that the only answer to our racial strife, the generation gap, and our national divisions is His divine love operating within us. He is offering to us the gift of His Spirit, the only One who can make us on tiptoe with love.

"The premise here is that an unknown but highly advanced group of beings have used their formidable scientific abilities to resurrect every human being who ever lived, on the shores of a multi-million mile long river. . . . The plot involves the quest of Sir Richard Burton and assorted others, ranging from a Neanderthal man Kazz to Hermann Goring, to find the source of the river and the base of the secret masters of the Riverworld. This odyssey format is perfect . . . Philip José Farmer is something special."

LUNA Monthly

TO YOUR SCATTERED BODIES GO

PHILIP JOSÉ FARMER

BERKLEY BOOKS, NEW YORK

This Berkley book contains the complete
text of the original hardcover edition.
It has been completely reset in a typeface
designed for easy reading, and was printed
from new film.

TO YOUR SCATTERED
BODIES GO

A Berkley Book / published by arrangement with
G. P. Putnam's Sons

PRINTING HISTORY
G. P. Putnam's Sons edition published 1971
Berkley Medallion edition / September 1971
Twenty-fourth printing / October 1983
Twenty-fifth printing / March 1984
Twenty-sixth printing / January 1985
Twenty-seventh printing / June 1985

ISBN: 0-425-08198-2

A BERKLEY BOOK TM ® 757,375
Berkley Books are published by The Berkley Publishing Group,
200 Madison Avenue, New York, New York 10016.
The name "BERKLEY" and the stylized "B" with design
are trademarks belonging to Berkley Publishing Corporation.

PRINTED IN THE UNITED STATES OF AMERICA

His wife had held him in her arms as if she could keep death away from him.

He had cried out, "My God, I am a dead man!"

The door to the room had opened, and he had seen a giant, black, one-humped camel outside and had heard the tinkle of the bells on its harness as the hot desert wind touched them. Then a huge black face topped by a great black turban had appeared in the doorway. The black eunuch had come in through the door, moving like a cloud, with a gigantic scimitar in his hand. Death, the Destroyer of Delights and the Sunderer of Society, had arrived at last.

Blackness. Nothingness. He did not even know that his heart had given out forever. Nothingness.

Then his eyes opened. His heart was beating strongly. He was strong, very strong! All the pain of the gout in his feet, the agony in his liver, the torture in his heart, all were gone.

It was so quiet he could hear the blood moving in his head. He was alone in a world of soundlessness.

A bright light of equal intensity was everywhere. He could see, yet he did not understand what he was seeing. What were these things above, beside, below him? Where was he?

He tried to sit up and felt, numbly, a panic. There was nothing to sit up upon because he was hanging in nothingness. The attempt sent him forward and over, very slowly, as if he were in a bath of thin treacle. A foot from his fingertips was a rod of bright red metal. The rod came from above, from infinity, and went on down to infinity. He tried to grasp it because it was the nearest solid object but something invisible was resisting him. It was as if lines of some force were pushing against him, repelling him.

Slowly, he turned over in a somersault. Then the resistance halted him with his fingertips about six inches from the rod. He straightened his body out and moved forward a fraction of an inch. At the same time, his body began to rotate on its longitudinal axis. He sucked in air with a loud sawing noise. Though he knew no hold existed for him, he could not help flailing his arms in panic to try to seize onto something.

Now he was face "down," or was it "up"? Whatever the direction, it was opposite to that toward which he had been looking when he had awakened. Not that this mattered. "Above" him and "below" him the view was the same. He was suspended in space, kept from falling by an invisible and unfelt cocoon. Six feet "below" him was the body of a woman with a very pale skin. She was naked and completely hairless. She seemed to be asleep. Her eyes were closed, and her breasts rose and fell gently. Her legs were together and straight out, and her arms were by her side. She turned slowly like a chicken on a spit.

The same force that was rotating her was also rotating him. He spun slowly away from her, saw other naked and hairless bodies, men, women, and children, opposite him in silent spinning rows. Above him was the rotating naked and hairless body of a Negro.

He lowered his head so that he could see along his own body. He was naked and hairless, too. His skin was smooth, and the muscles of his belly were ridged, and his thighs were packed with strong young muscles. The veins that had stood out like blue mole-ridges were gone. He no longer had the body of the enfeebled and sick sixty-nine-year-old man who had been dying only a moment ago. And the hundred or so scars were gone.

He realized then that there were no old men or women among the bodies surrounding him. All seemed to be about twenty-five years old, though it was difficult to determine the exact age, since the hairless heads and pubes made them seem older and younger at the same time.

He had boasted that he knew no fear. Now fear ripped

6

away the cry forming in his throat. His fear pressed down on him and squeezed the new life from him.

He had been stunned at first because he was still living. Then his position in space and the arrangement of his new environment had frozen his senses. He was seeing and feeling through a thick semiopaque window. After a few seconds, something snapped inside him. He could almost hear it, as if a window had suddenly been raised.

The world took a shape which he could grasp, though he could not comprehend it. Above him, on both sides, below him, as far as he could see, bodies floated. They were arranged in vertical and horizontal rows. The up-and-down ranks were separated by red rods, slender as broomsticks, one of which was twelve inches from the feet of the sleepers and the other twelve inches from their heads. Each body was spaced about six feet from the body above and below and on each side.

The rods came up from an abyss without bottom and soared into an abyss without ceiling. That grayness into which the rods and the bodies, up and down, right and left, disappeared was neither the sky nor the earth. There was nothing in the distance except the lackluster of infinity.

On one side was a dark man with Tuscan features. On his other side was an Asiatic Indian and beyond her a large Nordic-looking man. Not until the third revolution was he able to determine what was so odd about the man. The right arm, from a point just below the elbow, was red. It seemed to lack the outer layer of skin.

A few seconds later, several rows away, he saw a male adult body lacking the skin and all the muscles of the face.

There were other bodies that were not quite complete. Far away, glimpsed unclearly, was a skeleton and a jumble of organs inside it.

He continued turning and observing while his heart slammed against his chest with terror. By then he understood that he was in some colossal chamber and that the metal rods were radiating some force that somehow supported and revolved millions—maybe billions—of human beings.

7

Where was this place?

Certainly, it was not the city of Trieste of the Austro-Hungarian Empire of 1890.

It was like no hell or heaven of which he had ever heard or read, and he had thought that he was acquainted with every theory of the afterlife.

He had died. Now he was alive. He had scoffed all his life at a life-after-death. For once, he could not deny that he had been wrong. But there was no one present to say, "I told you so, you damned infidel!"

Of all the millions, he alone was awake.

As he turned at an estimated rate of one complete revolution per ten seconds, he saw something else that caused him to gasp with amazement. Five rows away was a body that seemed, at first glance, to be human. But no member of *Homo sapiens* had three fingers and a thumb on each hand and four toes on each foot. Nor a nose and thin black leathery lips like a dog's. Nor a scrotum with many small knobs. Nor ears with such strange convolutions.

Terror faded away. His heart quit beating so swiftly, though it did not return to normal. His brain unfroze. He must get out of this situation where he was as helpless as a hog on a turnspit. He would get to somebody who could tell him what he was doing here, how he had come here, why he was here.

To decide was to act.

He drew up his legs and kicked and found that the action, the reaction, rather, drove him forward a half-inch. Again, he kicked and moved against the resistance. But, as he paused, he was slowly moved back toward his original location. And his legs and arms were gently pushed toward their original rigid position.

In a frenzy, kicking his legs and moving his arms in a swimmer's breast stroke, he managed to fight toward the rod. The closer he got to it, the stronger the web of force became. He did not give up. If he did, he would be back where he had been and without enough strength to begin fighting again. It was not his nature to give up until all his strength had been expended.

He was breathing hoarsely, his body was coated with sweat, his arms and legs moved as if in a thick jelly, and his progress was imperceptible. Then, the fingertips of his left hand touched the rod. It felt warm and hard.

Suddenly, he knew which way was "down." He fell.

The touch had broken the spell. The webs of air around him snapped soundlessly, and he was plunging.

He was close enough to the rod to seize it with one hand. The sudden checking of his fall brought his hip up against the rod with a painful impact. The skin of his hand burned as he slid down the rod, and then his other hand clutched the rod, and he had stopped.

In front of him, on the other side of the rod, the bodies had started to fall. They descended with the velocity of a falling body on Earth, and each maintained its stretched-out position and the original distance between the body above and below. They even continued to revolve.

It was then that the puffs of air on his naked sweating back made him twist around on the rod. Behind him, in the vertical row of bodies that he had just occupied, the sleepers were also falling. One after the other, as if methodically dropped through a trapdoor, spinning slowly, they hurtled by him. Their heads missed him by a few inches. He was fortunate not to have been knocked off the rod and sent plunging into the abyss along with them.

In stately procession, they fell. Body after body shooting down on both sides of the rod, while the other rows of millions upon millions slept on.

For a while, he stared. Then he began counting bodies; he had always been a devoted enumerator. But when he had counted 3,001, he quit. After that he gazed at the cataract of flesh. How far up, how immeasurably far up, were they stacked? And how far down could they fall? Unwittingly, he had precipitated them when his touch had disrupted the force emanating from the rod.

He could not climb up the rod, but he could climb down it. He began to let himself down, and then he looked upward and he forgot about the bodies hurtling by him. Somewhere overhead, a humming was overriding the whooshing sound of the falling bodies.

A narrow craft, of some bright green substance and shaped like a canoe, was sinking between the column of the fallers and the neighboring column of suspended. The aerial canoe had no visible means of support, he thought, and it was a measure of his terror that he did not even think about his pun. No visible means of support. Like a magical vessel out of *The Thousand and One Nights*.

A face appeared over the edge of the vessel. The craft stopped, and the humming noise ceased. Another face was by the first. Both had long, dark and straight hair. Presently, the faces withdrew, the humming was renewed, and the canoe again descended toward him. When it was about five feet above him, it halted. There was a single small symbol on the green bow: a white spiral that exploded to the right. One of the canoe's occupants spoke in a language with many vowels and a distinct and frequently recurring glottal stop. It sounded like Polynesian.

Abruptly, the invisible cocoon around him reasserted itself. The falling bodies began to slow in their rate of descent and then stopped. The man on the rod felt the retaining force close in on him and lift him up. Though he clung desperately to the rod, his legs were moved up and then away and his body followed it. Soon he was looking downward. His hands were torn loose; he felt as if his grip on life, on sanity, on the world, had also been torn away. He began to drift upward and to revolve. He went by the aerial canoe and rose above it. The two men in the canoe were naked, dark-skinned as Yemenite Arabs, and handsome. Their features were Nordic, resembling those of some Icelanders he had known.

One of them lifted a hand which held a pencil-sized metal object. The man sighted along it as if he were going to shoot something from it.

The man floating in the air shouted with rage and hate and frustration and flailed his arms to swim toward the machine.

"I'll kill!" he screamed. "Kill! Kill!"

Oblivion came again.

10

*God was standing over him as he lay on the grass by the
waters and the weeping willows. He lay wide-eyed and as
weak as a baby just born. God was poking him in the ribs
with the end of an iron cane. God was a tall man of
middle age. He had a long black forked beard, and He was
wearing the Sunday best of an English gentleman of the
53rd year of Queen Victoria's reign.*

*"You're late," God said. "Long past due for the pay-
ment of your debt, you know."*

*"What debt?" Richard Francis Burton said. He passed
his fingertips over his ribs to make sure that all were still
there.*

*"You owe for the flesh," replied God, poking him again
with the cane. "Not to mention the spirit. You owe for the
flesh and the spirit, which are one and the same thing."*

*Burton struggled to get up onto his feet. Nobody, not
even God, was going to punch Richard Burton in the ribs
and get away without a battle.*

*God, ignoring the futile efforts, pulled a large gold
watch from His vest pocket, unsnapped its heavy
enscrolled gold lid, looked at the hands, and said, "Long
past due."*

God held out His other hand, its palm turned up.

"Pay up, sir. Otherwise, I'll be forced to foreclose."

"Foreclose on what?"

*Darkness fell. God began to dissolve into the darkness.
It was then that Burton saw that God resembled himself.
He had the same black straight hair, the same Arabic face
with the dark stabbing eyes, high cheekbones, heavy lips,
and the thrust-out, deeply cleft chin. The same long deep
scars, witnesses of the Somali javelin which pierced his*

jaws in that fight at Berbera, were on His cheeks. His hands and feet were small, contrasting with His broad shoulders and massive chest. And He had the long thick moustachios and the long forked beard that had caused the Bedouin to name Burton "the Father of Moustachios."

"You look like the Devil," Burton said, but God had become just another shadow in the darkness.

3

Burton was still sleeping, but he was so close to the surface of consciousness that he was aware that he had been dreaming. Light was replacing the night.

Then his eyes did open. And he did not know where he was.

A blue sky was above. A gentle breeze flowed over his naked body. His hairless head and his back and legs and the palms of his hands were against grass. He turned his head to the right and saw a plain covered with very short, very green, very thick grass. The plain sloped gently upward for a mile. Beyond the plain was a range of hills that started out mildly, then became steeper and higher and very irregular in shape as they climbed toward the mountains. The hills seemed to run for about two and a half miles. All were covered with trees, some of which blazed with scarlets, azures, bright greens, flaming yellows, and deep pinks. The mountains beyond the hills rose suddenly, perpendicularly, and unbelievably high. They were black and bluish-green, looking like a glassy igneous rock with huge splotches of lichen covering at least a quarter of the surface.

Between him and the hills were many human bodies. The closest one, only a few feet away, was that of the white woman who had been below him in that vertical row.

He wanted to rise up, but he was sluggish and numb. All he could do for the moment, and that required a strong effort, was to turn his head to the left. There were more naked bodies there on a plain that sloped down to a river perhaps 100 yards away. The river was about a mile wide, and on its other side was another plain, probably about a mile broad and sloping upward to foothills covered with more of the trees and then the towering precipitous black and bluish-green mountains. That was the east, he thought frozenly. The sun had just risen over the top of the mountain there.

Almost by the river's edge was a strange structure. It was a gray red-flecked granite and was shaped like a mushroom. Its broad base could not be more than five feet high, and the mushroom top had a diameter of about fifty feet.

He managed to rise far enough to support himself on one elbow.

There were more mushroom-shaped granites along both sides of the river.

Everywhere on the plain were unclothed bald-headed human beings, spaced about six feet apart. Most were still on their backs and gazing into the sky. Others were beginning to stir, to look around, or even sitting up.

He sat up also and felt his head and face with both hands. They were smooth.

His body was not that wrinkled, ridged, bumpy, withered body of the sixty-nine-year-old which had lain on his deathbed. It was the smooth-skinned and powerfully muscled body he had when he was twenty-five years old. The same body he had when he was floating between those rods in that dream. Dream? It had seemed too vivid to be a dream. It was *not* a dream.

Around his wrist was a thin band of transparent material. It was connected to a six-inch-long strap of the same material. The other end was clenched about a metallic arc, the handle of a grayish metal cylinder with a closed cover.

Idly, not concentrating because his mind was too sluggish, he lifted the cylinder. It weighed less than a pound, so it could not be of iron even if it was hollow. Its diameter was a foot and a half and it was over two and a half feet tall.

Everyone had a similar object strapped to his wrist.

Unsteadily, his heart beginning to pick up speed as his senses became unnumbed, he got to his feet.

Others were rising, too. Many had faces which were slack or congealed with an icy wonder. Some looked fearful. Their eyes were wide and rolling; their chests rose and fell swiftly; their breaths hissed out. Some were shaking as if an icy wind had swept over them, though the air was pleasantly warm.

The strange thing, the really alien and frightening thing, was the almost complete silence. Nobody said a word; there was only the hissing of breaths of those near him, a tiny slap as a man smacked himself on his leg; a low whistling from a woman.

Their mouths hung open, as if they were about to say something.

They began moving about, looking into each other's faces, sometimes reaching out to lightly touch another. They shuffled their bare feet, turned this way, turned back the other way, gazed at the hills, the trees covered with the huge vividly colored blooms, the lichenous and soaring mountains, the sparkling and green river, the mushroom-shaped stones, the straps and the gray metallic containers.

Some felt their naked skulls and their faces.

Everybody was encased in a mindless motion and in silence.

Suddenly, a woman began moaning. She sank to her knees, threw her head and her shoulders back, and she howled. At the same time, far down the riverbank, somebody else howled.

It was as if these two cries were signals. Or as if the two were double keys to the human voice and had unlocked it.

The men and women and children began screaming or sobbing or tearing at their faces with their nails or beating themselves on their breasts or falling on their knees and

14

lifting their hands in prayer or throwing themselves down and trying to bury their faces in the grass as if, ostrich-like, to avoid being seen, or rolling back and forth, barking like dogs or howling like wolves.

The terror and the hysteria gripped Burton. He wanted to go to his knees and pray for salvation from judgment. He wanted mercy. He did not want to see the blinding face of God appear over the mountains, a face brighter than the sun. He was not as brave and as guiltless as he had thought. Judgment would be so terrifying, so utterly *final*, that he could not bear to think about it.

Once, he had had a fantasy about standing before God after he had died. He had been little and naked and in the middle of a vast plain, like this, but he had been all alone. Then God, great as a mountain, had strode toward him. And he, Burton, had stood his ground and defied God.

There was no God here, but he fled anyway. He ran across the plain, pushing men and women out of the way, running around some, leaping over others as they rolled on the ground. As he ran, he howled, "No! No! No!" His arms windmilled to fend off unseen terrors. The cylinder strapped to his wrist whirled around and around.

When he was panting so that he could no longer howl, and his legs and arms were hung with weights, and his lungs burned, and his heart boomed, he threw himself down under the first of the trees.

After a while, he sat up and faced towards the plain. The mob noise had changed from screams and howls to a gigantic chattering. The majority were talking to each other, though it did not seem that anybody was listening. Burton could not hear any of the individual words. Some men and women were embracing and kissing as if they had been acquainted in their previous lives and now were holding each other to reassure each other of their identities and of their reality.

There were a number of children in the great crowd. Not one was under five years of age, however. Like their elders, their heads were hairless. Half of them were weeping, rooted to one spot. Others, also crying out, were running back and forth, looking into the faces above them,

15

obviously seeking their parents.

He was beginning to breathe more easily. He stood up and turned around. The tree under which he was standing was a red pine (sometimes wrongly called a Norway pine) about two hundred feet tall. Beside it was a tree of a type he had never seen. He doubted that it had existed on Earth. (He was sure that he was not on Earth, though he could not have given any specific reasons at that moment.) It had a thick, gnarled blackish trunk and many thick branches bearing triangular six-feet-long leaves, green with scarlet lacings. It was about three hundred feet high. There were also trees that looked like white and black oaks, firs, Western yew, and lodgepole pine.

Here and there were clumps of tall bamboo-like plants, and everywhere that there were no trees or bamboo was a grass about three feet high. There were no animals in sight. No insects and no birds.

He looked around for a stick or a club. He did not have the slightest idea what was on the agenda for humanity, but if it was left unsupervised or uncontrolled, it would soon be reverting to its normal state. Once the shock was over, the people would be looking out for themselves, and that meant that some would be bullying others.

He found nothing useful as a weapon. Then it occurred to him that the metal cylinder could be used as a weapon. He banged it against a tree. Though it had little weight, it was extremely hard.

He raised the lid, which was hinged inside at one end. The hollow interior had six snapdown rings of metal, three on each side and spaced so that each could hold a deep cup or dish or rectangular container of gray metal. All the containers were empty. He closed the lid. Doubtless he would find out in time what the function of the cylinder was.

Whatever else had happened, resurrection had not resulted in bodies of fragile misty ectoplasm. He was all bone and blood and flesh.

Though he still felt somewhat detached from reality, as if he had been disengaged from the gears of the world, he was emerging from his shock.

16

He was thirsty. He would have to go down and drink from the river and hope that it would not be poisoned. At this thought, he grinned wryly, and stroked his upper lip. His finger felt disappointed. That was a curious reaction, he thought, and then he remembered that his thick moustache was gone. Oh, yes, he had hoped that the riverwater would not be poisoned. What a strange thought! Why should the dead be brought back to life only to be killed again? But he stood for a long while under the tree. He hated to go back through that madly talking, hysterically sobbing crowd to reach the river. Here, away from the mob, he was free from much of the terror and the panic and the shock that covered them like a sea. If he ventured back, he would be caught up in their emotions again.

Presently, he saw a figure detach itself from the naked throng and walk toward him. He saw that it was not human.

It was then that Burton was sure that this Resurrection Day was not the one which any religion had stated would occur. Burton had not believed in the God portrayed by the Christians, Moslems, Hindus, or any faith. In fact, he was not sure that he believed in any Creator whatsoever. He had believed in Richard Francis Burton and a few friends. He was sure that when he died, the world would cease to exist.

4

Waking up after death, in this valley by this river, he had been powerless to defend himself against the doubts that existed in every man exposed to an early religious conditioning and to an adult society which preached its convictions at every chance.

17

Now, seeing the alien approach, he was sure that there was some other explanation for this event than a supernatural one. There was a physical, a scientific, reason for his being here; he did not have to resort to Judeo-Christian-Moslem myths for cause.

The creature, it, he—it undoubtedly was a male—was a biped about six feet eight inches tall. The pink-skinned body was very thin; there were three fingers and a thumb on each hand and four very long and thin toes on each foot. There were two dark red spots below the male nipples on the chest. The face was semihuman. Thick black eyebrows swept down to the protruding cheekbones and flared out to cover them with a brownish down. The sides of his nostrils were fringed with a thin membrane about a sixteenth of an inch long. The thick pad of cartilage on the end of his nose was deeply cleft. The lips were thin, leathery, and black. The ears were lobeless and the convolutions within were nonhuman. His scrotum looked as if it contained many small testes.

He had seen this creature floating in the ranks a few rows away in that nightmare place.

The creature stopped a few feet away, smiled, and revealed quite human teeth. He said, "I hope you speak English. However, I can speak with some fluency in Russian, Mandarin Chinese, or Hindustani."

Burton felt a slight shock, as if a dog or an ape had spoken to him.

"You speak Midwestern American English," he replied. "Quite well, too. Although too precisely."

"Thank you," the creature said. "I followed you because you seemed the only person with enough sense to get away from that chaos. Perhaps you have some explanation for this . . . what do you call it? . . . resurrection?"

"No more than you," Burton said. "In fact, I don't have any explanation for your existence, before or after resurrection."

The thick eyebrows of the alien twitched, a gesture which Burton was to find indicated surprise or puzzlement.

18

"No? That is strange. I would have sworn that not one of the six billion of Earth's inhabitants had not heard of or seen me on TV."

"TV?"

The creature's brows twitched again.

"You don't know what TV . . ."

His voice trailed, then he smiled again.

"Of course, how stupid of me! You must have died before I came to Earth!"

"When was that?"

The alien's eyebrows rose (equivalent to a human frown as Burton would find), and he said slowly, "Let's see. I believe it was, in your chronology, 2002 A.D. When did you die?"

"It must have been in 1890 A.D.," Burton said. The creature had brought back his sense that all this was not real. He ran his tongue around his mouth; the back teeth he had lost when the Somali spear ran through his cheeks were now replaced. But he was still circumcised, and the men on the riverbank—most of whom had been crying out in the Austrian-German, Italian, or the Slovenian of Trieste—were also circumcised. Yet, in his time, most of the males in that area would have been uncircumcised.

"At least," Burton added, "I remember nothing after October 20, 1890."

"*Aab!*" the creature said. "So, I left my native planet approximately 200 years before you died. My planet? It was a satellite of that star you Terrestrials call Tau Ceti. We placed ourselves in suspended animation, and, when our ship approached your sun, we were automatically thawed out, and . . . but you do not know what I am talking about?"

"Not quite. Things are happening too fast. I would like to get details later. What is your name?"

"Monat Grrautut. Yours?"

"Richard Francis Burton at your service."

He bowed slightly and smiled. Despite the strangeness of the creature and some repulsive physical aspects, Burton found himself warming to him.

"The late Captain Sir Richard Francis Burton," he

added. "Most recently Her Majesty's Consul in the Austro-Hungarian port of Trieste."

"Elizabeth?"

"I lived in the nineteenth century, not the sixteenth."

"A Queen Elizabeth reigned over Great Britain in the twentieth century," Monat said.

He turned to look toward the riverbank.

"Why are they so afraid? All the human beings I met were either sure that there would be no afterlife or else that they would get preferential treatment in the hereafter."

Burton grinned and said, "Those who denied the hereafter are sure they're in Hell because they denied it. Those who knew they would go to Heaven are shocked, I would imagine, to find themselves naked. You see, most of the illustrations of our afterlives showed those in Hell as naked and those in Heaven as being clothed. So, if you're resurrected bare-ass naked, you must be in Hell."

"You seem amused," Monat said.

"I wasn't so amused a few minutes ago," Burton said. "And I'm shaken. Very shaken. But seeing you here makes me think that things are not what people thought they would be. They seldom are. And God, if He's going to make an appearance, does not seem to be in a hurry about it. I think there's an explanation for this, but it won't match any of the conjectures I knew on Earth."

"I doubt we're on Earth," Monat said. He pointed upward with long slim fingers which bore thick cartilage pads instead of nails.

He said, "If you look steadily there, with your eyes shielded, you can see another celestial body near the sun. It is not the moon."

Burton cupped his hands over his eyes, the metal cylinder on his shoulder, and stared at the point indicated. He saw a faintly glowing body which seemed to be an eighth of the size of a full moon. When he put his hands down, he said, "A star?"

Monat said, "I believe so. I thought I saw several other very faint bodies elsewhere in the sky, but I'm not sure.

We will know when night comes."

"Where do you think we are?"

"I would not know."

Monat gestured at the sun.

"It is rising and so it will descend, and then night should come. I think that it would be best to prepare for the night. And for other events. It is warm and getting warmer, but the night may be cold and it might rain. We should build a shelter of some sort. And we should also think about finding food. Though I imagine that this device"—he indicated the cylinder—"will feed us."

Burton said, "What makes you think that?"

"I looked inside mine. It contains dishes and cups, all empty now, but obviously made to be filled."

Burton felt less unreal. The being—the Tau Cetan!—talked so pragmatically, so sensibly, that he provided an anchor to which Burton could tie his senses before they drifted away again. And, despite the repulsive alienness of the creature, he exuded a friendliness and an openness that warmed Burton. Moreover, any creature that came from a civilization which could span many trillions of miles of interstellar space must have very valuable knowledge and resources.

Others were beginning to separate themselves from the crowd. A group of about ten men and women walked slowly toward him. Some were talking, but others were silent and wide-eyed. They did not seem to have a definite goal in mind; they just floated along like a cloud driven by· a wind. When they got near Burton and Monat, they stopped walking.

A man trailing the group especially attracted Burton's scrutiny. Monat was obviously nonhuman but this fellow was subhuman or prehuman. He stood about five feet tall. He was squat and powerfully muscled. His head was thrust forward on a bowed and very thick neck. The forehead was low and slanting. The skull was long and narrow. Enormous supraorbital ridges shadowed dark brown eyes. The nose was a smear of flesh with arching nostrils, and the bulging bones of his jaws pushed his thin

21

lips out. He may have been covered with as much hair as an ape at one time, but now, like everybody else, he was stripped of hair.

The huge hands looked as if they could squeeze water from a stone.

He kept looking behind him as if he feared that someone was sneaking up on him. The human beings moved away from him when he approached them.

But then another man walked up to him and said something to the subhuman in English. It was evident that the man did not expect to be understood but that he was trying to be friendly. His voice, however, was almost hoarse. The newcomer was a muscular youth about six feet tall. He had a face that looked handsome when he faced Burton but was comically craggy in profile. His eyes were green.

The subhuman jumped a little when he was addressed. He peered at the grinning youth from under the bars of bone. Then he smiled, revealing large thick teeth, and spoke in a language Burton did not recognize. He pointed to himself and said something that sounded like *Kazzintuitruaabemss.* Later, Burton would find out that it was his name and it meant Man-Who-Slew-The-Long-White-Tooth.

The others consisted of five men and four women. Two of the men had known each other in Earthlife, and one of them had been married to one of the women. All were Italians or Slovenes who had died in Trieste, apparently about 1890, though he knew none of them.

"You there," Burton said, pointing to the man who had spoken in English. "Step forward. What is your name?"

The man approached him hesitantly. He said, "You're English, right?"

The man spoke with an American Midwest flatness.

Burton held out his hand and said, "Yaas. Burton here."

The fellow raised hairless eyebrows and said, "Burton?" He leaned forward and peered at Burton's face. "It's hard to say . . . it couldn't be . . ."

22

He straightened up. "Name's Peter Frigate. F-R-I-G-A-T-E."

He looked around him and then said in a voice even more strained, "It's hard to talk coherently. Everybody's in such a state of shock, you know. I feel as if I'm coming apart. But . . . here we are . . . alive again . . . young again . . . no hellfire . . . not yet, anyway. Born in 1918, died 2008 . . . because of what this extra-Terrestrial did . . . don't hold it against him . . . only defending himself, you know."

Frigate's voice died away to a whisper. He grinned nervously at Monat.

Burton said, "You know this . . . Monat Grrautut?"

"Not exactly," Frigate said. "I saw enough of him on TV, of course, and heard enough and read enough about him."

He held out his hand as if he expected it to be rejected. Monat smiled, and they shook hands.

Frigate said, "I think it'd be a good idea if we banded together. We may need protection."

"Why?" Burton said, though he knew well enough.

"You know how rotten most humans are," Frigate said. "Once people get used to being resurrected, they'll be fighting for women and food and anything that takes their fancy. And I think we ought to be buddies with this Neanderthal or whatever he is. Anyway, he'll be a good man in a fight."

Kazz, as he was named later on, seemed pathetically eager to be accepted. At the same time, he was suspicious of anyone who got too close.

A woman walked by then, muttering over and over in German, "My God! What have I done to offend Thee?"

A man, both fists clenched and raised to shoulder height, was shouting in Yiddish, "My beard! My beard!"

Another man was pointing at his genitals and saying in Slovenian, "They've made a Jew of me! A Jew! Do you think that . . . ? No, it couldn't be!"

Burton grinned savagely and said, "It doesn't occur to him that maybe They have made a Mohammedan out of

23

him or an Australian aborigine or an ancient Egyptian, all of whom practiced circumcision."

"What did he say?" asked Frigate. Burton translated; Frigate laughed.

A woman hurried by; she was making a pathetic attempt to cover her breasts and her pubic regions with her hands. She was muttering, "What will they think, what will they think?" And she disappeared behind the trees.

A man and a woman passed them; they were talking loudly in Italian as if they were separated by a broad highway.

"We can't be in Heaven . . . I know, oh my God, I know! . . . There was Giuseppe Zomzini and you know what a wicked man he was . . . he ought to burn in hellfire! I know, I know . . . he stole from the treasury, he frequented whorehouses, he drank himself to death . . . yet . . . he's here! . . . I know, I know . . ."

Another woman was running and screaming in German, "Daddy! Daddy! Where are you? It's your own darling Hilda!"

A man scowled at them and said repeatedly, in Hungarian, "I'm as good as anyone and better than some. To hell with them."

A woman said, "I wasted my whole life, my whole life. I did everything for them, and now . . ."

A man, swinging the metal cylinder before him as if it were a censer, called out, "Follow me to the mountains! Follow me! I know the truth, good people! Follow me! We'll be safe in the bosom of the Lord! Don't believe this illusion around you; follow me! I'll open your eyes!"

Others spoke gibberish or were silent, their lips tight as if they feared to utter what was within them.

"It'll take some time before they straighten out," Burton said. He felt that it would take a long time before the world became mundane for him, too.

"They may never know the truth," Frigate said.

"What do you mean?"

"They didn't know the Truth—capital T—on Earth, so why should they here? What makes you think we're going to get a revelation?"

24

Burton shrugged and said, "I don't. But I do think we ought to determine just what our environment is and how we can survive in it. The fortune of a man who sits, sits also."

He pointed toward the riverbank. "See those stone mushrooms? They seem to be spaced out at intervals of a mile. I wonder what their purpose is?"

Monat said, "If you had taken a close look at that one, you would have seen that its surface contains about 700 round indentations. These are just the right size for the base of a cylinder to fit in. In fact, there is a cylinder in the center of the top surface. I think that if we examine that cylinder, we may be able to determine their purpose. I suspect that it was placed there so we'd do just that."

5

A woman approached them. She was of medium height, had a superb shape, and a face that would have been beautiful if it had been framed by hair. Her eyes were large and dark. She made no attempt to cover herself with her hands. Burton was not the least bit aroused looking at her or any of the women. He was too deeply numbed.

The woman spoke in a well-modulated voice and an Oxford accent. "I beg your pardon, gentlemen. I couldn't help overhearing you. You're the only English voices I've heard since I woke up . . . here, wherever here is. I am an Englishwoman, and I am looking for protection. I throw myself on your mercy."

"Fortunately for you, madame," Burton said, "you come to the right men. At least, speaking for myself, I can assure you that you will get all the protection I can afford. Though, if I were like some of the English gentlemen I've known, you might not have fared so well. By the way, this

25

gentleman is not English. He's Yankee."

It seemed strange to be speaking so formally this day of all days, with all the wailing and shouting up and down the valley and everybody birth-naked and as hairless as eels.

The woman held out her hand to Burton. "I'm Mrs. Hargreaves," she said.

Burton took the hand and, bowing, kissed it lightly. He felt foolish, but, at the same time, the gesture strengthened his hold on sanity. If the forms of polite society could be preserved, perhaps the "rightness" of things might also be restored.

"The late Captain Sir Richard Francis Burton," he said, grinning slightly at the *late*. "Perhaps you've heard of me?"

She snatched her hand away and then extended it again.

"Yes, I've heard of you, Sir Richard."

Somebody said, "It can't be!"

Burton looked at Frigate, who had spoken in such a low tone.

"And why not?" he said.

"Richard Burton!" Frigate said. "Yes. I wondered, but without any hair? . . ."

"Yaas?" Burton drawled.

"Yaas!" Frigate said. "Just as the books said!"

"What are you talking about?"

Frigate breathed in deeply and then said, "Never mind now, Mr. Burton. I'll explain later. Just take it that I'm very shaken up. Not in my right mind. You understand that, of course."

He looked intently at Mrs. Hargreaves, shook his head, and said, "Is your name Alice?"

"Why, yes!" she said, smiling and becoming beautiful, hair or no hair. "How did you know? Have I met you? No, I don't think so."

"Alice Pleasance Liddell Hargreaves?"

"Yes!"

"I have to go sit down," the American said. He walked under the tree and sat down with his back to the trunk. His eyes looked a little glazed.

26

"Aftershock," Burton said.

He could expect such erratic behavior and speech from the others for some time. He could expect a certain amount of nonrational behavior from himself, too. The important thing was to get shelter and food and some plan for common defense.

Burton spoke in Italian and Slovenian to the others and then made the introductions. They did not protest when he suggested that they should follow him down to the river's edge.

"I'm sure we're all thirsty," he said. "And we should investigate that stone mushroom."

They walked back to the plain behind them. The people were sitting on the grass or milling about. They passed one couple arguing loudly and red-facedly. Apparently, they had been husband and wife and were continuing a life-long dispute. Suddenly, the man turned and walked away. The wife looked unbelievingly at him and then ran after him. He thrust her away so violently that she fell on the grass. He quickly lost himself in the crowd, but the woman wandered around, calling his name and threatening to make a scandal if he did not come out of hiding.

Burton thought briefly of his own wife, Isabel. He had not seen her in this crowd, though that did not mean that she was not in it. But she would have been looking for him. She would not stop until she found him.

He pushed through the crowd to the river's edge and then got down on his knees and scooped up water with his hands. It was cool and clear and refreshing. His stomach felt as if it were absolutely empty. After he had satisfied his thirst, he became hungry.

"The waters of the River of Life," Burton said. "The Styx? Lethe? No, not Lethe. I remember everything about my Earthly existence."

"I wish I could forget mine," Frigate said.

Alice Hargreaves was kneeling by the edge and dipping water with one hand while she leaned on the other arm. Her figure was certainly lovely, Burton thought. He wondered if she would be blonde when her hair grew out, if it grew out. Perhaps Whoever had put them here intended they should all be bald, forever, for some reason of Theirs.

They climbed upon the top of the nearest mushroom structure. The granite was a dense-grained gray flecked heavily with red. On its flat surface were seven hundred indentations, forming fifty concentric circles. The depression in the center held a metal cylinder. A little dark-skinned man with a big nose and receding chin was examining the cylinder. As they approached, he looked up and smiled.

"This one won't open," he said in German. "Perhaps it will later. I'm sure it's there as an example of what to do with our own containers."

He introduced himself as Lev Ruach and switched to a heavily accented English when Burton, Frigate, and Hargreaves gave their names.

"I was an atheist," he said, seeming to speak to himself more than to them. "Now, I don't know! This place is as big a shock to an atheist, you know, as to those devout believers who had pictured an afterlife quite different from this. Well, so I was wrong. It wouldn't be the first time."

He chuckled, and said to Monat, "I recognized you at once. It's a good thing for you that you were resurrected in a group mainly consisting of people who died in the nineteenth century. Otherwise, you'd be lynched."

"Why is that?" Burton asked.

"He killed Earth," Frigate said. "At least, I *think* he did."

"The scanner," Monat said dolefully, "was adjusted to kill only human beings. And it would not have exterminated all of mankind. It would have ceased operating after a predetermined number—unfortunately, a large number—had lost their lives. Believe me, my friends, I did not want to do that. You do not know what an agony it cost me to make the decision to press the button. But I had to protect *my* people. You forced my hand."

"It started when Monat was on a live show," Frigate said. "Monat made an unfortunate remark. He said that

28

his scientists had the knowledge and ability to keep people from getting old. Theoretically, using Tau Cetan techniques, a man could live forever. But the knowledge was not used on his planet; it was forbidden. The interviewer asked him if these techniques could be applied to Terrestrials. Monat replied that there was no reason why not. But rejuvenation was denied to his own kind for a very good reason, and this also applied to Terrestrials. By then, the government censor realized what was happening and cut off the audio. But it was too late."

"Later," Lev Ruach said, "the American government reported that Monat had misunderstood the question, that his knowledge of English had led him to make a misstatement. But it was too late. The people of America, and of the world, demanded that Monat reveal the secret of eternal youth."

"Which I did not have," said Monat. "Not a single one of our expedition had the knowledge. In fact, very few people on my planet had it. But it did no good to tell the people this. They thought I was lying. There was a riot, and a mob stormed the guards around our ship and broke into it. I saw my friends torn to pieces while they tried to reason with the mob. *Reason!*

"But I did what I did, not for revenge, but for a very different motive. I knew that, after we were killed, or even if we weren't, the U.S. government would restore order. And it would have the ship in its possession. It wouldn't be long before Terrestrial scientists would know how to duplicate it. Inevitably, the Terrestrials would launch an invasion fleet against our world. So, to make sure that Earth would be set back many centuries, maybe thousands of years, knowing that I must do the dreadful thing to save my own world, I sent the signal to the scanner to orbit. I would not have had to do that if I could have gotten to the destruct-button and blown up the ship. But I could not get to the control room. So, I pressed the scanner-activation button. A short time later, the mob blew off the door of the room in which I had taken refuge. I remember nothing after that."

Frigate said, "I was in a hospital in Western Samoa,

dying of cancer, wondering if I would be buried next to Robert Louis Stevenson. Not much chance, I was thinking. Still, I had translated the *Iliad* and the *Odyssey* into Samoan . . . Then, the news came. People all over the world were falling dead. The pattern of fatality was obvious. The Tau Cetan satellite was radiating something that dropped human beings in their tracks. The last I heard was that the U.S., England, Russia, China, France, and Israel were all sending up rockets to intercept it, blow it up. And the scanner was on a path which would take it over Samoa within a few hours. The excitement must have been too much for me in my weakened condition. I became unconscious. That is all I remember."

"The interceptors failed," Ruach said. "The scanner blew them up before they even got close."

Burton thought he had a lot to learn about post-1890, but now was not the time to talk about it. "I suggest we go up into the hills," he said. "We should learn what type of vegetation grows there and if it can be useful. Also, if there is any flint we can work into weapons. This Old Stone Age fellow must be familiar with stone-working. He can show us how."

They walked across the mile-broad plain and into the hills. On the way, several others joined their group. One was a little girl, about seven years old, with dark blue eyes and a beautiful face. She looked pathetically at Burton, who asked her in twelve languages if any of her parents or relatives were nearby. She replied in a language none of them knew. The linguists among them tried every tongue at their disposal, most of the European speeches and many of the African or Asiatic: Hebrew, Hindustani, Arabic, a Berber dialect, Romany, Turkish, Persian, Latin, Greek, Pushtu.

Frigate, who knew a little Welsh and Gaelic, spoke to her. Her eyes widened, and then she frowned. The words seemed to have a certain familiarity or similarity to her speech, but they were not close enough to be intelligible.

"For all we know," Frigate said, "she could be an ancient Gaul. She keeps using the word Gwenafra. Could that be her name?"

30

"We'll teach her English," Burton said. "And we'll call her Gwenafra." He picked up the child in his arms and started to walk with her. She burst into tears, but she made no effort to free herself. The weeping was a release from what must have been almost unbearable tension and a joy at finding a guardian. Burton bent his neck to place his face against her body. He did not want the others to see the tears in his eyes.

Where the plain met the hills, as if a line had been drawn, the short grass ceased and the thick, coarse espartolike grass, waist-high, began. Here, too, the towering pines, red pines and lodgepole pines, the oaks, the yew, the gnarled giants with scarlet and green leaves, and the bamboo grew thickly. The bamboo consisted of many varieties, from slender stalks only a few feet high to plants over fifty feet high. Many of the trees were overgrown with the vines bearing huge green, red, yellow, and blue flowers.

"Bamboo is the material for spear-shafts," Burton said, "pipes for conducting water, containers, the basic stuff for building houses, furniture, boats, charcoal even for making gunpowder. And the young stalks of some may be good for eating. But we need stone for tools to cut down and shape the wood."

They climbed over hills whose height increased as they neared the mountain. After they had walked about two miles as the crow flies, eight miles as the caterpillar crawls, they were stopped by the mountain. This rose in a sheer cliff-face of some blue-black igneous rock on which grew huge patches of a blue-green lichen. There was no way of determining how high it was, but Burton did not think that he was wrong in estimating it as at least 20,000 feet high. As far as they could see up and down the valley, it presented a solid front.

"Have you noticed the complete absence of animal life?" Frigate said. "Not even an insect."

Burton exclaimed. He strode to a pile of broken rock and picked up a fist-sized chunk of greenish stone. "Chert," he said. "If there's enough, we can make knives, spearheads, adzes, axes. And with them build houses,

31

boats, and many other things."

"Tools and weapons must be bound to wooden shafts," Frigate said. "What do we use as binding material?"

"Perhaps human skin," Burton said.

The others looked shocked. Burton gave a strange chirruping laugh, incongruous in so masculine-looking a man. He said, "If we're forced to kill in self-defense or lucky enough to stumble over a corpse some assassin has been kind enough to prepare for us, we'd be fools not to use what we need. However, if any of you feel self-sacrificing enough to offer your own epidermises for the good of the group, step forward! We'll remember you in our wills."

"Surely, you're joking," Alice Hargreaves said. "I can't say I particularly care for such talk."

Frigate said, "Hang around him, and you'll hear lots worse," but he did not explain what he meant.

6

Burton examined the rock along the base of the mountain. The blue-black densely grained stone of the mountain itself was some kind of basalt. But there were pieces of chert scattered on the surface of the earth or sticking out of the surface at the base. These looked as if they might have fallen down from a projection above, so it was possible that the mountain was not a solid mass of basalt. Using a piece of chert which had a thin edge, he scraped away a patch of the lichenous growth. The stone beneath it seemed to be a greenish dolomite. Apparently, the pieces of chert had come from the dolomite, though there was no evidence of decay or fracture of the vein.

The lichen could be *Parmelia saxitilis*, which also grew on old bones, including skulls, and hence, according to

The Doctrine of Signatures, was a cure for epilepsy and a healing salve for wounds.

Hearing stone banging away on stone, he returned to the group. All were standing around the subhuman and the American, who were squatting back to back and working on the chert. Both had knocked out rough handaxes. While the others watched, they produced six more. Then each took a large chert nodule and broke it into two with a hammerstone. Using one piece of the nodule, they began to knock long thin flakes from the outside rim of the nodule. They rotated the nodule and banged away until each had about a dozen blades.

They continued to work, one a type of man who had lived a hundred thousand years or more before Christ, the other the refined end of human evolution, a product of the highest civilization (technologically speaking) of Earth, and, indeed, one of the last men on Earth—if he was to be believed.

Suddenly, Frigate howled, jumped up, and hopped around holding his left thumb. One of his strokes had missed its target. Kazz grinned, exposing huge teeth like tombstones. He got up, too, and walked into the grass with his curious rolling gait. He returned a few minutes later with six bamboo sticks with sharpened ends and several with straight ends. He sat down and worked on one stick until he had split the end and inserted the triangular chipped-down point of an axehead into the split end. This he bound with some long grasses.

Within half an hour, the group was armed with handaxes, axes with bamboo hafts, daggers, and spears with wooden points and with stone tips.

By then Frigate's hand had quit hurting so much and the bleeding had stopped. Burton asked him how he happened to be so proficient in stone-working.

"I was an amateur anthropologist," he said. "A lot of people—a lot relatively speaking—learned how to make tools and weapons from stone as a hobby. Some of us got pretty good at it, though I don't think any modern ever got as skillful and as swift as a Neolithic specialist. Those guys did it all their lives, you know.

33

"Also, I just happen to know a lot about working bamboo, too, so I can be of some value to you."

They began walking back to the river. They paused a moment on top of a tall hill. The sun was almost directly overhead. They could see for many miles along the river and also across the river. Although they were too far away to make out any figures on the other side of the mile-wide stream, they could see the mushroom-shaped structures there. The terrain on the other side was the same as that on theirs. A mile-wide plain, perhaps two and a half miles of foothills covered with trees. Beyond, the straight-up face of an insurmountable black and bluish-green mountain.

North and south, the valley ran straight for about ten miles. Then it curved, and the river was lost to sight.

"Sunrise must come late and sunset early," Burton said. "Well, we must make the most of the bright hours."

At that moment, everybody jumped and many cried out. A blue flame arose from the top of each stone structure, soared up at least twenty feet, then disappeared. A few seconds later, a sound of distant thunder passed them. The boom struck the mountain behind them and echoed.

Burton scooped up the little girl in his arms and began to trot down the hill. Though they maintained a good pace, they were forced to walk from time to time to regain their breaths. Nevertheless, Burton felt wonderful. It had been so many years since he could use his muscles so profligately that he did not want to stop enjoying the sensation. He could scarcely believe that, only a short time ago, his right foot had been swollen with gout, and his heart had beaten wildly if he climbed a few steps.

They came to the plain and continued trotting, for they could see that there was much excitement around one of the structures. Burton swore at those in his way and pushed them aside. He got black looks but no one tried to push back. Abruptly, he was in the space cleared around the base. And he saw what had attracted them. He also smelled it.

34

Frigate, behind him, said, "Oh, my God!" and tried to retch on his empty stomach.

Burton had seen too much in his lifetime to be easily affected by grisly sights. Moreover, he could take himself to one remove from reality when things became too grim or too painful. Sometimes he made the move, the side-stepping of things-as-they-were, with an effort of will. Usually, it occurred automatically. In this case, the displacement was done automatically.

The corpse lay on its side and half under the edge of the mushroom top. Its skin was completely burned off, and the naked muscles were charred. The nose and ears, fingers, toes, and the genitals had been burned entirely away or were only shapeless stubs.

Near it, on her knees, was a woman mumbling a prayer in Italian. She had huge black eyes which would have been beautiful if they had not been reddened and puffy with tears. She had a magnificent figure which would have caught all his attention under different circumstances.

"What happened?" he said.

The woman stopped praying and looked at him. She got to her feet and whispered, "Father Giuseppe was leaning against the rock; he said he was hungry. He said he didn't see much sense in being brought back to life only to starve to death. I said that we wouldn't die, how could we? We'd been raised from the dead, and we'd be provided for. He said maybe we were in hell. We'd go hungry and naked forever. I told him not to blaspheme, of all people he should be the last to blaspheme. But he said that this was not what he'd been telling everybody for forty years would happen and then . . . and then . . ."

Burton waited a few seconds, and then said, "And then?"

"Father Giuseppe said that at least there wasn't any hellfire, but that that would be better than starving for eternity. And then the flames reached out and wrapped him inside them, and there was a noise like a bomb exploding, and then he was dead, burned to death. It was horrible, horrible."

Burton moved north of the corpse to get the wind behind him, but even here the stench was sickening. It was not the odor as much as the idea of death that upset him. The first day of the Resurrection was only half over and a man was dead. Did this mean that the resurrected were just as vulnerable to death as in Earthlife? If so, what sense was there to it?

Frigate had quit trying to heave on an empty stomach. Pale and shaking, he got to his feet and approached Burton. He kept his back turned to the dead man.

"Hadn't we better get rid of that?" he said, jerking his thumb over his shoulder.

"I suppose so," Burton said coolly. "It's too bad his skin is ruined, though."

He grinned at the American. Frigate looked even more shocked.

"Here," Burton said. "Grab hold of his feet, I'll take the other end. We'll toss him into the river."

"The river?" Frigate said.

"Yaas. Unless you want to carry him into the hills and chop out a hole for him there."

"I can't," Frigate said, and walked away. Burton looked disgustedly after him and then signalled to the subhuman. Kazz grunted and shuffled forward to the body with that peculiar walking-on-the-side-of-his-feet gait. He stooped over and, before Burton could get hold of the blackened stumps of the feet, Kazz had lifted the body above his head, walked a few steps to the edge of the river, and tossed the corpse into the water. It sank immediately and was moved by the current along the shore. Kazz decided that this was not good enough. He waded out after it up to his waist and stooped down, submerging himself for a minute. Evidently he was shoving the body out into the deeper part.

Alice Hargreaves had watched with horror. Now she said, "But that's the water we'll be drinking!"

"The river looks big enough to purify itself," Burton said. "At any rate, we have more things to worry about than proper sanitation procedures."

Burton turned when Monat touched his shoulder and

36

said, "Look at that!" The water was boiling about where the body should be. Abruptly, a silvery white-finned back broke the surface.

"It looks as if your worry about the water being contaminated is in vain," Burton said to Alice Hargreaves. "The river has scavengers. I wonder . . . I wonder if it's safe to swim."

At least, the subhuman had gotten out without being attacked. He was standing before Burton, brushing the water off his hairless body, and grinning with those huge teeth. He was frighteningly ugly. But he had the knowledge of a primitive man, knowledge which had already been handy in a world of primitive conditions. And he would be a damned good man to have at your back in a fight. Short though he was, he was immensely powerful. Those heavy bones afforded a broad base for heavy muscles. It was evident that he had, for some reason, become attached to Burton. Burton liked to think the savage, with a savage's instincts, "knew" that Burton was the man to follow if he would survive. Moreover, a subhuman or prehuman, being closer to the animals, would also be more psychic. So he would detect Burton's own well-developed psychic powers and would feel an affinity to Burton, even though he was *Homo sapiens*.

Then Burton reminded himself that his reputation for psychism had been built up by himself and that he was half-charlatan. He had talked about his powers so much, and had listened to his wife so much, that he had come to believe in them himself. But there were moments when he remembered that his "powers" were at least half-fake.

Nevertheless, he was a capable hypnotist, and he did believe that his eyes radiated a peculiar extra-sensory power, when he wished them to do so. It may have been this that attracted the half-man.

"The rock discharged a tremendous energy," Lev Ruach said. "It must have been electrical. But why? I can't believe that the discharge was purposeless."

Burton looked across the mushroom-shape of the rock. The gray cylinder in the center depression seemed to be undamaged by the discharge. He touched the stone. It was

37

no warmer than might have been expected from its exposure to the sun.

Lev Ruach said, "Don't touch it! There might be another . . ." and he stopped when he saw his warning was too late.

"Another discharge?" Burton said. "I don't think so. Not for some time yet, anyway. That cylinder was left here so we could learn something from it."

He put his hands on the top edge of the mushroom structure and jumped forward. He came up and onto the top with an ease that gladdened him. It had been so many years since he had felt so young and so powerful. Or so hungry.

A few in the crowd cried out to him to get down off the rock before the blue flames came again. Others looked as if they hoped that another discharge would occur. The majority were content to let him take the risks.

Nothing happened, although he had not been too sure he would not be incinerated. The stone felt only pleasantly warm on his bare feet.

He walked over the depressions to the cylinder and put his fingers under the rim of the cover. It rose easily. His heart beating with excitement, he looked inside it. He had expected the miracle, and there it was. The racks within held six containers, each of which was full.

He signalled to his group to come up. Kazz vaulted up easily. Frigate, who had recovered from his sickness, got onto the top with an athlete's ease. If the fellow did not have such a queasy stomach, he might be an asset, Burton thought. Frigate turned and pulled up Alice, who came over the edge at the ends of his hands.

When they crowded around him, their heads bent over the interior of the cylinder, Burton said, "It's a veritable grail! Look! Steak, a thick juicy steak! Bread and butter! Jam! Salad! And what's that? A package of cigarettes? Yaas! And a cigar! And a cup of bourbon, very good stuff by its odor! Something . . . what is it?"

"Looks like sticks of gum," Frigate said. "Unwrapped. And that must be a . . . what? A lighter for the smokes?"

"Food!" a man shouted. He was a large man, not a

38

member of what Burton thought of as "his group." He had followed them, and others were scrambling up on the rock. Burton reached down past the containers into the cylinder and gripped the small silvery rectangular object on the bottom. Frigate had said this might be a lighter. Burton did not know what a "lighter" was, but he suspected that it provided flame for the cigarettes. He kept the object in the palm of his hand and with the other he closed the lid. His mouth was watering, and his belly was rumbling. The others were just as eager as he; their expressions showed that they could not understand why he was not removing the food.

The large man said, in a loud blustery Triestan Italian, "I'm hungry, and I'll kill anybody who tries to stop me! Open that!"

The others said nothing, but it was evident that they expected Burton to take the lead in the defense. Instead, he said, "Open it yourself," and turned away. The others hesitated. They had seen and smelled the food. Kazz was drooling. But Burton said, "Look at that mob. There'll be a fight here in a minute. I say, let them fight over their morsels. Not that I'm avoiding a battle, you understand," he added, looking fiercely at them. "But I'm certain that we'll all have our own cylinders full of food by supper time. These cylinders, call them grails, if you please, just need to be left on the rock to be filled. That is obvious, that's why this grail was placed here."

He walked to the edge of the stone near the water and got off. By then the top was jammed with people and more were trying to get on. The large man had seized a steak and bitten into it, but someone had tried to snatch it away from him. He yelled with fury and, suddenly, rammed through those between him and the river. He went over the edge and into the water, emerging a moment later. In the meantime, men and women were screaming and striking each other over the rest of the food and goods in the cylinder.

The man who had jumped into the river floated off on his back while he ate the rest of the steak. Burton watched him closely, half-expecting him to be seized by fish. But

39

he drifted on down the stream, undisturbed.

The rocks to the north and south, on both sides of the river, were crowded with struggling humans.

Burton walked until he was free of the crowd and sat down. His group squatted by him or stood up and watched the writhing and noisy mass. The grailstone looked like a toadstool engulfed in pale maggots. Very noisy maggots. Some of them were now also red, because blood had been spilled.

The most depressing aspect of the scene was the reaction of the children. The younger ones had stayed back from the rock, but they knew that there was food in the grail. They were crying from hunger and from terror caused by the screaming and fighting of the adults on the stone. The little girl with Burton was dry-eyed, but she was shaking. She stood by Burton and put her arms around his neck. He patted her on the back and murmured encouraging words which she could not understand but the tone of which helped to quiet her.

The sun was on its descent. Within about two hours it would be hidden by the towering western mountain, though a genuine dusk presumably would not happen for many hours. There was no way to determine how long the day was here. The temperature had gone up, but sitting in the sun was not by any means unbearable, and the steady breeze helped cool them off.

Kazz made signs indicating that he would like a fire and also pointed at the tip of a bamboo spear. No doubt he wanted to fire-harden the tip.

Burton had inspected the metal object taken from the grail. It was of a hard silvery metal, rectangular, flat, about two inches long and three-tenths across. It had a small hole in one end and a slide on the other. Burton put his thumbnail against the projection at the end of the slide and pushed. The slide moved downward about two-sixteenths of an inch, and a wire about one-tenth of an inch in diameter and a half-inch long slid out of the hole in the end. Even in the bright sunlight, it glowed whitely. He touched the tip of the wire to a blade of grass; the blade shriveled up at once. Applied to the tip of the bamboo spear, it burned a tiny hole. Burton pushed the slide back into its original position, and the wire withdrew, like the hot head of a brazen turtle, into the silvery shell.

Both Frigate and Ruach wondered aloud at the power contained in the tiny pack. To make the wire that hot required much voltage. How many charges would the battery or the radioactive pile that must be in it give? How could the lighter's power pack be renewed?

There were many questions that could not be immediately answered or, perhaps, never. The greatest was how they could have been brought back to life in rejuvenated bodies. Whoever had done it possessed a science that was godlike. But speculation about it, though it would give them something to talk about, would solve nothing.

After a while, the crowd dispersed. The cylinder was left on its side on top of the grailstone. Several bodies were sprawled there, and a number of men and women who got off the rock were hurt. Burton went through the crowd. One woman's face had been clawed, especially around her right eye. She was sobbing with no one to pay attention to her. Another man was sitting on the ground and holding his groin, which had been raked with sharp fingernails.

Of the four lying on top of the stone, three were unconscious. These recovered with water dashed into their faces from the grail. The fourth, a short slender man, was dead. Someone had twisted his head until his neck had broken.

Burton looked up at the sun again and said, "I don't know exactly when supper time will occur. I suggest we return not too long after the sun goes down behind the mountain. We will set our grails, or glory buckets, or lunchpails, or whatever you wish to call them, in these depressions. And then we'll wait. In the meantime . . ."

He could have tossed this body into the river, too, but he had now thought of a use, perhaps uses, for it. He told the others what he wanted, and they got the corpse down off the stone and started to carry it across the plain. Frigate and Galeazzi, a former importer of Trieste, took

41

the first turn. Frigate had evidently not cared for the job, but when Burton asked him if he would, he nodded. He picked up the man's feet and led with Galeazzi holding the dead man under the armpits. Alice walked behind Burton with the child's hand in hers. Some in the crowd looked curiously or called out comments or questions, but Burton ignored them. After half a mile, Kazz and Monat took over the corpse. The child did not seem to be disturbed by the dead man. She had been curious about the first corpse, instead of being horrified by its burned appearance.

"If she really is an ancient Gaul," Frigate said, "she may be used to seeing charred bodies. If I remember correctly, the Gauls burned sacrifices alive in big wicker baskets at religious ceremonies. I don't remember what god or goddess the ceremonies were in honor of. I wish I had a library to refer to. Do you think we'll ever have one here? I think I would go nuts if I didn't have books to read."

"That remains to be seen," Burton said. "If we're not provided with a library, we'll make our own. If it's possible to do so."

He thought that Frigate's question was a silly one, but then not everybody was quite in their right minds at this time.

At the foothills, two men, Rocco and Brontich, succeeded Kazz and Monat. Burton led them past the trees through the waist-high grass. The saw-edged grass scraped their legs. Burton cut off a stalk with his knife and tested the stalk for toughness and flexibility. Frigate kept close to his elbow and seemed unable to stop chattering. Probably, Burton thought, he talked to keep from thinking about the two deaths.

"If every one who has ever lived has been resurrected here, think of the research to be done! Think of the historical mysteries and questions you could clear up! You could talk to John Wilkes Booth and find out if Secretary of War Stanton really was behind the Lincoln assassination. You might ferret out the identity of Jack the Ripper. Find out if Joan of Arc actually did belong to a witch cult. Talk to Napoleon's Marshal Ney; see if he did

42

escape the firing squad and become a schoolteacher in America. Get the true story on Pearl Harbor. See the face of the Man in the Iron Mask, if there ever was such a person. Interview Lucrezia Borgia and those who knew her and determine if she was the poisoning bitch most people think she was. Learn the identity of the assassin of the two little princes in the Tower. Maybe Richard III did kill them.

"And you, Richard Francis Burton, there are many questions about your own life that your biographers would like to have answered. Did you really have a Persian love you were going to marry and for whom you were going to renounce your true identity and become a native? Did she die before you could marry her, and did her death really embitter you, and did you carry a torch for her the rest of your life?"

Burton glared at him. He had just met the man and here he was, asking the most personal and prying questions. Nothing excused this.

Frigate backed away, saying, "And . . . and . . . well, it'll all have to wait, I can see that. But did you know that your wife had extreme unction administered to you shortly after you died and that you were buried in a Catholic cemetery—you, the infidel?"

Lev Ruach, whose eyes had been widening while Frigate was rattling on, said, "You're Burton, the explorer and linguist? The discoverer of Lake Tanganyika? The one who made a pilgrimage to Mecca while disguised as a Moslem? The translator of *The Thousand and One Nights*?"

"I have no desire to lie nor need to. I am he."

Lev Ruach spat at Burton, but the wind carried it away. "You son of a bitch!" he cried. "You foul Nazi bastard! I read about you! You were, in many ways, an admirable person, I suppose! But you were an anti-Semite!"

43

7

Burton was startled. He said, "My enemies spread that baseless and vicious rumor. But anybody acquainted with the facts and with me would know better. And now, I think you'd . . ."

"I suppose you didn't write *The Jew, The Gypsy, and El Islam*?" Ruach said, sneering.

"I did," Burton replied. His face was red, and when he looked down, he saw that his body was also flushed. "And now, as I started to say before you so boorishly interrupted me, I think you had better go. Ordinarily, I would be at your throat by now. A man who talks to me like that has to defend his words with deeds. But this is a strange situation, and perhaps you are overwrought. I do not know. But if you do not apologize now, or walk off, I am going to make another corpse."

Ruach clenched his fists and glared at Burton; then he spun around and stalked off.

"What is a Nazi?" Burton said to Frigate.

The American explained as best he could. Burton said, "I have much to learn about what happened after I died. That man is mistaken about me. I'm no Nazi. England, you say, became a second-class power? Only fifty years after my death? I find that difficult to believe."

"Why would I lie to you?" Frigate said. "Don't feel bad about it. Before the end of the twentieth century, she had risen again, and in a most curious way, though it was too late . . ."

Listening to the Yankee, Burton felt pride for his country. Although England had treated him more than shabbily during his lifetime, and although he had always wanted to get out of the island whenever he had been on it, he would defend it to the death. And he had been devoted to the Queen.

Abruptly, he said, "If you guessed my identity, why didn't you say something about it?"

"I wanted to be sure. Besides, we've not had much time for social intercourse," Frigate said. "Or any other kind, either," he added, looking sidewise at Alice Hargreaves' magnificent figure.

"I know about *her*, too," he said, "if she's the woman I think she is."

"That's more than I do," Burton replied. He stopped. They had gone up the slope of the first hill and were on its top. They lowered the body to the ground beneath a giant red pine.

Immediately, Kazz, chert knife in his hand, squatted down by the charred corpse. He raised his head upward and uttered a few phrases in what must have been a religious chant. Then, before the others could object, he had cut into the body and removed the liver.

Most of the group cried out in horror. Burton grunted. Monat stared.

Kazz's big teeth bit into the bloody organ and tore off a large chunk. His massively muscled and thickly boned jaws began chewing, and he half-closed his eyes in ecstasy. Burton stepped up to him and held out his hand, intending to remonstrate. Kazz grinned broadly and cut off a piece and offered it to Burton. He was very surprised at Burton's refusal.

"A cannibal!" Alice Hargreaves said. "Oh, my God, a bloody, stinking cannibal! And this is the promised afterlife!"

"He's no worse than our own ancestors," Burton said. He had recovered from the shock, and was even enjoying—a little—the reaction of the others. "In a land where there seems to be precious little food, his action is eminently practical. Well, our problem of burying a corpse without proper digging tools is solved. Furthermore, if we're wrong about the grails being a source of food, we may be emulating Kazz before long!"

"Never!" Alice said. "I'd die first!"

45

"That is exactly what you would do," Burton replied, coolly. "I suggest we retire and leave him to his meal. It doesn't do anything for my own appetite, and I find his table manners as abominable as those of a Yankee frontiersman's. Or a country prelate's," he added for Alice's benefit.

They walked out of sight of Kazz and behind one of the great gnarled trees. Alice said, "I don't want him around. He's an animal, an abomination! Why, I wouldn't feel safe for a second with him around!"

"You asked me for protection," Burton said. "I'll give it to you as long as you are a member of this party. But you'll also have to accept my decisions. One of which is that the apeman remains with us. We need his strength and his skills, which seem to be very appropriate for this type of country. We've become primitives; therefore, we can learn from a primitive. He stays."

Alice looked at the others with silent appeal. Monat twitched his eyebrows. Frigate shrugged his shoulders and said, "Mrs. Hargreaves, if you can possibly do it, forget your mores, your conventions. We're not in a proper upper-class Victorian heaven. Or, indeed, in any sort of heaven ever dreamed of. You can't think and behave as you did on Earth. For one thing, you come from a society where women covered themselves from neck to foot in heavy garments, and the sight of a woman's knee was a stirring sexual event. Yet, you seem to suffer no embarrassment because you're nude. You are as poised and dignified as if you wore a nun's habit."

Alice said, "I don't like it. But why should I be embarrassed? Where all are nude, none are nude. It's the thing to do, in fact, the only thing that can be done. If some angel were to give me a complete outfit, I wouldn't wear it. I'd be out of style. And my figure is good. If it weren't I might be suffering more."

The two men laughed, and Frigate said, "You're fabulous, Alice. Absolutely. I may call you Alice? Mrs. Hargreaves seems so formal when you're nude."

She did not reply but walked away and disappeared

46

behind a large tree. Burton said, "Something will have to be done about sanitation in the near future. Which means that somebody will have to decide the health policies and have the power to make regulations and enforce them. How does one form legislative, judicial, and executive bodies from the present state of anarchy?"

"To get to more immediate problems," Frigate said, "what do we do about the dead man?"

He was only a little less pale than a moment ago when Kazz had made his incisions with his chert knife.

Burton said, "I'm sure that human skin, properly tanned, or human gut, properly treated, will be far superior to grass for making ropes or bindings. I intend to cut off some strips. Do you want to help me?"

Only the wind rustling the leaves and the tops of the grass broke the silence. The sun beat down and brought out sweat which dried rapidly in the wind. No bird cried, no insect buzzed. And then the shrill voice of the little girl shattered the quiet. Alice's voice answered her, and the little girl ran to her behind the tree.

"I'll try," the American said. "But I don't know. I've gone through more than enough for one day."

"You do as you please then," Burton said. "But anybody who helps me gets first call on the use of the skin. You may wish you could have some in order to bind an axehead to a haft."

Frigate gulped audibly and then said, "I'll come."

Kazz was still squatting in the grass by the body, holding the bloody liver with one hand and the bloody stone knife with the other. Seeing Burton, he grinned with stained lips and cut off a piece of liver. Burton shook his head. The others, Galeazzi, Brontich, Maria Tucci, Filipo Rocco, Rosa Nalini, Caterina Capone, Fiorenza Fiorri, Babich, and Giunta, had retreated from the grisly scene. They were on the other side of a thick-trunked pine and talking subduedly in Italian.

Burton squatted down by the body and applied the point of the knife, beginning just above the right knee and continuing to the collarbone. Frigate stood by him and stared. He became even more pale, and his trembling increased. But he stood firm until two long strips had been lifted from the body.

"Care to try your hand at it?" Burton said. He rolled the body over on its side so that other, even longer, strips could be taken. Frigate took the bloody-tipped knife and set to work, his teeth gritted.

"Not so deep," Burton said and, a moment later, "Now you're not cutting deeply enough. Here, give me the knife. Watch!"

"I had a neighbor who used to hang up his rabbits behind his garage and cut their throats right after breaking their necks," Frigate said. "I watched once. That was enough."

"You can't afford to be fastidious or weak-stomached," Burton said. "You're living in the most primitive of conditions. You have to be a primitive to survive, like it or not."

Brontich, the tall skinny Slovene who had once been an innkeeper, ran up to them. He said, "We just found another of those big mushroom-shaped stones. About forty yards from here. It was hidden behind some trees down in a hollow."

Burton's first delight in hectoring Frigate had passed. He was beginning to feel sorry for the fellow. He said, "Look, Peter, why don't you go investigate the stone? If there is one here, we can save ourselves a trip back to the river."

He handed Frigate his grail. "Put this in a hole on the stone, but remember exactly which hole you put it in. Have the others do that, too. Make sure that they know where they put their own grails. Wouldn't want to have any quarrels about that, you know."

Strangely, Frigate was reluctant to go. He seemed to feel that he had disgraced himself by his weakness. He stood there for a moment, shifting his weight from one leg to another and sighing several times. Then, as Burton continued to scrape away at the underside of the skinstrips, he walked away. He carried the two grails in one hand and his stone axehead in the other.

Burton stopped working after the American was out of sight. He had been interested in finding out how to cut off strips, and he might dissect the body's trunk to remove the entrails. But he could do nothing at this time about preserving the skin or guts. It was possible that the bark of the oak-like trees might contain tannin which could be used with other materials to convert human skin into leather. By the time that was done, however, these strips would have rotted. Still, he had not wasted his time. The efficiency of the stone knives was proven, and he had reinforced his weak memory of human anatomy. When they were juveniles in Pisa, Richard Burton and his brother Edward had associated with the Italian medical students of the university. Both of the Burton youths had learned much from the students and neither had abandoned their interest in anatomy. Edward became a surgeon, and Richard had attended a number of lectures and public and private dissections in London. But he had forgotten much of what he had learned.

Abruptly, the sun went past the shoulder of the mountain. A pale shadow fell over him, and, within a few minutes, the entire valley was in the dusk. But the sky was a bright blue for a long time. The breeze continued to flow at the same rate. The moisture-laden air became a little cooler. Burton and the Neanderthal left the body and followed the sounds of the others' voices. These were by the grailstone of which Brontich had spoken. Burton wondered if there were others near the base of the mountain, strung out at approximate distances of a mile. This one lacked the grail in the center depression, however. Perhaps this meant that it was not ready to operate. He did not think so. It could be assumed that Whoever had made the grailstones had placed grails in the center holes of those on the river's edge because the resurrectees would be using these first. By the time they found the inland stones, they would know how to use them.

The grails were set on the depressions of the outmost circle. Their owners stood or sat around, talking but with their minds on the grails. All were wondering when—or perhaps if—the next blue flames would come. Much of their conversation was about how hungry they were. The rest was mainly surmise about how they had come here, Who had put them here, where They were, and what was being planned for them. A few spoke of their lives on Earth.

Burton sat down beneath the wide-flung and densely leaved branches of the gnarled black-trunked "irontree." He felt tired, as all, except Kazz, obviously did. His empty belly and his stretched-out nerves kept him from dozing off, although the quiet voices and the rustle of leaves conduced to sleep. The hollow in which the group waited was formed by a level space at the junction of four hills and was surrounded by trees. Though it was darker than on top of the hills, it also seemed to be a little warmer. After a while, as the dusk and the chill increased, Burton organized a firewood-collecting party. Using the knives and handaxes, they cut down many mature bamboo plants and gathered piles of grass. With the white-hot wire of the lighter, Burton started a fire of leaves and grass. These were green, and so the fire was smoky and unsatisfactory until the bamboo was put on.

Suddenly, an explosion made them jump. Some of the women screamed. They had forgotten about watching the grailstone. Burton turned just in time to see the blue flames soar up about twenty feet. The heat from the discharge could be felt by Brontich, who was about twenty feet from it.

Then the noise was gone, and they stared at the grails. Burton was the first upon the stone again; most of them did not care to venture on the stone too soon after the flames. He lifted the lid of his grail, looked within, and whooped with delight. The others climbed up and opened their own grails. Within a minute, they were seated near the fire, eating rapidly, exclaiming with ecstasy, pointing out to each other what they'd found, laughing, and joking. Things were not so bad after all. Whoever was responsible for this was taking care of them.

There was food in plenty, even after fasting all day, or, as Frigate put it, "probably fasting for half of eternity."

50

He meant by this, as he explained to Monat, that there was no telling how much time had elapsed between 2008 A.D. and today. This world wasn't built in a day, and preparing humanity for resurrection would take more than seven days. That is, if all of this had been brought about by scientific means, not by supernatural.

Burton's grail had yielded a four-inch cube of steak; a small ball of dark bread; butter; potatoes and gravy; lettuce with salad dressing of an unfamiliar but delicious taste. In addition, there was a five-ounce cup containing an excellent bourbon and another small cup with four ice cubes in it.

There was more, all the better because unexpected. A small briar pipe. A sack of pipe tobacco. Three panatela-shaped cigars. A plastic package with ten cigarettes.

"Unfiltered!" Frigate said.

There was also one small brown cigarette which Burton and Frigate smelled and said, at the same time, "Marihuana!"

Alice, holding up a small metallic scissors and a black comb, said, "Evidently we're going to get our hair back. Otherwise, there'd be no need for these. I'm so glad! But do . . . They . . . really expect me to use this?"

She held out a tube of bright red lipstick.

"Or me?" Frigate said, also looking at a similar tube.

"They're eminently practical," Monat said, turning over a packet of what was obviously toilet paper. Then he pulled out a sphere of green soap.

Burton's steak was very tender, although he would have preferred it rare. On the other hand, Frigate complained because it was not cooked enough.

"Evidently, these grails do not contain menus tailored for the individual owner," Frigate said. "Which may be why we men also get lipstick and the women got pipes. It's a mass production."

"Two miracles in one day," Burton said. "That is, if they are such. I prefer a rational explanation and intend to get it. I don't think anyone can, as yet, tell me how we were resurrected. But perhaps you twentieth-centurians have a reasonable theory for the seemingly magical

51

appearance of these articles in a previously empty container?"

"If you compare the exterior and interior of the grail," Monat said, "you will observe an approximate five-centimeter difference in depth. The false bottom must conceal a molar circuitry which is able to convert energy to matter. The energy, obviously, comes during the discharge from the rocks. In addition to the e-m converter, the grail must hold molar templates . . . ? molds . . . ? which form the matter into various combinations of elements and compounds.

"I'm safe in my speculations, for we had a similar converter on my native planet. But nothing as miniature as this, I assure you."

"Same on Earth," Frigate said. "They were making iron out of pure energy before 2002 A.D., but it was a very cumbersome and expensive process with an almost microscopic yield."

"Good," Burton said. "All this has cost us nothing. So far . . ."

He fell silent for a while, thinking of the dream he had when awakening.

"Pay up," God had said. "You owe for the flesh."

What had that meant? On Earth, at Trieste, in 1890, he had been dying in his wife's arms and asking for . . . what? Chloroform? Something. He could not remember. Then, oblivion. And he had awakened in that nightmare place and had seen things that were not on Earth nor, as far as he knew, on this planet. But that experience had been no dream.

8

They finished eating and replaced the containers in the racks within the grails. Since there was no water nearby, they would have to wait until morning to wash the containers. Frigate and Kazz, however, had made several buckets out of sections of the giant bamboo. The American volunteered to walk back to the river, if some of them would go with him, and fill the sections with water. Burton wondered why the fellow volunteered. Then, looking at Alice, he knew why. Frigate must be hoping to find some congenial female companionship. Evidently he took it for granted that Alice Hargreaves preferred Burton. And the other women, Tucci, Malini, Capone, and Fiorri, had made their choices of, respectively, Galleazzi, Brontich, Rocco, and Giunta. Babich had wandered off, possibly for the same reason that Frigate had for wishing to leave.

Monat and Kazz went with Frigate. The sky was suddenly crowded with gigantic sparks and great luminous gas clouds. The glitter of jampacked stars, some so large they seemed to be broken-off pieces of Earth's moon, and the shine of the clouds, awed them and made them feel pitifully microscopic and ill-made.

Burton lay on his back on a pile of tree leaves and puffed on a cigar. It was excellent, and in the London of his day would have cost at least a shilling. He did not feel so minute and unworthy now. The stars were inanimate matter, and he was alive. No star could ever know the delicious taste of an expensive cigar. Nor could it know the ecstasy of holding a warm well-curved woman next to it.

On the other side of the fire, half or wholly lost in the grasses and the shadows, were the Triestans. The liquor had uninhibited them, though part of their sense of freedom may have come from joy at being alive and young again. They giggled and laughed and rolled back and forth in the grass and made loud noises while kissing. And then, couple by couple, they retreated into the darkness. Or at least, made no more loud noises.

The little girl had fallen asleep by Alice. The firelight flickered over Alice's handsome aristocratic face and bald head and on the magnificent body and long legs. Burton suddenly knew that all of him had been resurrected. He definitely was not the old man who, during the last sixteen

53

years of his life, had paid so heavily for the many fevers and sicknesses that had squeezed him dry in the tropics. Now he was young again, healthy, and possessed by the old clamoring demon.

Yet he had given his promise to protect her. He could make no move, say no word which she could interpret as seductive.

Well, she was not the only woman in the world. As a matter of fact, he had the whole world of women, if not at his disposal, at least available to be asked. That is, he did if everybody who had died on Earth was on this planet. She would be only one among many billions (possibly thirty-six billion, if Frigate's estimate was correct). But there was, of course, no such evidence that this was the case.

The hell of it was that Alice might as well be the only one in the world, at this moment, anyway. He could not get up and walk off into the darkness looking for another woman, because that would leave her and the child unprotected. She certainly would not feel safe with Monat and Kazz, nor could he blame her. They were so terrifyingly ugly. Nor could he entrust her to Frigate—if Frigate returned tonight, which Burton doubted—because the fellow was an unknown quantity.

Burton suddenly laughed loudly at his situation. He had decided that he might as well stick it out for tonight. This thought set him laughing again, and he did not stop until Alice asked him if he was all right.

"More right than you will ever know," he said, turning his back to her. He reached into his grail and extracted the last item. This was a small flat stick of chicle-like substance. Frigate, before leaving, had remarked that their unknown benefactors must be American. Otherwise, they would not have thought of providing chewing gum.

After stubbing out his cigar on the ground, Burton popped the stick into his mouth. He said, "This has a strange but rather delicious taste. Have you tried yours?"

"I am tempted, but I imagine I'd look like a cow chewing her cud."

"Forget about being a lady," Burton said. "Do you

54

think that beings with the power to resurrect you would have vulgar tastes?"

Alice smiled slightly, said, "I really wouldn't know," and placed the stick in her mouth. For a moment, they chewed idly, looking across the fire at each other. She was unable to look him full in the eyes for more than a few seconds at a time.

Burton said, "Frigate mentioned that he knew you. *Of* you, rather. Just who are you, if you will pardon my unseemly curiosity?"

"There are no secrets among the dead," she replied lightly. "Or among the ex-dead, either."

She had been born Alice Pleasance Liddell on April 25, 1852. (Burton was thirty then). She was the direct descendant of King Edward III and his son, John of Gaunt. Her father was dean of Christ Church College of Oxford and co-author of a famous Greek-English lexicon. (Liddell and Scott! Burton thought.) She had had a happy childhood, an excellent education, and had met many famous people of her times: Gladstone, Matthew Arnold, the Prince of Wales, who was placed under her father's care while he was at Oxford. Her husband had been Reginald Gervis Hargreaves, and she had loved him very much. He had been a "country gentleman," liked to hunt, fish, play cricket, raise trees, and read French literature. She had three sons, all captains, two of whom died in the Great War of 1914-1918. (This was the second time that day that Burton had heard of the Great War.)

She talked on and on as if drink had loosened her tongue. Or as if she wanted to place a barrier of conversation between her and Burton.

She talked of Dinah, the tabby kitten she had loved when she was a child, the great trees of her husband's arboretum, how her father, when working on his lexicon, would always sneeze at twelve o'clock in the afternoon, no one knew why . . . at the age of eighty, she was given an honorary Doctor of Letters by the American university, Columbia, because of the vital part she had played in the genesis of Mr. Dodgson's famous book. (She neglected to mention the title and Burton, though a voracious reader, did not recall any works by a Mr. Dodgson.)

"That was a golden afternoon indeed," she said, "despite the official meteorological report. On July 4, 1862, I was ten . . . my sisters and I were wearing black shoes, white openwork socks, white cotton dresses, and hats with large brims."

Her eyes were wide, and she shook now and then as if she were struggling inside herself, and she began to talk even faster.

"Mr. Dodgson and Mr. Duckworth carried the picnic baskets . . . we set off in our boat from Folly Bridge up the Isis, upstream for a change. Mr. Duckworth rowed stroke; the drops fell off his paddle like tears of glass on the smooth mirror of the Isis, and . . ."

Burton heard the last words as if they had been roared at him. Astonished, he gazed at Alice, whose lips seemed to be moving as if she were conversing at a normal speech level. Her eyes were now fixed on him, but they seemed to be boring through him into a space and a time beyond. Her hands were half-raised as if she were surprised at something and could not move them.

Every sound was magnified. He could hear the breathing of the little girl, the pounding of her heart and Alice's, the gurgle of the workings of Alice's intestines and of the breeze as it slipped across the branches of the trees. From far away, a cry came.

He rose and listened. What was happening? Why the heightening of senses? Why could he hear their hearts but not his? He was also aware of the shape and texture of the grass under his feet. Almost, he could feel the individual molecules of the air as they bumped into his body.

Alice, too, had risen. She said, "What is happening?" and her voice fell against him like a heavy gust of wind.

He did not reply, for he was staring at her. Now, it seemed to him, he could really *see* her body for the first time. And he could see *her,* too. The entire Alice.

Alice came toward him with her arms held out, her eyes half-shut, her mouth moist. She swayed, and she crooned, "Richard! Richard!"

Then she stopped; her eyes widened. He stepped toward

her, his arms out. She cried, "No!" and turned and ran into the darkness among the trees.

For a second, he stood still. It did not seem possible that she, whom he loved as he had never loved anybody, could not love him back.

She must be teasing him. That was it. He ran after her, and called her name over and over.

It must have been hours later when the rain fell against them. Either the effect of the drug had worn off or the cold water helped dispel it, for both seemed to emerge from the ecstasy and the dreamlike state at the same time. She looked up at him as lightning lit their features, and she screamed and pushed him violently.

He fell on the grass, but reached out a hand and grabbed her ankle as she scrambled away from him on all fours.

"What's the matter with you?" he shouted.

Alice quit struggling. She sat down, hid her face against her knees, and her body shook with sobs. Burton rose and placed his hand under her chin and forced her to look upward. Lightning hit nearby again and showed him her tortured face.

"You promised to protect me!" she cried out.

"You didn't act as if you wanted to be protected," he said. "I didn't promise to protect you against a natural human impulse."

"Impulse!" she said. "Impulse! My God, I've never done anything like this in my life! I've always been good! I was a virgin when I married, and I stayed faithful to my husband all my life! And now . . . a total stranger! Just like that! I don't know what got into me!"

"Then I've been a failure," Burton said, and laughed. But he was beginning to feel regret and sorrow. If only it had been her own will, her own wish, then he would not now be having the slightest bite of conscience. But that gum had contained some powerful drug, and it had made them behave as lovers whose passion knew no limits. She had certainly cooperated as enthusiastically as any experienced woman in a Turkish harem.

"You needn't feel the least bit contrite or self-

57

reproachful," he said gently. "You were possessed. Blame the drug."

"I did it!" she said. "I . . . I! I wanted to! Oh, what a vile low whore I am!"

"I don't remember offering you any money."

He did not mean to be heartless. He wanted to make her so angry that she would forget her self-abasement. And he succeeded. She jumped up and attacked his chest and face with her nails. She called him names that a high-bred and gentle lady of Victoria's day should never have known.

Burton caught her wrists to prevent further damage and held her while she spewed more filth at him. Finally, when she had fallen silent and had begun weeping again, he led her toward the camp site. The fire was wet ashes. He scraped off the top layer and dropped a handful of grass, which had been protected from the rain by the tree, onto the embers. By its light, he saw the little girl sleeping huddled between Kazz and Monat under a pile of grass beneath the irontree. He returned to Alice, who was sitting under another tree.

"Stay away," she said. "I never want to see you again! You have dishonored me, dirtied me! And after you gave your word to protect me!"

"You can freeze if you wish," he said. "I was merely going to suggest that we huddle together to keep warm. But, if you wish discomfort, so be it. I'll tell you again that what we did was generated by the drug. No, not generated. Drugs don't generate desires or actions; they merely allow them to be released. Our normal inhibitions were dissolved, and neither one of us can blame himself or the other.

"However, I'd be a liar if I said I didn't enjoy it, and you'd be a liar if you claimed you didn't. So, why gash yourself with the knives of conscience?"

"I'm not a beast like you! I'm a good Christian God-fearing virtuous woman!"

"No doubt," Burton said dryly. "However, let me stress again one thing. I doubt if you would have done what you did if you had not wished in your heart to do so. The drug

58

suppressed your inhibitions, but it certainly did not put in your mind the idea of what to do. The idea was already there. Any action that resulted from taking the drug came from you, from what you wanted to do."

"I know that!" she screamed. "Do you think I'm some stupid simple serving girl? I have a brain! I know what I did and why! It's just that I never dreamed that I could be such . . . such a *person*! But I must have been! Must *be*!"

Burton tried to console her, to show her that everyone had certain unwished-for elements in their nature. He pointed out that the dogma of original sin surely covered this; she was human; therefore, she had dark desires in her. And so forth. The more he tried to make her feel better, the worse she felt. Then, shivering with cold, and tired of the useless arguments, he gave up. He crawled in between Monat and Kazz and took the little girl in his arms. The warmth of the three bodies and the cover of the grass pile and the feel of the naked bodies soothed him. He went to sleep with Alice's weeping coming to him faintly through the grass cover.

9

When he awoke, he was in the gray light of the false dawn, which the Arabs called the *wolf's tail*. Monat, Kazz, and the child were still sleeping. He scratched for a while at the itchy spots caused by the rough-edged grass and then crawled out. The fire was out; water drops hung from the leaves of the trees and the tips of the grass blades. He shivered with the cold. But he did not feel tired nor have any ill effects from the drug, as he had expected. He found a pile of comparatively dry bamboo under some grass beneath a tree. He rebuilt the fire with this and in a short time was comfortable. Then he saw the bamboo containers, and he drank water from one. Alice was sitting up in a mound of grass and staring sullenly at him. Her skin was ridged with goosebumps.

"Come and get warm!" he said.

She crawled out, stood up, walked over to the bamboo bucket, bent down, scooped up water, and splashed it over her face. Then she squatted down by the fire, warming her hands over a small flame. If everybody is naked, how quickly even the most modest lose their modesty, he thought.

A moment later, Burton heard the rustle of grass to the east. A naked head, Peter Frigate's, appeared. He strode from the grass, and was followed by the naked head of a woman. Emerging from the grass, she revealed a wet but beautiful body. Her eyes were large and a dark green, and her lips were a little too thick for beauty. But her other features were exquisite.

Frigate was smiling broadly. He turned and pulled her into the warmth of the fire with his hand.

"You look like the cat who ate the canary," Burton said. "What happened to your hand?"

Peter Frigate looked at the knuckles of his right hand. They were swelled, and there were scratches on the back of the hand.

"I got into a fight," he said. He pointed a finger at the woman, who was squatting near Alice and warming herself. "It was a madhouse down by the river last night. That gum must contain a drug of some sort. You wouldn't believe what people were doing. Or would you? After all, you're Richard Francis Burton. Anyway, all women, including the ugly ones, were occupied, one way or another. I got scared at what was going on and then I got mad. I hit two men with my grail, knocked them out. They were attacking a ten-year-old girl. I may have killed them; I hope I did. I tried to get the girl to come with me, but she ran away into the night.

"I decided to come back here. I was beginning to react pretty badly from what I'd done to those two men even if they deserved it. The drug was responsible; it must have released a lifetime of rage and frustration. So I started

60

back here and then I came across two more men, only these were attacking a woman, this one. I think she wasn't resisting the idea of intercourse so much as she was their idea of simultaneous attack, if you know what I mean. Anyway, she was screaming, or trying to, and struggling, and they had just started to hit her. So I hit them with my fist and kicked them and then banged away on them with my grail.

"Then I took the woman, her name's Loghu, by the way, that's all I know about her since I can't understand a word of her language, and she went with me."

He grinned again. "But we never got there."

He quit grinning, and shuddered.

"Then we woke up with the rain and lightning and thunder coming down like the wrath of God. I thought that maybe, don't laugh, that it was Judgment Day, that God had given us free rein for a day so He could let us judge ourselves. And now we were going to be cast into the pit."

He laughed tightly and said, "I've been an agnostic since I was fourteen years old, and I died one at the age of ninety, although I was thinking about calling in a priest then. But the little child that's scared of the Old Father God and Hellfire and Damnation, he's still down there, even in the old man. Or in the young man raised from the dead."

"What happened?" Burton said. "Did the world end in a crack of thunder and a stroke of lightning? You're still here, I see, and you've not renounced the delights of sin in the person of this woman."

"We found a grailstone near the mountains. About a mile west of here. We got lost, wandered around, cold, wet, jumping every time the lightning struck nearby. Then we found the grailstone. It was jammed with people, but they were exceptionally friendly, and there were so many bodies it was very warm, even if some rain did leak down through the grass. We finally went to sleep, long after the rain quit. When I woke up, I searched through the grass until I found Loghu. She got lost during the night, somehow. She seemed pleased to see me, though, and I like

61

her. There's an affinity between us. Maybe I'll find out why when she learns to speak English. I tried that and French and German and tags of Russian, Lithuanian, Gaelic, all the Scandinavian tongues, including Finnish, classical Nahuatl, Arabic, Hebrew, Onondaga Iroquois, Ojibway, Italian, Spanish, Latin, modern and Homeric Greek, and a dozen others. Result: a blank look."

"You must be quite a linguist," Burton said.

"I'm not fluent in any of those," Frigate said. "I can read most of them but can speak only a few everyday phrases. Unlike you, I am not master of thirty-nine languages—including pornography."

The fellow seemed to know much about himself, Burton thought. He would find out just how much at a later time.

"I'll be frank with you, Peter," Burton said. "Your account of your aggressiveness amazed me. I had not thought you capable of attacking and beating that many men. Your queasiness . . ."

"It was the gum, of course. It opened the door of the cage."

Frigate squatted down by Loghu and rubbed his shoulder against hers. She looked at him out of slightly slanted eyes. The woman would be beautiful once her hair grew out.

Frigate continued, "I'm so timorous and queasy because I am afraid of the anger, the desire to do violence, that lies not too deeply within me. I fear violence because I am violent. I fear what will happen if I am not afraid. Hell, I've known that for forty years. Much good the knowledge has done me!"

He looked at Alice and said, "Good morning!"

Alice replied cheerily enough, and she even smiled at Loghu when she was introduced. She would look at Burton, and she would answer his direct questions. But she would not chat with him or give him anything but a stern face.

Monat, Kazz, and the little girl, all yawning, came to the fireside. Burton prowled around the edges of the camp and found that the Triestans were gone. Some had left

62

their grails behind. He cursed them for their carelessness and thought about leaving the grails in the grass to teach them a lesson. But he eventually placed the cylinders in depressions on the grailstone.

If their owners did not return, they would go hungry unless someone shared their food with them. In the meantime, the food in their grails would have to be untouched. He would be unable to open them. They had discovered yesterday that only the owner of a grail could open it. Experimentation with a long stick had determined also that the owner had to touch the grail with his fingers or some part of his body before the lid would open. It was Frigate's theory that a mechanism in the grail was keyed to the peculiar configuration of skin voltage of the owner. Or perhaps the grail contained a very sensitive detector of the individual's brain waves.

The sky had become bright by then. The sun was still on the other side of the 20,000-foot high eastern mountain. Approximately a half hour later, the grailrock spurted blue flame with a roll of thunder. Thunder from the stones along the river echoed against the mountain.

The grails yielded bacon and eggs, ham, toast, butter, jam, milk, a quarter of a cantaloupe, cigarettes, and a cupful of dark brown crystals which Frigate said was instant coffee. He drank the milk in one cup, rinsed it out in water in a bamboo container, and set it by the fire. When the water was boiling, he put a teaspoonful of the crystals into the water and stirred it. The coffee was delicious, and there were enough crystals to provide six cups. Then Alice put the crystals into the water before heating it over the fire and found that it was not necessary to use the fire. The water boiled within three seconds after the crystals were placed into the cold water.

After eating, they washed out the containers and replaced them in the grails. Burton strapped his grail onto his wrist. He intended to explore, and he certainly was not going to leave the grail on the stone. Though it could do no one but himself any good, vicious people might take it just for the pleasure of seeing him starve.

Burton started his language lessons with the little girl

and Kazz, and Frigate got Loghu to sit in on them. Frigate suggested that a universal language should be adopted because of the many many languages and dialects, perhaps fifty to sixty thousand, that mankind had used in his several million years of existence and which he was using along the river. That is, provided that all of mankind had been resurrected. After all, all he knew about was the few square miles he had seen. But it would be a good idea to start propagating Esperanto, the synthetic language invented by the Polish oculist, Doctor Zamenhof, in 1887. Its grammar was very simple and absolutely regular, and its sound combinations, though not as easy for everybody to pronounce as claimed, were still relatively easy. And the basis of the vocabulary was Latin with many words from English and German and other West European languages.

"I had heard about it before I died," Burton said. "But I never saw any samples of it. Perhaps it may become useful. But, in the meantime, I'll teach these two English."

"But most of the people here speak Italian or Slovenian!" Frigate said.

"That may be true, though we haven't any survey as yet. However, I don't intend to stay here, you can be sure of that."

"I could have predicted that," Frigate muttered. "You always did get restless; you had to move on."

Burton glared at Frigate and then started the lessons. For about fifteen minutes, he drilled them in the identification and pronunciation of nineteen nouns and a few verbs: fire, bamboo, grail, man, woman, girl, hand, feet, eye, teeth, eat, walk, run, talk, danger, I, you, they, us. He intended that he should learn as much from them as they from him. In time, he would be able to speak their tongues, whatever they were.

The sun cleared the top of the eastern range. The air became warmer, and they let the fire die. They were well into the second day of resurrection. And they knew almost nothing about this world or what their eventual fate was supposed to be or Who was determining their fate.

Lev Ruach stuck his big-nosed face through the grass and said, "May I join you?"

Burton nodded, and Frigate said, "Sure, why not?"

Ruach stepped out of the grass. A short, pale-skinned woman with great brown eyes and lovely delicate features followed him. Ruach introduced her as Tanya Kauwitz. He had met her last night, and they had stayed together, since they had a number of things in common. She was of Russian-Jewish descent, was born in 1958 in the Bronx, New York City, had become an English schoolteacher, married a businessman who made a million and dropped dead when she was forty-five, leaving her free to marry a wonderful man with whom she had been in love for fifteen years. Six months later, she was dead of cancer. Tanya, not Lev, gave this information and in one sentence.

"It was hell down on the plains last night," Lev said. "Tanya and I had to run for our lives into the woods. So I decided that I would find you and ask if we could stay with you. I apologize for my hasty remarks of yesterday, Mr. Burton. I think that my observations were valid, but the attitudes I was speaking of should be considered in the context of your other attitudes."

"We'll go into that some other time," Burton said. "At the time I wrote that book, I was suffering from the vile and malicious lies of the money lenders of Damascus, and they . . ."

"Certainly, Mr. Burton," Ruach said. "As you say, later. I just wanted to make the point that I consider you to be a very capable and strong person, and I would like to join your group. We're in a state of anarchy, if you can call anarchy a state, and many of us need protection."

Burton did not like to be interrupted. He scowled and said, "Please permit me to explain myself. I . . ."

Frigate stood up and said, "Here come the others. Wonder where they've been?"

Only four of the original nine had come back, however. Maria Tucci explained that they had wandered away together after chewing the gum, and eventually ended up by one of the big bonfires on the plains. Then many things

65

had happened; there had been fights and attacks by men on women, men on men, women on men, women on women, and even attacks on children. The group had split up in the chaos, she had met the other three only an hour ago while she was searching in the hills for the grailstone.

Lev added some details. The result of chewing the narcotic gum had been tragic, amusing, or gratifying, depending, apparently, upon individual reaction. The gum had had an aphrodisiac effect upon many, but it also had many other effects. Consider the husband and wife, who had died in Opcina, a suburb of Trieste, in 1899. They had been resurrected within six feet of each other. They had wept with joy at being reunited when so many couples had not been. They thanked God for their good luck, though they also had made some loud comments that this world was not what they had been promised. But they had had fifty years of married bliss and now looked forward to being together for eternity.

Only a few minutes after both had chewed the gum, the man had strangled his wife, heaved her body into the river, picked up another woman in his arms, and run off into the darkness of the woods with her.

Another man had leaped upon a grailstone and delivered a speech that lasted all night, even through the rain. To the few who could hear, and the even fewer who listened, he had demonstrated the principles of a perfect society and how these could be carried out in practice. By dawn, he was so hoarse he could only croak a few words. On Earth, he had seldom bothered to vote.

A man and a woman, outraged at the public display of carnality, had forcefully tried to separate couples. The results: bruises, bloody noses, split lips, and two concussions, all theirs. Some men and women had spent the night on their knees praying and confessing their sins.

Some children had been badly beaten, raped, or murdered, or all three. But not everybody had succumbed to the madness. A number of adults had protected the children, or tried to.

Ruach described the despair and disgust of a Croat Moslem and an Austrian Jew because their grails contained pork. A Hindu screamed obscenities because his grail offered him meat.

A fourth man, crying out that they were in the hands of devils, had hurled his cigarettes into the river.

Several had said to him, "Why didn't you give us the cigarettes if you didn't want them?"

"Tobacco is the invention of the devil; it was the weed created by Satan in the Garden of Eden!"

A man said, "At least you could have shared the cigarettes with us. It wouldn't hurt you."

"I would like to throw all the evil stuff into the river!" he had shouted.

"You're an insufferable bigot and crazy to boot," another had replied, and struck him in the mouth. Before the tobacco-hater could get up off the ground, he was hit and kicked by four others.

Later, the tobacco-hater had staggered up and, weeping with rage, cried, "What have I done to deserve this, O Lord, my God! I have always been a good man. I gave thousands of pounds to charities, I worshiped in Thy temple three times a week, I waged a lifelong war against sin and corruption, I . . ."

"I know you!" a woman had shouted. She was a tall blue-eyed girl with a handsome face and well-curved figure. "I know you! Sir Robert Smithson!"

He had stopped talking and had blinked at her. "I don't know *you*!"

"You wouldn't! But you should! I'm one of the thousands of girls who had to work sixteen hours a day, six and a half days a week, so you could live in your big house on the hill and dress in fine clothes and so your horses and dogs could eat far better than I could! I was one of your factory girls! My father slaved for you, my mother slaved for you, my brothers and sisters, those who weren't too sick or who didn't die because of too little or too bad food, dirty beds, drafty windows, and rat bites, slaved for you. My father lost a hand in one of your machines, and you kicked him out without a penny. My mother died of the white plague. I was coughing out my life, too, my fine baronet, while you stuffed yourself with rich foods and sat in easy chairs and dozed off in your big expensive church pew and gave thousands to feed the poor unfortunates in Asia and to send missionaries to convert the poor heathens in Africa. I coughed out my lungs, and I had to go a-whoring to make enough money to feed my kid sisters and brothers. And I caught syphilis, you bloody pious bastard, because you wanted to wring out every drop of sweat and blood I had and those poor devils like me had! I died in prison because' you told the police they should deal harshly with prostitution. You . . . you . . . !"

Smithson had gone red at first, then pale. Then he had drawn himself up straight, scowling at the woman, and said, "You whores always have somebody to blame for your unbridled lusts, your evil ways. God knows that I followed His ways."

He had turned and had walked off, but the woman ran after him and swung her grail at him. It came around swiftly; somebody shouted; he spun and ducked. The grail almost grazed the top of his head.

Smithson ran past the woman before she could recover and quickly lost himself in the crowd. Unfortunately, Ruach said, very few understood what was going on because they couldn't speak English.

"Sir Robert Smithson," Burton said. "If I remember correctly, he owned cotton mills and steelworks in Manchester. He was noted for his philanthropies and his good works among the heathens. Died in 1870 or thereabouts at the age of eighty."

"And probably convinced that he would be rewarded in Heaven," Lev Ruach said. "Of course, it would never have occurred to him that he was a murderer many times over."

"If he hadn't exploited the poor, someone else would have done so."

"That is an excuse used by many throughout men's history," Lev said. "Besides, there *were* industrialists in your country who saw to it that wages and conditions in their factories were improved. Robert Owen was one, I believe."

10

"I don't see much sense in arguing about what went on in the past," Frigate said. "I think we should do something about our present situation."

Burton stood up. "You're right, Yank! We need roofs over our heads, tools, God knows what else! But first, I think we should take a look at the cities of the plains and see what the citizens are doing there."

At that moment, Alice came through the trees on the hill above them. Frigate saw her first. He burst out laughing. "The latest in ladies' wear!"

She had cut lengths of the grass with her scissors and plaited them into a two-piece garment. One was a sort of poncho which covered her breasts and the other a skirt which fell to her calves.

The effect was strange, though one that she should have expected. When she was naked, the hairless head still did not detract too much from her femaleness and her beauty. But with the green, bulky, and shapeless garments, her face suddenly became masculine and ugly.

The other women crowded around her and examined the weaving of the grass lengths and the grass belt that secured the skirt.

"It's very itchy, very uncomfortable," Alice said. "But it's decent. That's all I can say for it."

"Apparently you did not mean what you said about your unconcern with nudity in a land where all are nude," Burton said.

Alice stared coolly and said, "I expect that everybody will be wearing these. Every decent man and woman, that is."

"I supposed that Mrs. Grundy would rear her ugly head here," Burton replied.

"It was a shock to be among so many naked people," Frigate said. "Even though nudity on the beach and in the private home became commonplace in the late '80's. But it didn't take long for everyone to get used to it. Everyone except the hopelessly neurotic, I suppose."

Burton swung around and spoke to the other women. "What about you ladies? Are you going to wear these ugly and scratchy haycocks because one of your sex suddenly decides that she has private parts again? Can something that has been so public become private?"

Loghu, Tanya, and Alice did not understand him because he spoke in Italian. He repeated in English for the benefit of the last two.

Alice flushed and said, "What I wear is my business. If anybody else cares to go naked when I'm decently covered, well . . . !"

Loghu had not understood a word, but she understood what was going on. She laughed and turned away. The other women seemed to be trying to guess what each one intended to do. The ugliness and the uncomfortableness of the clothing were not the issues.

"While you females are trying to make up your minds," Burton said, "it would be nice if you would take a bamboo pail and go with us to the river. We can bathe, fill the pails with water, find out the situation in the plains, and then return here. We may be able to build several houses—or temporary shelters—before nightfall."

They started down the hills, pushing through the grass and carrying their grails, chert weapons, bamboo spears and buckets. They had not gone far before they encountered a number of people. Apparently, many plains dwellers had decided to move out. Not only that, some had also found chert and had made tools and weapons. These had learned the technique of working with stone from somebody, possibly from other primitives in the area. So far, Burton had seen only two specimens of non-*Homo sapiens*, and these were with him. But wherever the techniques had been learned, they had been put to good use. They passed two half-completed bamboo huts. These were round, one-roomed, and would have conical roofs thatched with the huge triangular leaves from the irontrees and with the long hill grass. One man, using a chert adze and axe, was building a short-legged bamboo bed.

Except for a number erecting rather crude huts or lean-tos without stone tools at the edge of the plains, and for a number swimming in the river, the plain was deserted. The bodies from last night's madness had been removed. So far, no one had put on a grass skirt, and many stared at Alice or even laughed and made raucous comments. Alice turned red, but she made no move to get rid of her clothes. The sun was getting hot, however, and she was scratching under her breast garment and under her skirt. It was a measure of the intensity of the irritation that she, raised by strict Victorian upper-class standards, would scratch in public.

However, when they got to the river, they saw a dozen heaps of stuff that turned out to be grass dresses. These had been left on the edge of the river by the men and women now laughing, splashing, and swimming in the river.

It was certainly a contrast to the beaches he knew. These were the same people who had accepted the bathing machines, the suits that covered them from ankle to neck, and all the other modest devices, as absolutely moral and vital to the continuation of the proper society—theirs. Yet, only one day after finding themselves here, they were swimming in the nude. And enjoying it.

Part of the acceptance of their unclothed state came from the shock of the resurrection. In addition, there was not much they could do about it that first day. And there had been a leavening of the civilized with savage peoples, or tropical civilized peoples, who were not particularly shocked by nudity.

He called out to a woman who was standing to her waist in the water. She had a coarsely pretty face and sparkling blue eyes.

71

"That is the woman who attacked Sir Robert Smithson," Lev Ruach said. "I believe her name is Wilfreda Allport."

Burton looked at her curiously and with appreciation of her splendid bust. He called out, "How's the water?"

"Very nice!" she said, smiling.

He unstrapped his grail, put down the container, which held his chert knife and handaxe, and waded in with his cake of green soap. The water felt as if it was about ten degrees below his body temperature. He soaped himself while he struck up a conversation with Wilfreda. If she still harbored any resentment about Smithson, she did not show it. Her accent was heavily North Country, perhaps Cumberland.

Burton said to her, "I heard about your little to-do with the late great hypocrite, the baronet. You should be happy now, though. You're healthy and young and beautiful again, and you don't have to toil for your bread. Also, you can do for love what you had to do for money."

There was no use beating around the bush with a factory girl. Not that she had any.

Wilfreda gave him a stare as cool as any he had received from Alice Hargreaves. She said, "Now, haven't you the ruddy nerve? English, aren't you? I can't place your accent, London, I'd say, with a touch of something foreign."

"You're close," he said, laughing. "I'm Richard Burton, by the way. How would you like to join our group? We've banded together for protection, we're going to build some houses this afternoon. We've got a grailstone all to ourselves up in the hills."

Wilfreda looked at the Tau Cetan and the Neanderthal. "They're part of your mob, now? I heard about 'em; they say the monster's a man from the stars, come along in 2000 A.D., they do say."

"He won't hurt you," Burton said. "Neither will the subhuman. What do you say?"

"I'm only a woman," she said. "What do I have to offer?"

"All a woman has to offer," Burton said, grinning.

72

Surprisingly, she burst out laughing. She touched his chest and said, "Now ain't you the clever one? What's the matter, you can't get no girl of your own?"

"I had one and lost her," Burton said. That was not entirely true. He was not sure what Alice intended to do. He could not understand why she continued to stay with his group if she was so horrified and disgusted. Perhaps it was because she preferred the evil she knew to the evil she did not know. At the moment, he himself felt only disgust at her stupidity, but he did not want her to go. That love he had experienced last night may have been caused by the drug, but he still felt a residue of it. Then why was he asking this woman to join them? Perhaps it was to make Alice jealous. Perhaps it was to have a woman to fall back upon if Alice refused him tonight. Perhaps . . . he did not know why.

Alice stood upon the bank, her toes almost touching the water. The bank was, at this point, only an inch above the water. The short grass continued from the plain to form a solid mat that grew down on the river bed. Burton could feel the grass under his feet as far as he could wade. He threw his soap onto the bank and swam out for about forty feet and dived down. Here the current suddenly became stronger and the depth much greater. He swam down, his eyes open, until the light failed and his ears hurt. He continued on down and then his fingers touched bottom. There was grass there, too.

When he swam back to where the water was up to his waist, he saw that Alice had shed her clothes. She was in closer to the shore, but squatting so that the water was up to her neck. She was soaping her head and face.

He called to Frigate, "Why don't you come in?"

"I'm guarding the grails," Frigate said.

"Very good!"

Burton swore under his breath. He should have thought of that and appointed somebody as a guard. He wasn't in actuality a good leader, he tended to let things go to pot, to permit them to disintegrate. Admit it. On Earth he had been the head of many expeditions, none of which had been distinguished by efficiency or strong management.

Yet, during the Crimean War, when he was head of Beatson's Irregulars, training the wild Turkish cavalry, the Bashi-Bazouks, he had done quite well, far better than most. So he should not be reprimanding himself . . .

Lev Ruach climbed out of the water and ran his hands over his skinny body to take off the drops. Burton got out, too, and sat down beside him. Alice turned her back on him, whether on purpose or not he had no way of knowing, of course.

"It's not just being young again that delights me," Lev said in his heavily accented English. "It's having this leg back."

He tapped his right knee.

"I lost it in a traffic accident on the New Jersey Turnpike when I was fifty years old."

He laughed and said, "There was an irony to the situation that some might call fate. I had been captured by Arabs two years before when I was looking for minerals in the desert, in the state of Israel, you understand . . ."

"You mean Palestine?" Burton said.

"The Jews founded an independent state in 1948," Lev said. "You wouldn't know about that, of course. I'll tell you all about it some time. Anyway, I was captured and tortured by Arab guerrillas. I won't go into the details; it makes me sick to recall it. But I escaped that night, though not before bashing in the heads of two with a rock and shooting two more with a rifle. The others fled, and I got away. I was lucky. An army patrol picked me up. However, two years later, when I was in the States, driving down the Turnpike, a truck, a big semi, I'll describe that later, too, cut in front of me and jackknifed and I crashed into it. I was badly hurt, and my right leg was amputated below the knee. But the point of this story is that the truck driver had been born in Syria. So, you see the Arabs were out to get me, and they did, though they did not kill me. That job was done by our friend from Tau Ceti. Though I can't say he did anything to humanity except hurry up its doom."

"What do you mean by that?" Burton said.

"There were millions dying from famine, even the

States were on a strictly rationed diet, and pollution of our water, land, and air was killing other millions. The scientists said that half of Earth's oxygen supply would be cut off in ten years because the phytoplankton of the oceans—they furnished half the world's oxygen, you know—were dying. The oceans were polluted."

"The *oceans?*"

"You don't believe it? Well, you died in 1890, so you find it hard to credit. But some people were predicting in 1968 exactly what did happen in 2008. I believed them, I was a biochemist. But most of the population, especially those who counted, the masses and the politicians, refused to believe until it was too late. Measures were taken as the situation got worse, but they were always too weak and too late and fought against by groups that stood to lose money, if effective measures were taken. But it's a long sad story, and if we're to build houses, we'd best start immediately after lunch."

Alice came out of the river and ran her hands over her body. The sun and the breeze dried her off quickly. She picked up her grass clothes but did not put them back on. Wilfreda asked her about them. Alice replied that they made her itch too much, but she would keep them to wear at night if it got too cold. Alice was polite to Wilfreda but obviously aloof. She had overheard much of the conversation and so knew that Wilfreda had been a factory girl who had become a whore and then had died of syphilis. Or at least Wilfreda thought that the disease had killed her. She did not remember dying. Undoubtedly, as she had said cheerily, she had lost her mind first.

Alice, hearing this, moved even further away. Burton grinned, wondering what she would do if she knew that he had suffered from the same disease, caught from a slave girl in Cairo when he had been disguised as a Moslem during his trip to Mecca in 1853. He had been "cured" and his mind had not been physically affected, though his mental suffering had been intense. But the point was that resurrection had given everybody a fresh, young, and undiseased body, and what a person had been on Earth should not influence another's attitude toward them.

Should not was not, however, *would* not.

He could not really blame Alice Hargreaves. She was the product of her society—like all women, she was what men had made her—and she had strength of character and flexibility of mind to lift herself above some of the prejudices of her time and her class. She had adapted to the nudity well enough, and she was not openly hostile or contemptuous of the girl. She had performed an act with Burton that went against a-lifetime of overt and covert indoctrination. And that was on the night of the first day of her life after death, when she should have been on her knees singing hosannas because she had "sinned" and promising that she would never "sin" again as long as she was not put in hellfire.

As they walked across the plain, he thought about her, turning his head now and then to look back at her. That hairless head made her face look so much older but the hairlessness made her look so childlike below the navel. They all bore this contradiction, old man or woman above the neck, young child below the bellybutton.

He dropped back until he was by her side. This put him behind Frigate and Loghu. The view of Loghu would yield some profit even if his attempt to talk to Alice resulted in nothing. Loghu had a beautifully rounded posterior; her buttocks were like two eggs. And she swayed as enchantingly as Alice.

He spoke in a low voice, "If last night distressed you so much, why do you stay with me?"

Her beautiful face became twisted and ugly.

"I am not staying with *you*! I am staying with the *group*! Moreover, I've been thinking about last night, though it pains me to do so. I must be fair. It was the narcotic in that hideous gum that made both of us behave the . . . way we did. At least, I know it was responsible for my behavior. And I'm giving you the benefit of the doubt."

"Then there's no hope of repetition?"

"How can you ask that! Certainly not! How dare you?"

"I did not force you," he said. "As I have pointed out, you did what you would do if you were not restrained by

76

your inhibitions. Those inhibitions are good things—under certain circumstances, such as being the lawful wedded wife of a man you love in the England of Earth. But Earth no longer exists, not as we knew it. Neither does England. Neither does English society. And if all of mankind has been resurrected and is scattered along this river, you still may never see your husband again. You are no longer married. Remember . . . *til death do us part?* You have died, and, therefore, parted. Moreover, *there is no giving into marriage in heaven.*"

"You are a blasphemer, Mr. Burton. I read about you in the newspapers, and I read some of your books about Africa and India and that one about the Mormons in the States. I also heard stories, most of which I found hard to believe, they made you out to be so wicked. Reginald was very indignant when he read your *Kasidah.* He said he'd have no such foul atheistic literature in his house, and he threw all your books into the furnace."

"If I'm so wicked, and you feel you're a *fallen* woman, why don't you leave?"

"Must I repeat everything? The next group might have even worse men in it. And, as you have been so kind to point out, you did not force me. Anyway, I'm sure that you have some kind of heart beneath that cynical and mocking air. I saw you weeping when you were carrying Gwenafra and she was crying."

"You have found me out," he said, grinning. "Very well. So be it. I will be chivalrous, I will not attempt to seduce you or to molest you in any way. But the next time you see me chewing the gum, you would do well to hide. Meanwhile, I give my word of honor; you have nothing to fear from me as long as I am not under the influence of the gum."

Her eyes widened, and she stopped. "You plan to use it again?"

"Why not? It apparently turned some people into violent beasts, but it had no such effect on me. I feel no craving for it, so I doubt it's habit-forming. I used to smoke a pipe of opium now and then, you know, and I did not become addicted to it, so I don't suppose I have a

77

psychological weakness for drugs."

"I understood that you were very often deep in your cups, Mister Burton. You and that nauseating creature, Mr. Swinburne . . ."

She stopped talking. A man had called out to her, and, though she did not understand Italian, she understood his obscene gesture. She blushed all over but walked briskly on. Burton glared at the man. He was a well-built brown-skinned youth with a big nose, a weak chin, and close-set eyes. His speech was that of the criminal class of the city of Bologna, where Burton had spent much time while investigating Etruscan relics and graves. Behind him were ten men, most of them as unprepossessing and as wicked-looking as their leader, and five women. It was evident that the men wanted to add more women to the group. It was also evident that they would like to get their hands on the stone weapons of Burton's group. They were armed only with their grails or with bamboo sticks.

11

Burton spoke sharply, and his people closed up. Kazz did not understand his words, but he sensed at once what was happening. He dropped back to form the rearguard with Burton. His brutish appearance and the handaxe in his huge fist checked the Bolognese somewhat. They followed the group, making loud comments and threats, but they did not get much closer. When they reached the hills, however, the leader of the gang shouted a command, and it attacked.

The youth with the close-set eyes, yelling, swinging his grail at the end of the strap, ran at Burton. Burton gauged the swing of the cylinder and then launched his bamboo spear just as the grail was arcing outward. The stone tip went into the man's solar plexus, and he fell on his side with the spear sticking in him. The subhuman struck a swinging grail with a stick, which was knocked out of his hand. He leaped inward and brought the edge of the handaxe against the top of the head of his attacker, and that man went down with a bloody skull.

Little Lev Ruach threw his grail into the chest of a man and ran up and jumped on him. His feet drove into the face of the man, who was getting up again. The man went backward; Ruach bounded up and gashed the man's shoulder with his chert knife. The man, screaming, got to his feet and raced away.

Frigate did better than Burton had expected him to, since he had turned pale and begun shaking when the gang had first challenged them. His grail was strapped to his left wrist while his right held a handaxe. He charged into the group, was hit on the shoulder with a grail, the impact of which was lessened when he partially blocked it with his grail, and he fell to his side. A man lifted a bamboo stick with both hands to bring it down on Frigate, but he rolled away, bringing his grail up and blocking the stick as it came down. Then he was up, his head butting into the man and carrying him back. Both went down, Frigate on top, and his stone axe struck the man twice on the temple.

Alice had thrown her grail into the face of a man and then stabbed at him with the fire-sharpened end of her bamboo spear. Loghu ran around to the side of the man and hit him across the head with her stick so hard that he dropped to his knees.

The fight was over in sixty seconds. The other men fled with their women behind them. Burton turned the screaming leader onto his back and pulled his spear out of the pit of his stomach. The tip had not gone in more than half an inch.

The man got to his feet and, clutching the streaming wound, staggered off across the plains. Two of the gang were unconscious but would probably survive. The man Frigate had attacked was dead.

The American had turned from pale to red and then back to pale. But he did not look contrite or sickened. If his expression held anything, it was elation. And relief.

He said, "That was the first man I've ever killed! The first!"

"I doubt that it'll be the last," Burton said. "Unless you're killed first."

Ruach, looking at the corpse, said, "A dead man looks just as dead here as on Earth. I wonder where those who are killed in the afterlife go?"

"If we live long enough, we might find out. You two women gave a very fine account of yourselves."

Alice said, "I did what had to be done," and walked away. She was pale and shaking. Loghu, on the other hand, seemed exhilarated.

They got to the grailstone about a half-hour before noon. Things had changed. Their quiet little hollow contained about sixty people, many of whom were working on pieces of chert. One man was holding a bloody eye into which a chip of stone had flown. Several more were bleeding from the face or holding smashed fingers.

Burton was upset but he could do nothing about it. The only hope for regaining the quiet retreat was that the lack of water would drive the intruders away. That hope went quickly. A woman told him that there was a small cataract about a mile and a half to the west. It fell from the top of the mountain down the tip of an arrowhead-shaped canyon and into a large hole which it had only half-filled. Eventually, it should spill out and take a course through the hills and spread out on the plain. Unless, of course, stone from the mountain base was brought down to make a channel for the stream.

"Or we make waterpipes out of the big bamboo," Frigate said.

They put their grails on the rock, each carefully noting the exact location of his, and they waited. He intended to move on after the grails were filled. A location halfway between the cataract and the grailstone would be advantageous, and they might not be so crowded.

The blue flames roared out above the stone just as the sun reached its zenith. This time, the grails yielded an antipasto salad, Italian black bread with melted garlic butter, spaghetti and meatballs, a cupful of dry red wine, grapes, more coffee crystals, ten cigarettes, a marihuana stick, a cigar, more toilet paper and a cake of soap, and four chocolate creams. Some people complained that they did not like Italian food, but no one refused to eat.

The group, smoking their cigarettes, walked along the base of the mountain to the cataract. This was at the end of the triangular canyon, where a number of men and women had set up camp around the hole. The water was icy cold. After washing out their containers, drying them, and refilling the buckets, they went back in the direction of the grailstone. After a half a mile, they chose a hill covered by pines except for the apex, on which a great irontree grew. There was plenty of bamboo of all sizes growing around them. Under the direction of Kazz and of Frigate, who had spent a few years in Malaysia, they cut down bamboo and built their huts. These were round buildings with a single door and a window in the rear and a conical thatched roof. They worked swiftly and did not try for nicety, so that by dinnertime everything except the roofs was finished. Frigate and Monat were picked to stay behind as guards while the others took the grails to the stone. Here they found about 300 people constructing lean-tos and huts. Burton had expected this. Most people would not want to walk a half mile every day three times a day for their meals. They would prefer to cluster around the grailstones. The huts here were arranged haphazardly and closer than necessary. There was still the problem of getting fresh water, which was why he was surprised that there were so many here. But he was informed by a pretty Slovene that a source of water had been found closeby only this afternoon. A spring ran from a cave almost in a straight line up from the rock. Burton investigated. Water had broken out from a cave and was trickling down the face of the cliff into a basin about fifty feet wide and eight deep.

He wondered if this was an afterthought on the part of Whoever had created this place. .

He returned just as the blue flames thundered.

Kazz suddenly stopped to relieve himself. He did not

bother to turn away; Loghu giggled; Tanya turned red; the Italian women were used to seeing men leaning against buildings wherever the fancy took them; Wilfreda was used to anything; Alice, surprisingly, ignored him as if he were a dog. And that might explain her attitude. To her, Kazz was not human and so could not be expected to act as humans were expected to act.

There was no reason to reprimand Kazz for this just now, especially when Kazz did not understand his language. But he would have to use sign language the next time Kazz proceeded to relieve himself while they were sitting around and eating. Everybody had to learn certain limits, and anything that upset others while they were eating should be forbidden. And that, he thought, included quarreling during mealtimes. To be fair, he would have to admit that he had participated in more than his share of dinner disputes in his lifetime.

He patted Kazz on top of the breadloaf-shaped skull as he passed him. Kazz looked at him and Burton shook his head, figuring that Kazz would find out why when he learned to speak English. But he forgot his intention, and he stopped and rubbed the top of his own head. Yes, there was a very fine fuzz there.

He felt his face, which was as smooth as ever. But his armpits were fuzzy. The pubic area was, however, smooth. That might be a slower growth than scalp hair, though. He told the others, and they inspected themselves and each other. It was true. Their hair was returning, at least, on their heads and their armpits. Kazz was the exception. His hair was growing out all over him except on his face.

The discovery made them jubilant. Laughing, joking, they walked along the base of the mountain in the shadow. They turned east then and waded through the grass of four hills before coming up the slope of the hill they were beginning to think of as home. Halfway up it, they stopped, silent. Frigate and Monat had not returned their calls.

After telling them to spread out and to proceed slowly, Burton led them up the hill. The huts were deserted, and several of the little huts had been kicked or trampled. He

82

felt a chill, as if a cold wind had blown on him. The silence, the damaged huts, the complete absence of the two, was foreboding.

A minute later, they heard a halloo and turned to look down the hill. The skin-heads of Monat and Frigate appeared in the grasses and then they were coming up the hill. Monat looked grave, but the American was grinning. His face was bruised over the cheek, and the knuckles of both hands were torn and bloody.

"We just got back from chasing off four men and three women who wanted to take over our huts," he said. "I told them they could build their own, and that you'd be back right away and beat hell out of them if they didn't take off. They understood me all right, they spoke English. They had been resurrected at the grailstone a mile north of ours along the river. Most of the people there were Triestans of your time, but about ten, all together, were Chicagoans who'd died about 1985. The distribution of the dead sure is funny, isn't it? There's a random choice operating along here, I'd say.

"Anyway, I told them what Mark Twain said the devil said, *You Chicagoans think you're the best people here whereas the truth is you're just the most numerous.* That didn't go over very well, they seemed to think that I should be buddy-buddies with them because I was an American. One of the women offered herself to me if I'd change sides and take their part in appropriating the huts. She was the one who was living with two of the men. I said no. They said they'd take the huts anyway, and over my dead body if they had to.

"But they talked more brave than they were. Monat scared them just by looking at them. And we did have the stone weapons and spears. Still, their leader was whipping them up into rushing us, when I took a good hard look at one of them.

"His head was bald so he didn't have that thick straight black hair, and he was about thirty-five when I first knew him, and he wore thick shell-rimmed glasses then, and I hadn't seen him for fifty-four years. But I stepped up closer, and I looked into his face, which was grinning just like I remembered it, like the proverbial skunk, and I said, *'Lem? Lem Sharkko!* It is *Lem Sharkko,* isn't it?'

"His eyes opened then, and he grinned even more, and he took my hand, *my hand,* after all he'd done to me, and he cried out as if we were long-lost brothers, 'It is, it is! It's Pete Frigate! My God, Pete Frigate!'

"I was almost glad to see him and for the same reason he said he was glad to see me. But then I told myself, 'This is the crooked publisher that cheated you out of $4,000 when you were just getting started as a writer and ruined your career for years. This is the slimy schlock dealer who cheated you and at least four other writers out of a lot of money and then declared bankruptcy and skipped. And then he inherited a lot of money from an uncle and lived very well indeed, thus proving that crime *did* pay. This is the man you have not forgotten, not only because of what he did to you and others but because of so many other crooked publishers you ran into later on.' "

Burton grinned and said, "I once said that priests, politicians, and publishers would never get past the gates of heaven. But I was wrong, that is, if this is heaven."

"Yeah, I know," Frigate said. "I've never forgotten that you said that. Anyway, I put down my natural joy at seeing a familiar face again, and I said, 'Sharkko . . .' "

"With a name like that, he got you to trust him?" Alice said.

"He told me it was a Czech name that meant *trustworthy.* Like everything else he told me, it was a lie. Anyway, I had just about convinced myself that Monat and I should let them take over. We'd retire and then we'd run them out when you came back from the grailstone. That was the smart thing to do. But when I recognized Sharkko, I got so *mad!* I said, grinning, 'Gee, it's really great to see your face after all these years. Especially here where there are no cops or courts!'

"And I hit him right in the nose! He went over flat on his back, with his nose spouting blood. Monat and I rushed the others, and I kicked one, and then another hit me on the cheek with his grail. I was knocked silly, but Monat knocked one out with the butt of his spear and cracked the ribs of another; he's skinny but he's awful fast, and what he doesn't know about self-defense—or offense! Sharkko got up then and I hit with my other fist, but only a glancing blow along his jaw. It hurt my fist more than it hurt his jaw. He spun around and took off, and I went after him. The others took off, too, with Monat beating them on the tail with his spear. I chased Sharkko up the next hill and caught him on the downslope and punched him but good! He crawled away, begging for mercy, which I gave him with a kick in the rear that rolled him howling all the way down the hill."

Frigate was still shaking with reaction, but he was pleased.

"I was afraid I was going to turn chicken there for a while," he said. "After all, all that had been so long ago and in another world, and maybe we're here to forgive our enemies—and some of our friends—and be forgiven. But on the other hand, I thought, maybe we're here so we can give a little back of what we had to take on Earth. What about it, Lev? Wouldn't you like a chance to turn Hitler over a fire? Very slowly over a fire?"

"I don't think you could compare a crooked publisher to Hitler," Ruach said. "No, I wouldn't want to turn him over a fire. I might want to starve him to death, or feed him just enough to keep him alive. But I wouldn't do that. What good would it do? Would it make him change his mind about anything, would he then believe that Jews were human beings? No, I would do nothing to him if he were in my power except kill him so he couldn't hurt others. But I'm not so sure that killing would mean he'd stay dead. Not here."

"You're a real Christian," Frigate said, grinning.

"I thought you were my friend!" Ruach said.

12

This was the second time that Burton had heard the name Hitler. He intended to find out all about him, but at the moment everybody would have to put off talking to finish the roofs on the huts. They all pitched in, cutting off more grass with the little scissors they had found in their grails, or climbing the irontrees and tearing off the huge triangular green and scarlet-laced leaves. The roofs left much to be desired. Burton meant to search around for a professional thatcher and learn the proper techniques. The beds would have to be, for the time being, piles of grass on top of which were piles of the softer irontree leaves. The blankets would be another pile of the same leaves.

"Thank God, or Whoever, that there is no insect life," Burton said.

He lifted the gray metal cup which still held two ounces of the best scotch he had ever tasted.

"Here's to Whoever. If he had raised us just to live on an exact duplicate of Earth, we'd be sharing our beds with ten thousand kinds of biting, scratching, stinging, scraping, tickling, bloodsucking vermin."

They drank, and then they sat around the fire for a while and smoked and talked. The shadow darkened, the sky lost its blue, and the gigantic stars and great sheets, which had been dimly seen ghosts just before dusk, blossomed out. The sky was indeed a blaze of glory.

"Like a Sime illustration," Frigate said.

Burton did not know what a Sime was. Half of the conversation with the non-nineteenth centurians consisted of them explaining their reference and he explaining his.

Burton rose and went over to the other side of the fire and squatted by Alice. She had just returned from putting the little girl, Gwenafra, to bed in a hut.

Burton held out a stick of gum to Alice and said, "I just had half a piece. Would you care for the other half?"

She looked at him without expression and said, "No, thanks."

"There are eight huts," he said. "There isn't any doubt about who is sharing which hut with whom, except for Wilfreda, you, and me."

"I don't think there's any doubt about that," she said.

"Then you're sleeping with Gwenafra?"

She kept her face turned away from him. He squatted for a few seconds and then got up and went back to the other side and sat down by Wilfreda.

"You can move on, Sir Richard," she said. Her lip was curled. "Lord grab me, I don't like being second choice. You could of asked 'er where nobody could of seen you. I got some pride, too."

He was silent for a minute. His first impulse had been to lash out at her with a sharp-pointed insult. But she was right. He had been too contemptuous of her. Even if she had been a whore, she had a right to be treated as a human being. Especially since she maintained that it was hunger that had driven her to prostitution, though he had been skeptical about that. Too many prostitutes had to rationalize their profession; too many had justifying fantasies about their entrance into the business. Yet, her rage at Smithson and her behavior toward him indicated that she was sincere.

He stood up and said, "I didn't mean to hurt your feelings."

"Are you in love with her?" Wilfreda said, looking up at him.

"I've only told one woman that I ever loved her," he said.

"Your wife?"

"No. The girl died before I could marry her."

"And how long was you married?"

"Twenty-nine years, though it's none of your business."

"Lord grab me! All that time, and you never once told her you loved her!"

"It wasn't necessary," he said, and walked away. The hut he chose was occupied by Monat and Kazz. Kazz was snoring away; Monat was leaning on his elbow and smoking a marihuana stick. Monat preferred that to tobacco, because it tasted more like his native tobacco. However, he got little effect from it. On the other hand, tobacco sometimes gave him fleeting but vividly colored visions.

Burton decided to save the rest of his dreamgum, as he called it. He lit up a cigarette, knowing that marihuana would probably make his rage and frustration even darker. He asked Monat questions about his home, Ghuurrkh. He was intensely interested, but the marihuana betrayed him, and he drifted away while the Cetan's voice became fainter and fainter.

"*. . . cover your eyes now, boys!*" *Gilchrist said in his broad Scots speech.*

Richard looked at Edward; Edward grinned and put his hands over his eyes, but he was surely peeking through the spaces between his fingers. Richard placed his own hands over his eyes and continued to stand on tiptoe. Although he and his brother were standing on boxes, they still had to stretch to see over the heads of the adults in front of them.

The woman's head was in the stock by now; her long brown hair had fallen over her face. He wished he could see her expression as she stared down at the basket waiting for her, or for her head, rather.

"*Don't peek now, boys!*" *Gilchrist said again.*

There was a roll of drums, a single shout, and the blade raced downward, and then a concerted shout from the crowd, mingled with some screams and moans, and the head fell down. The neck spurted out blood and would never stop. It kept spurting out and covered the crowd and, though he was at least fifty yards from her, the blood struck him in the hands and seeped down between his fingers and over his face, filling his eyes and blinding him and making his lips sticky and salty. He screamed . . .

"Wake up, Dick!" Monat was saying. He was shaking

Burton by the shoulder. "Wake up! You must have been having a nightmare!"

Burton, sobbing and shivering, sat up. He rubbed his hands and then felt his face. Both were wet. But with perspiration, not with blood.

"I was dreaming," he said. "I was just six years old and in the city of Tours. In France, where we were living then. My tutor, John Gilchrist, took me and my brother Edward to see the execution of a woman who had poisoned her family. It was a *treat*, Gilchrist said.

"I was excited, and I peeked through my fingers when he told us not to watch the final seconds, when the blade of the guillotine came down. But I did; I had to. I remember getting a little sick at my stomach but that was the only effect the gruesome scene had on me. I seemed to have dislocated myself while I was watching it; it was as if I saw the whole thing through a thick glass, as if it were unreal. Or I was unreal. So I wasn't really horrified."

Monat had lit another marihuana. Its light was enough so that Burton could see him shaking his head. "How savage! You mean that you not only killed your criminals, you cut their heads off! In public! And you allowed children to see it!"

"They were a little more humane in England," Burton said. "They hung the criminals!"

"At least the French permitted the people to be fully aware that they were spilling the blood of their criminals," Monat said. "The blood was on their hands. But apparently this aspect did not occur to anyone. Not consciously, anyway. So now, after how many years —sixty-three?—you smoke some marihuana and you relive an incident which you had always believed did not harm you. But, this time, you recoil with horror. You screamed like a frightened child. You reacted as you should have reacted when you were a child. I would say that the marihuana dug away some deep layers of repression and uncovered the horror that had been buried there for sixty-three years."

"Perhaps," Burton said.

He stopped. There was thunder and lightning in the distance. A minute later, a rushing sound came, and then the patter of drops on the roof. It had rained about this time last night, about three in the morning, he would guess. And this second night, it was raining about the same time. The downpour became heavy, but the roof had been packed tightly, and no water dripped down through it. Some water did, however, come under the back wall, which was uphill. It spread out over the floor but did not wet them, since the grass and leaves under them formed a mat about ten inches thick.

Burton talked with Monat until the rain ceased approximately half an hour later. Monat fell asleep; Kazz had never awakened. Burton tried to get back to sleep but could not. He had never felt so alone, and he was afraid that he might slip back into the nightmare. After a while, he left the hut and walked to the one which Wilfreda had chosen. He smelled the tobacco before he got to the doorway. The tip of her cigarette glowed in the dark. She was a dim figure sitting upright in the pile of grass and leaves.

"Hello," she said. "I was hoping you would come."

"It's the instinct to own property," Burton said.

"I doubt that it's an instinct in man," Frigate said. "Some people in the '60's—1960's, that is—tried to demonstrate that man had an instinct which they called the *territorial imperative*. But . . ."

"I like that phrase. It has a fine ring to it," Burton said.

"I knew you'd like it," Frigate said. "But Ardrey and others tried to prove that man not only had an instinct to claim a certain area of land as his own, he also was descended from a killer ape. And the instinct to kill was still strong in his heritage from the killer ape. Which explained national boundaries, patriotism both national and local, capitalism, war, murder, crime, and so forth. But the other school of thought, or of the temperamental inclination, maintained that all these are the results of culture, of the cultural continuity of societies dedicated from earliest times to tribal hostilities, to war, to murder,

90

to crime, and so forth. Change the culture, and the killer ape is missing. Missing because he was never there, like the little man on the stairs. The killer was the society, and society bred the new killers out of every batch of babies. But there were some societies, composed of preliterates, it is true, but still societies, that did not breed killers. And they were proof that man was not descended from a killer ape. Or I should say, he was perhaps descended from the ape but he did not carry the killing genes any longer, any more than he carried the genes for a heavy supraorbital ridge or a hairy skin or thick bones or a skull with only 650 cubic centimeters capacity."

"That is all very interesting," Burton said. "We'll go into the theory more deeply at another time. Let me point out to you, however, that almost every member of resurrected humanity comes from a culture which encouraged war and murder and crime and rape and robbery and madness. It is these people among whom we are living and with whom we have to deal. There may be a new generation some day. I don't know. It's too early to say, since we've only been here for seven days. But, like it or not, we are in a world populated by beings who quite often act *as if* they were killer apes."

"In the meantime, let's get back to our model."

They were sitting on bamboo stools before Burton's hut. On a little bamboo table in front of them was a model of a boat made from pine and bamboo. It had a double hull across the top of which was a platform with a low railing in the center. It had a single mast, very tall, with a fore-and-aft rig, a balloon jib sail, and a slightly raised bridge with a wheel. Burton and Frigate had used chert knives and the edge of the scissors to carve the model of the catamaran. Burton had decided to name the boat, when it was built, *The Hadji*. It would be going on a pilgrimage, though its goal was not Mecca. He intended to sail it up The River as far as it would go. (By now, the river had become The River.)

The two had been talking about the *territorial imperative* because of some anticipated difficulties in getting the boat built. By now the people in this area were somewhat settled. They had staked out their property and constructed their dwellings or were still working on them. These ranged all the way from lean-tos to relatively grandiose buildings that would be made of bamboo logs and stone, have four rooms, and be two stories high. Most of them were near the grailstones along The River and at the base of the mountain. Burton's survey, completed two days before, resulted in an estimate of about 260 to 261 people per square mile. For every square mile of flat plain on each side of The River, there were approximately 2.4 square miles of hills. But the hills were so high and irregular that their actual inhabitable area was about nine square miles. In the three areas that he had studied, he found that about one-third had built their dwellings close to the riverside grailstone and one-third around the inland grailstones. Two hundred and sixty-one persons per square mile seemed like a heavy population, but the hills were so heavily wooded and convoluted in topography that a small group living there could feel isolated. And the plain was seldom crowded except at mealtimes, because the plains people were in the woods or fishing along the edge of The River. Many were working on dugouts or bamboo boats with the idea of fishing in the middle of The River. Or, like Burton, of going exploring.

The stands of bamboo had disappeared, although it was evident that they would be quickly replaced. The bamboo had a phenomenal growth. Burton estimated that a fifty-foot-high plant could grow from start to finish in ten days.

His gang had worked hard and cut down all they thought they would need for the boat. But they wanted to keep thieves away, so they used more wood to erect a high fence. This was being finished the same day that the model was completed. The trouble was that they would have to build the boat on the plain. It could never be gotten through the woods and down the various hills if it were built on this site.

"Yeah, but if we move out and set up a new base, we'll run into opposition," Frigate had said. "There isn't a square inch of the high-grass border that isn't claimed. As it is, you have to trespass to get to the plain. So far, nobody has tried to be hard-nosed about their property rights, but this can change any day. And if you build the ship a little back from the high-grass border, you can get it out of the woods okay and between the huts. But you'd have to set up a guard night and day, otherwise your stuff will be stolen. Or destroyed. You know these barbarians."

He was referring to the huts wrecked while their owners were away and to the fouling of the pools below the cataract and the spring. He was also referring to the highly unsanitary habits of many of the locals. These would not use the little outhouses put up by various peoples for the public.

"We'll erect new houses and a boatyard as close to the border as we can get," Burton said. "Then we'll chop down any tree that gets in our way and we'll ram our way past anybody who refuses us right-of-way."

It was Alice who went down to some people who had huts on the border between the plain and the hills and talked them into making a trade. She did not tell anybody what she intended. She had known of three couples who were unhappy with their location because of lack of privacy. These made an agreement and moved into the huts of Burton's gang on the twelfth day after Resurrection, on a Thursday. By a generally agreed upon convention, Sunday, the first, was Resurrection Day. Ruach said he would prefer that the first day be called Saturday, or even better, just First Day. But he was in an area predominately Gentile—or ex-Gentile (but once a Gentile always a Gentile)—so he would go along with the others. Ruach had a bamboo stick on which he kept count of the days by notching it each morning. The stick was driven into the ground before his hut.

Transferring the lumber for the boat took four days of heavy work. By then, the Italian couples decided that they had had enough of *working their fingers to the bone*. After all, why get on a boat and go some place else when every place was probably just like this? They had obviously been raised from the dead so they could enjoy themselves. Otherwise, why the liquor, the cigarettes, the marihuana, the dreamgum, and the nudity?

93

They left without ill feelings on the part of anybody; in fact, they were given a going-away party. The next day, the twentieth of Year 1, A.R., two events occurred, one of which solved one puzzle and the other of which added one, though it was not very important.

The group went across the plain to the grailstone at dawn. They found two new people near the grailstone, both of them sleeping. They were easily aroused, but they seemed alarmed and confused. One was a tall brown-skinned man who spoke an unknown language. The other was a tall, handsome, well-muscled man with gray eyes and black hair. His speech was unintelligible until Burton suddenly understood that he was speaking English. It was the Cumberland dialect of the English spoken during the reign of King Edward I, sometimes called *Longshanks*. Once Burton and Frigate had mastered the sounds and made certain transpositions, they were able to carry on a halting conversation with him. Frigate had an extensive reading vocabulary of Early Middle English, but he had never encountered many of the words or certain grammatical usages.

John de Greystock was born in the manor of Greystoke in the Cumberland country. He had accompanied Edward I into France when the king invaded Gascony. There he had distinguished himself in arms, if he was to be believed. Later, he was summoned to Parliament as Baron Greystoke and then again went to the wars in Gascony. He was in the retinue of Bishop Anthony Bec, Patriarch of Jerusalem. In the 28th and 29th years of Edward's reign, he fought against the Scots. He died in 1305, without children, but he settled his manor and barony on his cousin, Ralph, son of Lord Grimthorpe in Yorkshire.

He had been resurrected somewhere along The River among a people about ninety percent early fourteenth-century English and Scottish and ten percent ancient Sybarites. The peoples across The River were a mixture of Mongols of the time of Kubla Khan and some dark people the identity of which Greystock did not know. His description fitted North American Indians.

The nineteenth day after Resurrection, the savages

across The River had attacked. Apparently they did so for no other reason than they wanted a good fight, which they got. The weapons were mostly sticks and grails, because there was little stone in the area. John de Greystock put ten Mongols out of commission with his grail and then was hit on the head with a rock and stabbed with the fire-hardened tip of a bamboo spear. He awoke, naked, with only his grail—or a grail—by this grailstone.

The other man told his story with signs and pantomime. He had been fishing when his hook was taken by something so powerful that it pulled him into the water. Coming back up, he had struck his head on the bottom of the boat and drowned.

The question of what happened to those who were killed in the afterlife was answered. Why they were not raised in the same area as in which they died was another question.

The second event was the failure of the grails to deliver the noonday meal. Instead, crammed inside the cylinders were six cloths. These were of various sizes and of many different colors, hues, and patterns. Four were obviously designed to be worn as kilts. They could be fastened around the body with magnetic tabs inside the cloth. Two were of thinner almost transparent material and obviously made as brassieres, though they could be used for other purposes. Though the cloth was soft and absorbent, it stood up under the roughest treatment and could not be cut by the sharpest chert or bamboo knife.

Mankind gave a collective whoop of delight on finding these "towels." Though men and women had by then become accustomed, or at least resigned, to nudity, the more aesthetic and the less adaptable had found the universal spectacle of human genitalia unbeautiful or even repulsive. Now, they had kilts and bras and turbans. The latter were used to cover up their heads while their hair was growing back in. Later, turbans became a customary headgear.

Hair was returning everywhere except on the face.

Burton was bitter about this. He had always taken pride in his long moustachios and forked beard; he claimed that their absence made him feel more naked than the lack of trousers.

Wilfreda had laughed and said, "I'm glad they're gone. I've always hated hair on men's faces. Kissing a man with a beard was like sticking my face in a bunch of broken bedsprings."

13

Sixty days had passed. The boat had been pushed across the plain on big bamboo rollers. The day of the launching had arrived. *The Hadji* was about forty feet long and essentially consisted of two sharp-prowed bamboo hulls fastened together with a platform, a bowsprit with a balloon sail and a single mast, fore-and-aft rigged, with sails of woven bamboo fibers. It was steered by a great oar of pine, since a rudder and steering wheel were not practicable. Their only material for ropes at this time was the grass, though it would not be long before leather ropes would be made from the tanned skin and entrails of some of the larger riverfish. A dugout fashioned by Kazz from a pine log was tied down to the foredeck.

Before they could get it into the water, Kazz made some difficulties. By now, he could speak a very broken and limited English and some oaths in Arabic, Baluchi, Swahili, and Italian, all learned from Burton.

"Must need . . . whacha call it? . . . *wallah*! . . . what it word? . . . kill somebody before place boat on river . . . you know . . . *merda* . . . need word, Burton-*naq* . . . you give, Burton-*naq* . . . word . . . word . . . kill man so god, *Kabburqanaqruebemss* . . . water god . . . no sink boat . . . get angry . . . drown us . . . eat us."

"Sacrifice?" Burton said.

"Many bloody thanks, Burton-*naq*. Sacrifice! Cut

96

throat . . . put on boat . . . rub it on wood . . . then water god not mad at us . . ."

"We don't do that," Burton said.

Kazz argued but finally agreed to get on the boat. His face was long, and he looked very nervous. Burton, to ease him, told him that this was not Earth. It was a different world, as he could see at a quick glance around him and especially at the stars. The gods did not live in this valley. Kazz listened and smiled, but he still looked as if he expected to see the hideous green-bearded face and bulging fishy eyes of *Kabburqanaqruebemss* rising from the depths.

The plain was crowded around the boat that morning. Everybody was there for many miles around, since anything out of the usual was entertainment. They shouted and laughed and joked. Though some of the comments were derisive, all were in good humor. Before the boat was rolled off the bank into The River, Burton stood up on its "bridge," a slightly raised platform, and held up his hand for silence. The crowd's chatter died away, and he spoke in Italian.

"Fellow lazari, friends, dwellers in the valley of the Promised Land! We leave you in a few minutes . . ."

"If the boat doesn't capsize!" Frigate muttered.

". . . to go up The River, against the wind and the current. We take the difficult route because the difficult always yields the greatest reward, if you believe what the moralists on Earth told us, and you know now how much to believe them!"

Laughter. With scowls here and there from die-hard religionists.

"On Earth, as some of you may know, I once led an expedition into deepest and darkest Africa to find the headwaters of the Nile. I did not find them, though I came close, and I was cheated out of the rewards by a man who owed everything to me, a Mister John Hanning Speke. If I should encounter him on my journey upriver, I will know how to deal with him . . ."

"Good God!" Frigate said. "Would you have him kill himself again with remorse and shame?"

". . . but the point is that this River may be one far far greater than any Nile, which as you may or may not know, was the longest river on Earth, despite the erroneous claims of Americans for their Amazon and Missouri-Mississippi complexes. Some of you have asked why we should set out for a goal that lies we know not how far away or that might not even exist. I will tell you that we are setting sail because the Unknown exists and we would make it the Known. That's all! And here, contrary to our sad and frustrating experience on Earth, money is not required to outfit us or to keep us going. King Cash is dead, and good riddance to him! Nor do we have to fill out hundreds of petitions and forms and beg audiences of influential people and minor bureaucrats to get permission to pass up The River. There are no national borders . . ."

". . . as yet," Frigate said.

". . . nor passports required nor officials to bribe. We just build a boat without having to obtain a license, and we sail off without a by-your-leave from any muckamuck, high, middle or low. We are free for the first time in man's history. Free! And so we bid you adieu, for I will not say goodbye . . ."

". . . you never would," Frigate muttered.

". . . because we may be back a thousand years or so from now! So I say adieu, the crew says adieu, we thank you for your help in building the boat and for your help in launching us. I hereby hand over my position as Her British Majesty's Consul at Trieste to whomever wishes to accept it and declare myself to be a free citizen of the world of The River! I will pay tribute to none; owe fealty to none; to myself only will I be true!"

> "Do what thy manhood bids thee do, from none
> but self expect applause;
> "He noblest lives and noblest dies who makes and
> keeps his self-made laws," Frigate chanted.

Burton glanced at the American but did not stop his speech. Frigate was quoting lines from Burton's poem, *The Kasidah of Haji Abdu Al-Yazdi*. It was not the first

98

time that he had quoted from Burton's prose or poetry. And though Burton sometimes found the American to be irritating, he could not become too angry at a man who had admired him enough to memorize his words.

A few minutes later, when the boat was pushed into The River by some men and women and the crowd was cheering, Frigate quoted him again. He looked at the thousands of handsome youths by the waters, their skins bronzed by the sun, their kilts and bras and turbans wind-moved and colorful, and he said,

> "Ah! gay the day with shine of sun, and bright the breeze, and blithe the throng
> "Met on the River-bank to play, when I was young, when I was young."

The boat slid out, and its prow was turned by the wind and the current downstream, but Burton shouted orders, and the sails were pulled up, and he turned the great handle of the paddle so that the nose swung around and then they were beating to windward. The *Hadji* rose and fell in the waves, the water hissing as it was cut by the twin prows. The sun was bright and warm, the breeze cooled them off, they felt happy but also a little anxious as the familiar banks and faces faded away. They had no maps nor travelers' tales to guide them; the world would be created with every mile forward.

That evening, as they made their first beaching, an incident occurred that puzzled Burton. Kazz had just stepped ashore among a group of curious people, when he became very excited. He began to jabber in his native tongue and tried to seize a man standing near. The man fled and was quickly lost in the crowd.

When asked by Burton what he was doing, Kazz said, "He not got . . . uh . . . whacha call it? . . . it . . . it . . ." and he pointed at his forehead. Then he traced several unfamiliar symbols in the air. Burton meant to pursue the matter, but Alice, suddenly wailing, ran up to a man. Evidently, she had thought he was a son who had been killed in World War I. There was some confusion. Alice admitted that she had made a mistake. By then, other business came up. Kazz did not mention the matter again, and Burton forgot about it. But he was to remember.

Exactly 415 days later, they had passed 24,900 grailrocks on the right bank of The River. Tacking, running against wind and current, averaging sixty miles a day, stopping during the day to charge their grails and at night to sleep, sometimes stopping all day so they could stretch their legs and talk to others besides the crew, they had journeyed 24,900 miles. On Earth, that distance would have been about once around the equator. If the Mississippi-Missouri, Nile, Congo, Amazon, Yangtze, Volga, Amur, Hwang, Lena, and Zambezi had been put end to end to make one great river, it still would not have been as long as that stretch of The River they had passed. Yet The River went on and on, making great bends, winding back and forth. Everywhere were the plains along the stream, the tree-covered hills behind, and, towering, impassable, unbroken, the mountain range.

Occasionally, the plains narrowed, and the hills advanced to The River-edge. Sometimes, The River widened and became a lake, three miles, five miles, six miles across. Now and then, the line of the mountains curved in toward each other, and the boat shot through canyons where the narrow passage forced the current to boil through and the sky was a blue thread far far above and the black walls pressed in on them.

And, always, there was humankind. Day and night, men, women, and children thronged the banks of The River and in the hills were more.

By then, the sailors recognized a pattern. Humanity had been resurrected along The River in a rough chronological and national sequence. The boat had passed by the area that held Slovenes, Italians, and Austrians who had died in the last decade of the nineteenth century, had passed by Hungarians, Norwegians, Finns, Greeks, Albanians, and Irish. Occasionally, they put in at areas which held peoples from other times and places. One was a twenty-mile stretch containing Australian aborigines who had never seen a European while on Earth. Another hundred-mile length was populated by Tocharians (Loghu's people). These had lived around the time of Christ in what later became Chinese Turkestan. They represented the easternmost extension of Indo-European speakers in ancient times; their culture had flourished for a while, then died before the encroachment of the desert and invasions of barbarians.

Through admittedly hasty and uncertain surveys, Burton had determined that each area was, in general, comprised of about 60 percent of a particular nationality and century, 30 percent of some other people, usually from a different time, and 10 percent from any time and place.

All men had awakened from death circumcised. All women had been resurrected as virgins. For most women, Burton commented, this state had not lasted beyond the first night on this planet.

So far, they had neither seen nor heard of a pregnant woman. Whoever had placed them here must have sterilized them, and with good reason. If mankind could reproduce, the Rivervalley would be jammed solid with bodies within a century.

At first, there had seemed to be no animal life but man. Now it was known that several species of worms emerged from the soil at night. And The River contained at least a hundred species of fish, ranging from creatures six inches long to the sperm whale-sized fish, the "riverdragon," which lived on the bottom of The River a thousand feet down. Frigate said that the animals were there for a good purpose. The fish scavenged to keep The River waters clean. Some types of worm ate waste matter and corpses. Other types served the normal function of earthworms.

Gwenafra was a little taller. All the children were growing up. Within twelve years, there would not be an infant or adolescent within the valley, if conditions everywhere conformed to what the voyagers had so far seen.

Burton, thinking of this, said to Alice, "This Reverend Dodgson friend of yours, the fellow who loved only little girls. He'll be in a frustrating situation then, won't he?"

"Dodgson was no pervert," Frigate said. "But what about those whose only sexual objects are children? What will they do when there are no more children? And what will those who got their kicks by mistreating or torturing animals do? You know, I've regretted the absence of animals. I love cats and dogs, bears, elephants, most animals. Not monkeys, they're too much like humans. But I'm glad they're not here. They can't be abused now. All the poor helpless animals who were in pain or going hungry or thirsty because of some thoughtless or vicious human being. Not now."

He patted Gwenafra's blonde hair which was almost six inches long.

"I felt much the same about all the helpless and abused little ones, too."

"What kind of a world is it that doesn't have children?" Alice said. "For that matter, what kind without animals? If they can't be mistreated or abused any more, they can't be petted and loved."

"One thing balances out another in this world," Burton said. "You can't have love without hate, kindness without malice, peace without war. In any event, we don't have a choice in the matter. The invisible Lords of this world have decreed that we do not have animals and that women no longer bear children. So be it."

The morning of the 416th day of their journey was like every morning. The sun had risen above the top of the range on their left. The wind from upRiver was an estimated fifteen miles per hour, as always. The warmth rose steadily with the sun and would reach the estimated 85 degrees Fahrenheit at approximately 2 in the afternoon. The catamaran, *The Hadji*, tacked back and forth. Burton stood on the "bridge" with both hands on the long thick pine tiller on his right, while the wind and the sun beat on his darkly tanned skin. He wore a scarlet and black checked kilt reaching almost to his knees and a necklace made of the convoluted shiny-black vertebrae of the hornfish. This was a six-foot long fish with a six-inch long horn that projected unicornlike from its forehead. The hornfish lived about a hundred feet below the surface

102

and was brought in on a line with difficulty. But its vertebrae made beautiful necklaces, its skin, properly tanned, made sandals and armor and shields or could be worked into tough pliable ropes and belts. Its flesh was delicious. But the horn was the most valuable item. It tipped spears or arrows or went into a wood handle to make a stiletto.

On a stand near him, encased in the transparent bladder of a fish, was a bow. It was made of the curved bones protruding from the sides of the mouth of the whale-sized dragonfish. When the ends of each had been cut so that one fitted into the other, a double recurved bow was the result. Fitted with a string from the gut of the dragonfish, this made a bow that only a very powerful man could fully draw. Burton had run across one forty days ago and offered its owner forty cigarettes, ten cigars, and thirty ounces of whiskey for it. The offer was turned down. So Burton and Kazz came back late that night and stole the bow. Or, rather, made a trade, since Burton felt compelled to leave his yew bow in exchange.

Since then, he had rationalized that he had every right to steal the bow. The owner had boasted that he had murdered a man to get the bow. So taking it from him was taking it from a thief and a killer. Nevertheless, Burton suffered from thrusts of conscience when he thought about it, which was not often.

Burton took *The Hadji* back and forth across the narrowing channel. For about five miles, The River had widened out to a three and a half mile broad lake, and now it was forming into a narrow channel less than half a mile across. The channel curved and disappeared between the walls of a canyon.

There the boat would creep along because it would be bucking an accelerated current and the space allowed for tacking was so limited. But he had been through similar straits many times and so was not apprehensive about this. Still, every time it happened, he could not help thinking of the boat as being reborn. It passed from a lake, a womb, through a tight opening and out into another lake. It was a bursting of waters in many ways, and there was always the

103

chance of a fabulous adventure, of a revelation, on the other side.

The catamaran turned away from a grailstone, only twenty yards off. There were many people on the right-side plain, which was only half a mile across here. They shouted at the boat or waved or shook their fists or shouted obscenities, unheard but understood by Burton because of so many experiences. But they did not seem hostile; it was just that strangers were always greeted by the locals in a varied manner. The locals here were a short, dark-skinned, dark-haired, thin-bodied people. They spoke a language that Ruach said was probably proto-Hamite-Semitic. They had lived on Earth somewhere in North Africa or Mesopotamia when those countries had been much more fertile. They wore the towels as kilts but the women went bare-breasted and used the "bras" as neckscarfs or turbans. They occupied the right bank for sixty grailstones, that is, sixty miles. The people before them had been strung out for eighty grailstones and had been tenth-century A.D. Ceylonese with a minority of pre-Columbian Mayans.

"The mixing bowl of Time," Frigate called the distribution of humanity. "The greatest anthropological and social experiment ever."

His statements were not too far-fetched. It did look as if the various peoples had been mixed up so that they might learn something from each other. In some cases, the alien groups had managed to create various social lubricants and lived in relative amity. In other cases, there was a slaughter of one side by the other, or a mutual near-extermination, or slavery, of the defeated.

For some time, after the resurrection, anarchy had been the usual rule. People had "milled around" and formed little groups for defense in very small areas. Then the natural leaders and power seekers had come to the front, and the natural followers had lined up behind the leaders of their choice—or of the leaders' choice, in many cases.

One of the several political systems that had resulted was that of "grail slavery." A dominant group in an area held the weaker prisoners. They gave the slave enough to eat because the grail of a dead slave became useless. But they took the cigarettes, the cigars, the marihuana, the dreamgum, the liquor, and the tastier food.

At least thirty times, *The Hadji* had started to put into a grailstone and had come close to being seized by grail slavers. But Burton and the others were on the alert for signs of slave states. Neighboring states often warned them. Twenty times, boats had put out to intercept them instead of trying to lure them ashore, and *The Hadji* had narrowly escaped being run down or boarded. Five times, Burton had been forced to turn back and sail downstream. His catamaran had always outrun the pursuers, who were reluctant to chase him outside their borders. Then *The Hadji* had sneaked back at night and sailed past the slavers.

A number of times, *The Hadji* had been unable to put into shore because the slave states occupied both banks for very long stretches. Then the crew went on half-rations or, if they were lucky, caught enough fish to fill their bellies.

The proto-Hamite-Semites of this area had been friendly enough after they were assured that the crew of *The Hadji* had no evil intentions. An eighteenth-century Muscovite had warned them that there were slave states on the other side of the channel. He did not know too much about them because of the precipitous mountains. A few boats had sailed through the channel and almost none had returned. Those that did brought news of evil men on the other side.

So *The Hadji* was loaded with bamboo shoots, dried fish, and supplies saved over a period of two weeks from the grails.

There was still about half an hour before the strait would be entered. Burton kept half his mind on his sailing and half on the crew. They were sprawled on the foredeck, taking in the sun or else sitting with their backs against the roofed coaming which they called the "fo'c'sle."

John de Greystock was affixing the thin carved bones of a hornfish to the butt of an arrow. The bones served quite well as feathers in a world where birds did not exist.

105

Greystock, or Lord Greystoke, as Frigate insisted on calling him for some private self-amusing reason, was a good man in a fight or when hard work was needed. He was an interesting, if almost unbelievably vulgar, talker, full of anecdotes of the campaigns in Gascony and on the border, of his conquests of women, of gossip about Edward Longshanks, and of course, of information about his times. But he was also very hard-headed and narrow-minded in many things—from the viewpoint of a later age—and not overly clean. He claimed to have been very devout in Earthlife, and he probably told the truth, otherwise, he would not have been honored by being attached to the retinue of the Patriarch of Jerusalem. But now that his faith had been discredited, he hated priests. And he was apt to drive any he met into a fury with his scorn, hoping that they would attack him. Some did, and he came close to killing them. Burton had cautiously reprimanded him for this (you did not speak harshly to de Greystock unless you wished to fight to the death with him), pointing out that when they were guests in a strange land, and immensely outnumbered by their hosts, they should act as guests. De Greystock admitted that Burton was right, but he could not keep from baiting every priest he met. Fortunately, they were not often in areas where there were Christian priests. Moreover, there were very few of these who admitted that they had been such.

Beside him, talking earnestly, was his current woman, born Mary Rutherfurd in 1637, died Lady Warwickshire in 1674. She was English but of an age 300 years later than his, so there were many differences in their attitudes and actions. Burton did not give them much longer to stay together.

Kazz was sprawled out on the deck with his head in the lap of Fatima, a Turkish woman whom the Neanderthal had met forty days ago during a lunch stop. Fatima, as Frigate had said, seemed to be "hung up on hair." That was his explanation for the obsession of the seventeenth-century wife of a baker of Ankara for Kazz. She found everything about him stimulating but it was the hairiness that sent her into ecstasies. Everybody was pleased about

106

this, most of all Kazz. He had not seen a single female of his own species during their long trip, though he had heard about some. Most women shied away from him because of his hairy and brutish appearance. He had had no permanent female companionship until he met Fatima.

Little Lev Ruach was leaning against the forward bulkhead of the fo'c'sle, where he was making a slingshot from the leather of a hornfish. A bag by his side contained about thirty stones picked up during the last twenty days. By his side, talking swiftly, incessantly exposing her long white teeth, was Esther Rodriguez. She had replaced Tanya, who had been henpecking Lev before *The Hadji* set off. Tanya was a very attractive and petite woman but she seemed unable to keep from "remodeling" her men; Lev found out that she had "remodeled" her father and uncle and two brothers and two husbands. She tried to do the same for, or to, Lev, usually in a loud voice so that other males in the neighborhood could benefit by her advice. One day, just as *The Hadji* was about to sail, Lev had jumped aboard, turned, and said, "Goodbye, Tanya. I can't stand any more reforming from The Bigmouth from The Bronx. Find somebody else, somebody that's perfect."

Tanya had gasped, turned white, and then started screaming at Lev. She still was screaming, judging by her mouth, long after *The Hadji* had sailed out of earshot. The others laughed and congratulated Lev, but he only smiled sadly. Two weeks later, in an area predominantly ancient Libyan, he met Esther, a fifteenth-century Sephardic Jewess.

"Why don't you try your luck with a Gentile?" Frigate had said.

Lev had shrugged his narrow shoulders. "I have. But sooner or later you get into a big fight, and they lose their temper and call you a goddam kike. The same thing also happens with my Jewish women, but from them I can take it."

"Listen, friend," the American said. "There are billions of Gentiles along this river who've never heard of a Jew. They can't be prejudiced. Try one of them."

107

"I'll stick to the evil I know."

"You mean you're stuck to it," Frigate said.

Burton sometimes wondered why Ruach stayed with the boat. He had never made any more references to *The Jew, The Gypsy, and El Islam,* though he often questioned Burton about other aspects of his past. He was friendly enough but had a certain indefinable reserve. Though small, he was a good man in a fight and he had been invaluable in teaching Burton judo, karate, and jukado. His sadness, which hung about him like a thin mist even when he was laughing, or making love, according to Tanya, came from mental scars. These resulted from his terrible experiences in concentration camps in Germany and Russia, or so he claimed. Tanya had said that Lev was born sad; he inherited all the genes of sorrow from the time when his ancestors sat down by the willows of Babylon.

Monat was another case of sadness, though he could come out of it fully at times. The Tau Cetan kept looking for one of his own kind, for one of the thirty males and females who had been torn apart by the lynch mob. He did not give himself much chance. Thirty in an estimated thirty-five to thirty-six billion strung out along a river that could be ten million miles long made it improbable that he would ever see even one. But there was hope.

Alice Hargreaves was sitting forward of the fo'c'sle, only the top of her head in his view, and looking at the people on the banks whenever the boat got close enough for her to make out individual faces. She was searching for her husband, Reginald, and also for her three sons and for her mother and father and her sisters and brothers. For any dear familiar face. The implications were that she would leave the boat as soon as this happened. Burton had not commented on this. But he felt a pain in his chest when he thought of it. He wished that she would leave and yet he did not wish it. To get her out of his sight would eventually be to get her out of his mind. It was inevitable. But he did not want the inevitable. He felt for her as he had for his Persian love, and to lose her, too, would be to suffer the same long-lived torture.

Yet he had never said a word about how he felt to her. He talked to her, jested with her, showed her a concern that he found galling because she did not return it, and, in the end, got her to relax when with him. That is, she would relax if there were others around. When they were alone, she tightened up.

She had never used the dreamgum since that first night. He had used it for a third time and then hoarded his share and traded it for other items. The last time he had chewed it, with the hope of an unusually ecstatic lovemaking with Wilfreda, he had been plunged back into the horrible sickness of the "little irons," the sickness that had almost killed him during his expedition to Lake Tanganyika. Speke had been in the nightmare, and he had killed Speke. Speke had died in a hunting "accident" which everybody had thought was a suicide even if they had not said so. Speke, tormented by remorse because he had betrayed Burton, had shot himself. But in the nightmare, he had strangled Speke when Speke bent over to ask him how he was. Then, just as the vision faded, he had kissed Speke's dead lips.

14

Well, he had known that he had loved Speke at the same time that he hated him, justifiably hated him. But the knowledge of his love had been very fleeting and infrequent and it had not affected him. During the dreamgum nightmare, he had felt so horrified at the realization that love lay far beneath his hate that he had screamed. He awakened to find Wilfreda shaking him, demanding to know what had happened. Wilfreda had smoked opium or drunk it in her beer when on Earth, but here, after one session with dreamgum, she had been afraid to chew any more. Her horror came from seeing again the death of a younger sister from tuberculosis and, at the same time, reliving her first experience as a whore.

"It's a strange psychedelic," Ruach had told Burton. He had explained what the word meant. The discussion about that had gone on for a long time. "It seems to bring up traumatic incidents in a mixture of reality and symbolism. Not always. Sometimes it's an aphrodisiac. Sometimes, as they said, it takes you on a beautiful trip. But I would guess that dreamgum has been provided us for therapeutic, if not cathartic, reasons. It's up to us to find out just how to use it."

"Why don't you chew it more often?" Frigate had said.

"For the same reason that some people refused to go into psychotherapy or quit before they were through; I'm afraid."

"Yeah, me, too," Frigate said. "But some day, when we stop off some place for a long time, I'm going to chew a stick every night, so help me. Even if it scares hell out of me. Of course, that's easy to say now."

Peter Jairus Frigate had been born only twenty-eight years after Burton had died, yet the world between them was wide. They saw so many things so differently; they would have argued violently if Frigate was able to argue violently. Not on matters of discipline in the group or in running the boat. But on so many matters of looking at the world. Yet, in many ways, Frigate was much like Burton, and it may have been this that had caused him to be so fascinated by Burton on Earth. Frigate had picked up in 1938 a soft-cover book by Fairfax Downey titled *Burton: Arabian Nights' Adventurer*. The front page illustration was of Burton at the age of fifty. The savage face, the high brow and prominent supraorbital ridges, the heavy black brows, the straight but harsh nose, the great scar on his cheek, the thick "sensual" lips, the heavy downdrooping moustache, the heavy forked beard, the essential broodingness and aggressiveness of the face, had caused him to buy the book.

"I'd never heard of you before, Dick," Frigate said. "But I read the book at once and was fascinated. There

110

was something about you, aside from the obvious daring-do of your life, your swordsmanship, mastery of many languages, disguises as a native doctor, native merchantman, as a pilgrim to Mecca, the first European to get out of the sacred city of Harar alive, discoverer of Lake Tanganyika and near-discoverer of the source of the Nile, co-founder of the Royal Anthropological Society, inventor of the term ESP, translator of the Arabian Nights, student of the sexual practices of the East, and so forth . . .

"Aside from all this, fascinating enough in itself, you had a special affinity for me. I went to the public library—Peoria was a small city but had many books on you and about you, donated by some admirer of yours who'd passed on—and I read these. Then I started to collect first editions by you and about you. I became a fiction writer eventually, but I planned to write a huge definitive biography of you, travel everywhere you had been, take photographs and notes of these places, found a society to collect funds for the preservation of your tomb . . ."

This was the first time Frigate had mentioned his tomb. Burton, startled, said, "Where?" Then, "Oh, of course! Mortlake! I'd forgotten! Was the tomb really in the form of an Arab tent, as Isabel and I had planned?"

"Sure. But the cemetery was swallowed up in a slum, the tomb was defaced by vandals, there were weeds up to your tocus and talk of moving the bodies to a more remote section of England, though by then it was hard to find a really remote section."

"And did you found your society and preserve my tomb?" Burton said.

He had gotten used to the idea by then of having been dead, but to talk with someone who had seen his tomb made his skin chill for a moment.

Frigate took a deep breath. Apologetically, he said, "No. By the time I was in a position to do that, I would have felt guilty spending time and money on the dead. The world was in too much of a mess. The living needed all the attention they could get. Pollution, poverty, oppression,

111

and so forth. These were the important things."

"And that giant definitive biography?"

Again, Frigate spoke apologetically. "When I first read about you, I thought I was the only one deeply interested in you or even aware of you. But there was an upsurge of interest in you in the '60's. Quite a few books were written about you and even one about your wife."

"Isabel? Someone wrote a book about her? Why?"

Frigate had grinned. "She was a pretty interesting woman. Very aggravating, I'll admit, pitifully superstitious and schizophrenic and self-fooling. Very few would ever forgive her for burning your manuscripts and your journals . . ."

"What?" Burton had roared. "Burn . . . ?"

Frigate nodded and said, "What your doctor, Grenfell Baker, described as 'the ruthless holocaust that followed his lamented death.' She burned your translation of *The Perfumed Garden,* claiming you would not have wanted to publish it unless you needed the money for it, and you didn't need it, of course, because you were now dead."

Burton was speechless for one of the few times in his life.

Frigate looked out of the corner of his eyes at Burton and grinned. He seemed to be enjoying Burton's distress.

"Burning *The Perfumed Garden* wasn't so bad, though bad enough. But to burn both sets of your journals, the private ones in which, supposedly, you let loose all your deepest thoughts and most burning hates, and even the public ones, the diary of daily events, well, *I* never forgave her! Neither did a lot of people. That was a great loss; only one of your notebooks, a small one, escaped, and that was burned during the bombing of London in World War II."

He paused and said, "Is it true that you converted to the Catholic Church on your deathbed, as your wife claimed?"

"I may have," Burton said. "Isabel had been after me for years to convert, though she never dared urge me directly. When I was so sick there, at last, I may have told her I would do so in order to make her happy. She was so grief-stricken, so distressed, so afraid my soul would burn in Hell."

"Then you did love her?" Frigate had said.

"I would have done the same for a dog," Burton replied.

"For somebody who can be so upsettingly frank and direct, you can be very ambiguous at times."

This conversation had taken place about two months after First Day, A.R. 1. The result had been something like that which Doctor Johnson would have felt on encountering another Boswell.

This had been the second stage of their curious relationship. Frigate became closer but, at the same time, more of an annoyance. The American had always been restrained in his comments on Burton's attitudes, undoubtedly because he did not want to anger him. Frigate made a very conscious effort not to anger anybody. But he also made unconscious efforts to antagonize them. His hostilities came out in many subtle, and some not so subtle, actions and words. Burton did not like this. He was direct, not at all afraid of anger. Perhaps, as Frigate pointed out, he was too eager for hostile confrontations.

One evening, as they were sitting around a fire under a grailstone, Frigate had spoken about Karachi. This village, which later became the capital of Pakistan, the nation created in 1947, had only 2,000 population in Burton's time. By 1970, its population was approximately 2,000,000. That led to Frigate's asking, rather indirectly, about the report Burton had made to his general, Sir Robert Napier, on houses of male prostitution in Karachi. The report was supposed to be kept in the secret files of the East India Army, but it was found by one of the many enemies of Burton. Though the report was never mentioned publicly, it had been used against him throughout his life. Burton had disguised himself as a native in order to get into the house and make observations that no European would have been allowed to make. He had been proud that he had escaped detection, and he had taken the unsavory job because he

113

was the only one who could do it and because his beloved leader, Napier, had asked him to.

Burton had replied to Frigate's questions somewhat surlily. Alice had angered him earlier that day—she seemed to be able to do so very easily lately—and he was thinking of a way to anger her. Now he seized upon the opportunity given him by Frigate. He launched into an uninhibited account of what went on in the Karachi houses. Ruach finally got up and walked away. Frigate looked as if he were sick, but he stayed. Wilfreda laughed until she rolled on the ground. Kazz and Monat kept stolid expressions. Gwenafra was sleeping on the boat, so Burton did not have to take her into account. Loghu seemed to be fascinated but also slightly repulsed.

Alice, his main target, turned pale and then, later, red. Finally, she rose and said, "Really, Mr. Burton, I had thought you were low before. But to brag of this . . . this . . . you are utterly contemptible, degenerate, and repulsive. Not that I believe a word of what you've been telling me. I can't believe that anybody would behave as you claim you did and then boast about it. You are living up to your reputation as a man who likes to shock others no matter what damage it does to his own reputation."

She had walked off into the darkness.

Frigate had said, "Sometime, maybe, you will tell me how much of that is true. I used to think as she did. But when I got older, more evidence about you was turned up, and one biographer made a psychoanalysis of you based on your own writing and various documentary sources."

"And the conclusions?" Burton said mockingly.

"Later, Dick," Frigate said. "Ruffian Dick," he added, and he, too, left.

Now, standing at the tiller, watching the sun beat down on the group, listening to the hissing of water cut by the two sharp prows, and the creaking of rigging, he wondered what lay ahead on the other side of the canyonlike channel. Not the end of The River, surely. That would probably go on forever. But the end of the group might be near. They had been cooped up too long together. Too many days had been spent on the narrow deck with too

114

little to do except talk or help sail the ship. They were rubbing each other raw and had been doing it for a long time. Even Wilfreda had been quiet and unresponsive lately. Not that he had been too stimulating. Frankly, he was tired of her. He did not hate her or wish her any ill. He was just tired of her, and the fact that he could have her and not have Alice Hargreaves made him even more tired of her.

Lev Ruach was staying away from him or speaking as little as possible, and Lev was arguing even more with Esther about his dietary habits and his daydreaming and why didn't he ever talk to her?

Frigate was mad at him about something. But Frigate would never come out and say anything, the coward, until he was driven into a corner and tormented into a mindless rage. Loghu was angry and scornful of Frigate because he was as sullen with her as with the others. Loghu was also angry with him, Burton, because he had turned her down when they had been alone gathering bamboo in the hills several weeks ago. He had told her no, adding that he had no moral scruples against making love to her, but that he would not betray Frigate or any other member of the crew. Loghu said that it was not that she did not love Frigate; it was just that she needed a change now and then. Just as Frigate did.

Alice had said that she was about to give up hope of ever seeing anybody she knew again. They must have passed an estimated 44,370,000 people, at least, and not once had she seen anybody she had known on Earth. She had seen some that she had mistaken for old acquaintances. And she admitted that she had only seen a small percentage of the 44,370,000 at close range or even at far range. But that did not matter. She was getting abysmally depressed and weary of sitting on this cramped foredeck all day with her only exercise handling the tiller or the rigging or opening and closing her lips with conversation, most of it inane.

Burton did not want to admit it, but he was afraid that she might leave. She might just get off at the next stop, walk off onto the shore with her grail and few belongings, and say goodbye. See you in a hundred years or so. Perhaps. The chief thing keeping her on the boat so far had been Gwenafra. She was raising the little ancient Briton as a Victorian-lady-cum-post-Resurrection-mores-child. This was a most curious mixture, but not any more curious than anything else along The River.

Burton himself was weary of the eternal voyaging on the little vessel. He wanted to find some hospitable area and settle down there to rest, then to study, to engage in local activities, to get his land legs back, and allow the drive to get out and away to build up again. But he wanted to do it with Alice as his hutmate.

"The fortune of the man who sits also sits," he muttered. He would have to take action with Alice; he had been a gentleman long enough. He would woo her; he would take her by storm. He had been an aggressive lover when a young man, then he had gotten used to being the loved, not the lover, after he got married. And his old habit patterns, old neural circuits, were still with him. He was an old person in a new body.

The Hadji entered the dark and turbulent channel. The blue-black rock walls rose on both sides and the boat went down a curve and the broad lake behind was lost. Everybody was busy then, jumping to handle the sails as Burton took *The Hadji* back and forth in the quarter-mile wide stream and against a current that raised high waves. The boat rose and dipped sharply and heeled far over when they changed course abruptly. It often came within a few feet of the canyon walls, where the waves slapped massively against the rock. But he had been sailing the boat so long that he had become a part of it, and his crew had worked with him so long that they could anticipate his orders, though they never acted ahead of them.

The passage took about thirty minutes. It caused anxiety in some—no doubt of Frigate and Ruach being worried—but it also exhilarated all of them. The boredom and the sullenness were, temporarily, at least, gone.

The Hadji came out into the sunshine of another lake. This was about four miles wide and stretched northward as far as they could see. The mountains abruptly fell

116

away; the plains on both sides resumed the usual mile width.

There were fifty or so craft in view, ranging from pine dugouts to two-masted bamboo boats. Most of them seemed to be engaged in fishing. To the left, a mile away, was the ubiquitous grailstone, and along the shore were dark figures. Behind them, on the plain and hills, were bamboo huts in the usual style of what Frigate called Neo-Polynesian or, sometimes, Post-Mortem Riparian Architecture.

On the right, about half a mile from the exit of the canyon, was a large log fort. Before it were ten massive log docks with a variety of large and small boats. A few minutes after *The Hadji* appeared, drums began beating. These could be hollow logs or drums made with tanned fishskin or human skin. There was already a crowd in front of the fort, but a large number swarmed out of it and from a collection of huts behind it. They piled into the boats, and these cast off.

On the left bank, the dark figures were launching dugouts, canoes, and single-masted boats.

It looked as if both shores were sending boats out in a competition to seize *The Hadji* first.

Burton took the boat back and forth as required, cutting in between the other boats several times. The men on the right were closer; they were white and well armed, but they made no effort to use their bows. A man standing in the prow of a warcanoe with thirty paddlers shouted at them, in German, to surrender.

"You will not be harmed!"

"We come in peace!" Frigate bawled at him.

"He knows that!" Burton said. "It's evident that we few aren't going to attack them!"

Drums were beating on both sides of The River now. It sounded as if the lake shores were alive with drums. And the shores were certainly alive with men, all armed. Other boats were being put out to intercept them. Behind them, the boats that had first gone out were pursuing but losing distance.

Burton hesitated. Should he bring *The Hadji* on around

117

and go back through the channel and then return at night? It would be a dangerous maneuver, because the 20,000-foot high walls would block out the light from the blazing stars and gas sheets. They would be almost blind.

And this craft did seem to be faster than anything the enemy had. So far, that is. Far in the distance, tall sails were coming swiftly toward him. Still, they had the wind and current behind them, and if he avoided them, could they outstrip him when they, too, had to tack?

All the vessels he had seen so far had been loaded with men, thus slowing them down. Even a boat that had the same potentialities as *The Hadji* would not keep up with her if she were loaded with warriors.

He decided to keep on running upRiver.

Ten minutes later, as he was running close-hauled, another large warcanoe cut across his path. This held sixteen paddlers on each side and supported a small deck in the bow and the stern. Two men stood on each deck beside a catapult mounted on a wooden pedestal. The two in the bow placed a round object which sputtered smoke in the pocket of the catapult. One pulled the catch, and the arm of the machine banged against the crossbeam. The canoe shuddered, and there was a slight halt in the deep rhythmic grunting of the paddlers. The smoking object flew in a high arc until it was about twenty feet in front of *The Hadji* and ten feet above the water. It exploded with a loud noise and much black smoke, quickly cleared away by the breeze.

Some of the women screamed, and a man shouted. He thought, there is sulfur in this area. Otherwise, they would not have been able to make gunpowder.

He called to Loghu and Esther Rodriquez to take over at the tiller. Both women were pale, but they seemed calm enough, although neither woman had ever experienced a bomb.

Gwenafra had been put inside the fo'c's'le. Alice had a yew bow in her hand and a quiver of arrows strapped to her back. Her pale skin contrasted shockingly with the red lipstick and the green eyelid-makeup. But she had been through at least ten running battles on the water, and her

118

nerves were as steady as the chalk cliffs of Dover. Moreover, she was the best archer of the lot. Burton was a superb marksman with a firearm but he lacked practice with the bow. Kazz could draw the riverdragon-horn bow even deeper than Burton, but his marksmanship was abominable. Frigate claimed it would never be very good; like most preliterates, he lacked a development of the sense of perspective.

The catapult men did not fit another bomb to the machine. Evidently, the bomb had been a warning to stop. Burton intended to stop for nothing. Their pursuers could have shot them full of arrows several times. That they had refrained meant that they wanted *The Hadji* crew alive.

The canoe, water boiling from its prow, paddles flashing in the sun, paddlers grunting in unison, passed closely to the stern of *The Hadji*. The two men on the foredeck leaped outward, and the canoe rocked. One man splashed into the water, his fingertips striking the edge of the deck. The other landed on his knees on the edge. He gripped a bamboo knife between his teeth; his belt held two sheaths, one with a small stone axe and the other with a hornfish stiletto. For a second, as he tried to grab onto the wet planking and pull himself up, he stared upward into Burton's eyes. His hair was a rich yellow, his eyes were a pale blue, and his face was classically handsome. His intention was probably to wound one or two of the crew and then to dive off, maybe with a woman in his arms. While he kept *The Hadji* crew busy, his fellows would sail up and engage *The Hadji* and pour aboard, and that would be that.

He did not have much chance of carrying out his plan, probably knew it, and did not care. Most men still feared death because the fear was in the cells of their bodies, and they reacted instinctively. A few had overcome their fear, and others had never really felt it.

Burton stepped up and banged the man on the side of the head with his axe. The man's mouth opened; the bamboo knife fell out; he collapsed face down on the deck. Burton picked up the knife, untied the man's belt, and shoved him off into the water with his foot. At that, a

119

roar came from the men in the warcanoe, which was turning around. Burton saw that the shore was coming up fast, and he gave orders to tack. The vessel swung around, and the boom swung by. Then they were beating across The River, with a dozen boats speeding toward them. Three were four-man dugouts, four were big warcanoes, and five were two-masted schooners. The latter held a number of catapults and many men on the decks.

Halfway across The River, Burton ordered *The Hadji* swung around again. The maneuver allowed the sailships to get much closer, but he had calculated for that. Now, sailing close-hauled again, *The Hadji* cut water between the two schooners. They were so close that he could clearly see the features of all aboard both craft. They were mostly Caucasian, though they ranged from very dark to Nordic pale. The captain of the boat on the portside shouted in German at Burton, demanding that he surrender.

"We will not harm you if you give up, but we will torture you if you continue to fight!"

He spoke German with an accent that sounded Hungarian.

For reply, Burton and Alice shot arrows. Alice's shaft missed the captain but hit the helmsman, and he staggered back and fell over the railing. The craft immediately veered. The captain sprang to the wheel, and Burton's second shaft went through the back of his knee.

Both schooners struck slantingly with a great crash and shot off with much tearing up of timbers, men screaming and falling onto the decks or falling overboard. Even if the boats did not sink, they would be out of action.

But just before they hit, their archers had put a dozen flaming arrows into the bamboo sails of *The Hadji*. The shafts carried dry grass which had been soaked with turpentine made from pine resin, and these, fanned by the wind, spread the flames quickly.

Burton took the tiller back from the women and shouted orders. The crew dipped fired-clay vessels and their open grails into The River and then threw the water on the flames. Loghu, who could climb like a monkey,

120

went up the mast with a rope around her shoulder. She let the rope down and pulled up the containers of water.

This permitted the other schooners and several canoes to draw close. One was on a course which would put it directly in the path of *The Hadji*. Burton swung the boat around again, but it was sluggish because of Loghu's weight on the mast. It wheeled around, the boom swung wildly as the men failed to keep control of its ropes, and more arrows struck the sail and spread more fire. Several arrows thunked into the deck. For a moment, Burton thought that the enemy had changed his mind and was trying to down them. But the arrows were just misdirected.

Again, *The Hadji* sliced between two schooners. The captains and the crew of both were grinning. Perhaps they had been bored for a long time and were enjoying the pursuit. Even so, the crews ducked behind the railings, leaving the officers, helmsmen, and the archers to receive the fire from *The Hadji*. There was a strumming, and dark streaks with red heads and blue tails went halfway through the sails in two dozen places, a number drove into the mast or the boom, a dozen hissed into the water, one shot by Burton a few inches from his head.

Alice, Ruach, Kazz, de Greystock, Wilfreda, and he had shot while Esther handled the tiller. Loghu was frozen halfway up the mast, waiting until the arrow fire quit. The five arrows found three targets of flesh, a captain, a helmsman, and a sailor who stuck his head up at the wrong time for him.

Esther screamed, and Burton spun. The warcanoe had come out from behind the schooner and was a few feet in front of *The Hadji's* bow. There was no way to avoid a collision. The two men on the platform were diving off the side, and the paddlers were standing up or trying to stand up so they could get overboard. Then *The Hadji* smashed into its port near the bow, cracking it open, turning it over, and spilling its crew into The River. Those on *The Hadji* were thrown forward, and de Greystock went into the water. Burton slid on his face and chest and knees, burning off the skin.

121

Esther had been torn from the tiller and rolled across the deck until she thumped against the edge of the fo'c'sle coaming. She lay there without moving.

Burton looked upward. The sail was blazing away beyond hope of being saved. Loghu was gone, so she must have been hurled off at the moment of impact. Then, getting up, he saw her and de Greystock swimming back to *The Hadji*. The water around them was boiling with the splashing of the dispossessed canoemen, many of whom, judging by their cries, could not swim.

Burton called to the men to help the two aboard while he inspected the damage. Both prows of the very thin twin hulls had been smashed open by the crash. Water was pouring inside. And the smoke from the burning sail and mast was curling around them, causing Alice and Gwenafra to cough.

Another warcanoe was approaching swiftly from the north; the two schooners were sailing close-hauled toward them.

They could fight and draw some blood from their enemies, who would be holding themselves back to keep from killing them. Or they could swim for it. Either way, they would be captured.

Loghu and de Greystock were pulled aboard. Frigate reported that Esther could not be brought back to consciousness. Ruach felt her pulse and opened her eyes and then walked back to Burton.

"She's not dead, but she's totally out."

Burton said, "You women know what will happen to you. It's up to you, of course, but I suggest you swim down as deeply as you can and draw in a good breath of water. You'll wake up tomorrow, good as new."

Gwenafra had come out from the fo'c'sle. She wrapped her arms around his waist and looked up, dry-eyed but scared. He hugged her with one arm and then said, "Alice! Take her with you!"

"Where?" Alice said. She looked at the canoe and back at him. She coughed again as more smoke wrapped around her and then she moved forward, upwind.

"When you go down."

He gestured at The River.

"I can't do that," she said.

"You wouldn't want those men to get her, too. She's only a little girl but they'll not stop for that."

Alice looked as if her face was going to crumple and wash away with tears. But she did not weep.

She said, "Very well. It's no sin now, killing yourself. I just hope . . ."

He said, "Yes."

He did not drawl the word; there was no time to drawl anything out. The canoe was within forty feet of them.

"The next place might be just as bad or worse than this one," Alice said. "And Gwenafra will wake up all alone. You know that the chances of us being resurrected at the same place are slight."

"That can't be helped," he said.

She clamped her lips, then opened them and said, "I'll fight until the last moment. Then . . ."

"It may be too late," he said. He picked up his bow and drew an arrow from his quiver. De Greystock had lost his bow, so he took Kazz's. The Neanderthal placed a stone in a sling and began whirling it. Lev picked up his sling and chose a stone for its pocket. Monat used Esther's bow, since he had lost his, also.

The captain of the canoe shouted in German, "Lay down your arms! You won't be harmed!"

He fell off the platform onto a paddler a second later as Alice's arrow went through his chest. Another arrow, probably de Greystock's, spun the second man off the platform and into the water. A stone hit a paddler in the shoulder, and he collapsed with a cry. Another stone struck glancingly off another paddler's head, and he lost his paddle.

The canoe kept on coming. The two men on the aft platform urged the crew to continue driving toward *The Hadji*. Then they fell with arrows in them.

Burton looked behind him. The two schooners were letting their sails drop now. Evidently they would slide on up to *The Hadji* where the sailors would throw their grappling hooks into it. But if they got too close, the

123

flames might spread to them.

The canoe rammed into *The Hadji* with fourteen of the original complement dead or too wounded to fight. Just before the canoe's prow hit, the survivors dropped their paddles and raised small round leather shields. Even so, two arrows went through two shields and into the arms of the men holding them. That still left twenty men against six men, five women, and a child.

But one was a five-foot high hairy man with tremendous strength and a big stone axe. Kazz jumped into the air just before the canoe rammed the starboard hull and came down in it a second after it had halted. His axe crushed two skulls and then drove through the bottom of the canoe. Water poured in, and de Greystock, shouting something in his Cumberland Middle English, leaped down beside Kazz. He held a stiletto in one hand and a big oak club with flint spikes in the other.

The others on *The Hadji* continued to shoot their arrows. Suddenly, Kazz and de Greystock were scrambling back onto the catamaran and the canoe was sinking with its dead, dying, and its scared survivors. A number drowned; the others either swam away or tried to get aboard *The Hadji*. These fell back with their fingers chopped off or stamped flat.

Something struck on the deck near him and then something else coiled around him. Burton spun and slashed at the leather rope which had settled around his neck. He leaped to one side to avoid another and yanked savagely at a third rope and pulled the man on the other end over the railing. The man, screaming, pitched out and struck the deck of *The Hadji* with his shoulder. Burton smashed in his face with his axe.

But now men were dropping from the decks of both schooners, and ropes were falling everywhere. The smoke and the flames added to the confusion, though they may have helped *The Hadji*'s crew more than the boarders.

Burton shouted at Alice to get Gwenafra and jump into The River. He could not find her and then had to parry the thrust of the big Black with a spear. The man seemed to have forgotten any orders to capture Burton; he looked as

124

if he meant to kill. Burton knocked the short spear aside and whirled, lashing the Black's neck. Burton continued to whirl, felt a sharp pain in his ribs, another in his shoulder, but knocked two men down and then was in the water. He fell between the schooner and *The Hadji,* went down, released the axe and pulled the stiletto from its sheath. When he came up, he was looking up at a tall, rawboned, redheaded man who was lifting the screaming Gwenafra above him with both hands. The man pitched her far out into the water.

Burton dived again and coming up saw Gwenafra's face only a few feet before him. It was gray, and her eyes were dull. Then he saw the blood darkening the water around her. She disappeared before he could get to her. He dived down after her, caught her and pulled her back up. A hornfish tip was stuck into her back.

He let her body go. He did not know why the man had killed her when he could have easily taken her prisoner. Perhaps Alice had stabbed her and the man had figured that she was as good as dead and so had tossed her over the side to the fishes.

A body shot out of the smoke, followed by another. One man was dead with a broken neck; the other was alive. Burton wrapped his arm around the man's neck and stabbed him at the juncture of jaw and ear. The man quit struggling and slipped down into the depths.

Frigate leaped out from the smoke, his face and shoulders bloody. He hit the water at a slant and dived deep. Burton swam toward him to help him. There was no use even trying to get back on the craft. It was solid with struggling bodies, and other canoes and dugouts were closing in.

Frigate's head rose out of the water. His skin was white where the blood was not pumping out over it. Burton swam to him and said, "Did the women get away?"

Frigate shook his head and then said, "Watch out!"

Burton upended to dive down. Something hit his legs; he kept on going down, but he could not carry out his intention of breathing in the water. He would fight until they had to kill him.

On coming up, he saw that the water was alive with men who had jumped in after him and Frigate. The American, half-conscious, was being towed to a canoe. Three men closed in on Burton, and he stabbed two, and then a man in a dugout reached down with a club and banged him on the head.

15

They were led ashore near a large building behind a wall of pine logs. Burton's head throbbed with pain at every step. The gashes in his shoulder and ribs hurt, but they had quit bleeding. The fortress was built of pine logs, had an overhanging second story, and many sentinels. The captives were marched through an entrance that could be closed with a huge log gate. They marched across sixty feet of grass-covered yard and through another large gateway into a hall about fifty feet long and thirty wide. Except for Frigate, who was too weak, they stood before a large round table of oak. They blinked in the dark and cool interior before they could clearly see the two men at the table.

Guards with spears, clubs, and stone axes were everywhere. A wooden staircase at one end of the hall led up to a runway with high railings. Women looked over the railings at them.

One of the men at the table was short and muscular. He had a hairy body, black curly hair, a nose like a falcon's, and brown eyes as fierce as a falcon's. The second man was taller, had blond hair, eyes the exact color of which was difficult to tell in the dusky light but were probably blue, and a broad Teutonic face. A paunch and the beginnings of jowls told of the food and liquor he had taken from the grails of slaves.

126

Frigate had sat down on the grass, but he was pulled up to his feet when the blond gave a signal. Frigate looked at the blond and said, "You look like Hermann Göring when he was young."

Then he dropped to his knees, screaming with pain from the impact of a spear butt over his kidneys.

The blond spoke in an English with a heavy German accent. "No more of that unless I order it. Let them talk."

He scrutinized them for several minutes, then said, "Yes, I am Hermann Göring."

"Who is Göring?" Burton said.

"Your friend can tell you later," the German said. "If there is a later for you. I am not angry about the splendid fight you put up. I admire men who can fight well. I can always use more spears, especially since you killed so many. I offer you a choice. You men, that is. Join me and live well with all the food, liquor, tobacco, and women you can possibly want. Or work for me as my slaves."

"For us," the other man said in English. "You forget, Hermann, dat I have yust as muck to say about dis as you."

Göring smiled, chuckled, and said, "Of course! I was only using the royal I, you might say. Very well, we. If you swear to serve *us,* and it will be far better for you if you do, you will swear loyalty to me, Hermann Göring, and to the one-time king of ancient Rome, Tullius Hostilius."

Burton looked closely at the man. Could he actually be the legendary king of ancient Rome? Of Rome when it was a small village threatened by the other Italic tribes, the Sabines, Aequi, and Volsci? Who, in turn, were being pressed by the Umbrians, themselves pushed by the powerful Etruscans? Was this really Tullius Hostilius, warlike successor to the peaceful Numa Pompilius? There was nothing to distinguish him from a thousand men whom Burton had seen on the streets of Siena. Yet, if he was what he claimed to be, he could be a treasure trove, historically and linguistically speaking. He would, since he was probably Etruscan himself, know that language, in addition to pre-Classical Latin, and Sabine, and perhaps

Campanian Greek. He might even have been acquainted with Romulus, supposed founder of Roma. What stories that man could tell!

"Well?" Göring said.

"What do we have to do if we join you?" Burton said.

"First, I . . . we . . . have to make sure that you are the caliber of man we want. In other words, a man who will unhesitatingly and immediately do anything that we order. We will give you a little test."

He gave an order and a minute later, a group of men was brought forward. All were gaunt, and all were crippled.

"They were injured while quarrying stone or building our walls," Göring said. "Except for two caught while trying to escape. They will have to pay the penalty. All will be killed because they are now useless. So, you should not hesitate about killing them to show your determination to serve us."

He added, "Besides, they are all Jews. Why worry about them?"

Campbell, the redhead who had thrown Gwenafra into The River, held out to Burton a large club studded with chert blades. Two guards seized a slave and forced him to his knees. He was a large blond with blue eyes and a Grecian profile; he glared at Göring and then spat at him.

Göring laughed. "He has all the arrogance of his race. I could reduce him to a quivering screaming mass begging for death if I wanted to. But I do not really care for torture. My compatriot would like to give him a taste of the fire, but I am essentially a humanitarian."

"I will kill in defense of my life or in defense of those who need protection," Burton said. "But I am not a murderer."

"Killing this Jew would be an act in defense of your life," Göring replied. "If you do not, you will die anyway. Only it will take you a long time."

"I will not," Burton said.

Göring sighed. "You English! Well, I would rather have you on my side. But if you don't want to do the rational thing, so be it. What about you?" he said to Frigate.

Frigate, who was still in agony, said, "Your ashes ended in a trash heap in Dachau because of what you did and what you were. Are you going to repeat the same criminal acts on this world?"

Göring laughed and said, "I know what happened to me. Enough of my Jewish slaves have told me."

He pointed at Monat. "What kind of a freak is that?"

Burton explained. Göring looked grave, then said, "I couldn't trust him. He goes into the slave camp. You, there, apeman. What do you say?"

Kazz, to Burton's surprise, stepped forward. "I kill for you. I don't want to be slave."

He took the club while the guards held their spears poised to run him through if he had other ideas for using it. He glared at them from under his shelving brows, then raised the club. There was a crack, and the slave pitched forward on the dirt. Kazz returned the club to Campbell and stepped aside. He did not look at Burton.

Göring said, "All the slaves will be assembled tonight, and they will be shown what will happen to them if they try to get away. The escapees will be roasted for a while, then put out of their misery. My distinguished colleague will personally handle the club. He likes that sort of thing."

He pointed at Alice. "That one. I'll take her."

Tullius stood up. "No, no. I like her. You take de oders, Hermann. I giw you bot' off dem. But sye, I want her wery muck. Sye look like, wat you say, aristocrat. A . . . queen?"

Burton roared, snatched a club from Campbell's hand, and leaped upon the table. Göring fell backward, the tip of the club narrowly missing his nose. At the same time, the Roman thrust a spear at Burton and wounded him in the shoulder. Burton kept hold of the club, whirled, and knocked the weapon out of Tullius' hand.

The slaves, shouting, threw themselves upon the guards. Frigate jerked a spear loose and brought the butt of it against Kazz's head. Kazz crumpled. Monat kicked a guard in the groin and picked up his spear.

Burton did not remember anything after that. He awoke several hours before dusk. His head hurt worse than before. His ribs and both shoulders were stiff with pain. He was lying on grass in a pine log enclosure with a diameter of about fifty yards. Fifteen feet above the grass, circling the interior of the wall, was a wooden walk on which armed guards paced.

He groaned when he sat up. Frigate, squatting near him, said, "I was afraid you'd never come out of it."

"Where are the women?" Burton said.

Frigate began to weep. Burton shook his head and said, "Quit blubbering. Where are they?"

"Where the hell do you think they are?" Frigate said. "Oh, my God!"

"Don't think about the women. There's nothing you can do for them. Not now, anyway. Why wasn't I killed after I attacked Göring?"

Frigate wiped away the tears and said, "Beats me. Maybe they're saving you, and me, for the fire. As an example. I wish they had killed us."

"What, so recently gained paradise and wish so soon to lose it?" Burton said. He began to laugh but quit because pains speared his head.

Burton talked to Robert Spruce, an Englishman born in 1945 in Kensington. Spruce said that it was less than a month since Göring and Tullius had seized power. For the time being, they were leaving their neighbors in peace. Eventually, of course, they would try to conquer the adjacent territories, including the Onondaga Indians' across The River. So far, no slave had escaped to spread word about Göring's intentions.

"But the people on the borders can see for themselves that the walls are being built by slaves," Burton said.

Spruce grinned wryly and said, "Göring has spread the word that these are all Jews, that he is only interested in enslaving Jews. So, what do they care? As you can see for yourself, that is not true. Half of the slaves are Gentile."

At dusk, Burton, Frigate, Ruach, de Greystock, and

130

Monat were taken from the stockade and marched down to a grailrock. There were about two hundred slaves there, guarded by about seventy Göringites. Their grails were placed on the rock, and they waited. After the blue flames roared, the grails were taken down. Each slave opened his, and guards removed the tobacco, liquor, and half of the food.

Frigate had gashes in his head and in his shoulder which needed sewing up, though the bleeding had stopped. His color had much improved, though his back and kidneys pained him.

"So now we're slaves," Frigate said. "Dick, you thought quite a lot of the institution of slavery. What do you think of it now?"

"That was *Oriental* slavery," Burton said. "In *this* type of slavery, there's no chance for a slave to gain his freedom. Nor is there any personal feeling, except hatred, between slave and owner. In the Orient, the situation was different. Of course, like any human institution, it had its abuses."

"You're a stubborn man," Frigate said. "Have you noticed that at least half the slaves are Jews? Late twentieth-century Israeli, most of them. That girl over there told me that Göring managed to start grail-slavery by stirring up anti-Semitism in this area. Of course, it had to exist before it could be aroused. Then, after he had gotten into power with Tullius' aid, he enslaved many of his former supporters."

He continued, "The hell of it is, Göring is not, relatively speaking, a genuine anti-Semite. He personally intervened with Himmler and others to save Jews. But he is something even worse than a genuine Jew-hater. He is an opportunist. Anti-Semitism was a tidal wave in Germany; to get any place, you had to ride the wave. So, Göring rode there, just as he rode here. An anti-Semite such as Goebbels or Frank believed in the principles they professed. Perverted and hateful principles, true, but still principles. Whereas big fat happy-go-lucky Göring did not really care one way or the other about the Jews. He just wanted to use them."

"All very well," Burton said, "but what has that got to do with me? Oh, I see! That look! You are getting ready to lecture me."

"Dick, I admire you as I have admired few men. I love you as one man loves another. I am as happy and delighted to have had the singular good luck to fall in with you as, say, Plutarch would be if he had met Alcibiades or Theseus. But I am not blind. I know your faults, which are many, and I regret them."

"Just which one is it this time?"

"That book. *The Jew, The Gypsy, and El Islam.* How could you have written it? A hate document full of bloody-minded nonsense, folk tales, superstitions! Ritual murders, indeed!"

"I was still angry because of the injustices I had suffered at Damascus. To be expelled from the consulate because of the lies of my enemies, among whom . . ."

"That doesn't excuse your writing lies about a whole group," Frigate said.

"Lies! I wrote the truth!"

"You may have thought they were truths. But I come from an age which definitely knows that they were not. In fact, no one in his right mind in your time would have believed that crap!"

"The facts are," Burton said, "that the Jewish moneylenders in Damascus were charging the poor a thousand percent interest on their loans. The facts are that they were inflicting this monstrous usury not only on the Moslem and Christian populace but on their own people. The facts are, that when my enemies in England accused me of anti-Semitism, many Jews in Damascus came to my defense. It is a fact that I protested to the Turks when they sold the synagogue of the Damascan Jews to the Greek Orthodox bishop so he could turn it into a church. It is a fact that I went out and drummed up eighteen Moslems to testify in behalf of the Jews. It is a fact that I protected the Christian missionaries from the Druzes. It is a fact that I warned the Druzes that that fat and oily Turkish swine, Rashid Pasha, was trying to incite them to revolt so he could massacre them. It is a fact that when I was recalled from my consular post, because of the lies of the Christian missionaries and priests, of Rashid Pasha, and of the Jewish usurers, thousands of Christians, Moslems, and Jews rallied to my aid, though it was too late then.

"It is also a fact that I don't have to answer to you or to any man for my actions!"

How like Frigate to bring up such an irrelevant subject at such an inappropriate time. Perhaps he was trying to keep from blaming himself by turning his fear and anger on Burton. Or perhaps he really felt that his hero had failed him.

Lev Ruach had been sitting with his head between his hands. He raised his head and said, hollowly, "Welcome to the concentration camp, Burton! This is your first taste of it. It's an old tale to me, one I was tired of hearing from the beginning. I was in a Nazi camp, and I escaped. I was in a Russian camp, and I escaped. In Israel, I was captured by Arabs, and I escaped.

"So, now, perhaps I can escape again. But to what? To another camp? There seems to be no end to them. Man is forever building them and putting the perennial prisoner, the Jew, or what have you, in them. Even here, where we have a fresh start, where all religions, all prejudices, should have been shattered on the anvil of resurrection, little is changed."

"Shut your mouth," a man near Ruach said. He had red hair so curly it was almost kinky, blue eyes, and a face that might have been handsome if it had not been for his broken nose. He was six feet tall and had a wrestler's body.

"Dov Targoff here," he said in a crisp Oxford accent. "Late commander in the Israeli Navy. Pay no attention to this man. He's one of the old-time Jews, a pessimist, a whiner. He'd rather wail against the wall than stand up and fight like a man."

Ruach choked, then said, "You arrogant sabra! I fought; I killed! And I am not a whiner! What are you doing now, you brave warrior? Aren't you a slave as much as the rest of us?"

133

"It's the old story," a woman said. She was tall and dark-haired and probably would have been a beauty if she had not been so gaunt. "The old story. We fight among ourselves while our enemies conquer. Just as we fought when Titus besieged Jerusalem and we killed more of our own people than we did the Romans. Just as . . ."

The two men turned against her, and all three argued loudly until a guard began beating them with a stick.

Later, through swollen lips, Targoff said, "I can't take much of this, much longer. Soon . . . well, that guard is mine to kill."

"You have a plan?" Frigate said, eagerly, but Targoff would not answer.

Shortly before dawn, the slaves were awakened and marched to the grailrock. Again, they were given a modicum of food. After eating, they were split up into groups and marched off to their different assignments. Burton and Frigate were taken to the northern border. They were put to work with a thousand other slaves, and they toiled naked all day in the sun. Their only rest was when they took their grails to the rock at noon and were fed.

Göring meant to build a wall between the mountain and The River; he also intended to erect a second wall which would run for the full ten-mile length of the lakeshore and a third wall at the southern end.

Burton and the others had to dig a deep trench and then pile the dirt taken from the hole into a wall. This was hard work, for they had only stone hoes with which to hack at the ground. Since the roots of the grass formed a thickly tangled complex of very tough material, they could be cut only with repeated blows. The dirt and roots were scraped up on wooden shovels and tossed onto large bamboo sleds. These were dragged by teams onto the top of the wall, where the dirt was shoveled off to make the wall even higher and thicker.

At night, the slaves were herded back into the stockade. Here, most of them fell asleep almost at once. But Targoff, the red-headed Israeli, squatted by Burton.

"The grapevine gives a little juice now and then," he

said. "I heard about the fight you and your crew made. I also heard about your refusal to join Göring and his swine."

"What do you hear about my infamous book?" Burton said.

Targoff smiled and said, "I never heard of it until Ruach brought it to my attention. Your actions speak for themselves. Besides, Ruach is very sensitive about such things. Not that you can really blame him after what he went through. But I do not think that you would behave as you did if you were what he said you are. I think you're a good man, the type we need. So . . ."

Days and nights of hard work and short rations followed. Burton learned through the grapevine about the women. Wilfreda and Fatima were in Campbell's apartment. Loghu was with Tullius. Alice had been kept by Göring for a week, then had been turned over to a lieutenant, a Manfred von Kreyscharft. Rumor was that Göring had complained of her coldness and had wanted to give her to his bodyguards to do with as they pleased. But von Kreyscharft had asked for her.

Burton was in agony. He could not endure the mental images of her with Göring and von Kreyscharft. He had to stop these beasts or at least die trying. Late that night, he crawled from the big hut he occupied with twenty-five men into Targoff's hut and woke him up.

"You said you knew that I must be on your side," he whispered. "When are you going to take me into your confidence? I might as well warn you now that, if you don't do so at once, I intend to foment a break among my own group and anybody else who will join us."

"Ruach has told me *more* about you," Targoff said. "I didn't understand, really, what he was talking about. Could a Jew trust anyone who wrote such a book? Or could such a man be trusted not to turn on them after the common enemy has been defeated?"

Burton opened his mouth to speak angrily, then closed it. For a moment, he was silent. When he spoke, he did so calmly. "In the first place, my actions on Earth speak louder than any of my printed words. I was the friend and

135

protector of many Jews; I had many Jewish friends."

"That last statement is always a preface to an attack on the Jews," Targoff said.

"Perhaps. However, even if what Ruach claims were true, the Richard Burton you see before you in this valley is not the Burton who lived on Earth. I think every man has been changed somewhat by his experience here. If he hasn't, he is incapable of change. He would be better off dead.

"During the four hundred and seventy-six days that I have lived on this River, I have learned much. I am not incapable of changing my mind. I listened to Ruach and Frigate. I argued frequently and passionately with them. And though I did not want to admit it at the time, I thought much about what they said."

"Jew-hate is something bred into the child," Targoff said. "It becomes part of the nerve. No act of will can get rid of it, unless it is not very deeply embedded or the will is extraordinarily strong. The bell rings, and Pavlov's dog salivates. Mention the word *Jew,* and the nervous system storms the citadel of the mind of the Gentile. Just as the word *Arab* storms mine. But I have a realistic basis for hating all Arabs."

"I have pled enough," Burton said. "You will either accept me or reject me. In either case, you know what I will do."

"I accept," Targoff said. "If you can change your mind, I can change mine. I've worked with you, eaten bread with you. I like to think I'm a good judge of character. Tell me, if you were planning this, what would you do?"

Targoff listened carefully. At the end of Burton's explanation, Targoff nodded. "Much like my plan. Now . . ."

16

The next day, shortly after breakfast, several guards came for Burton and Frigate. Targoff looked hard at Burton, who knew what Targoff was thinking. Nothing could be done except to march off to Göring's "palace." He was seated in a big wooden chair and smoking a pipe. He asked them to sit down and offered them cigars and wine.

"Every once in a while," he said, "I like to relax and talk with somebody besides my colleagues, who are not overly bright. I like especially to talk with somebody who lived *after* I died. And to men who were famous in their time. I've few of either type, so far."

"Many of your Israeli prisoners lived after you," Frigate said.

"Ah, the Jews!" Göring airily waved his pipe. "That is the trouble. They know me too well. They are sullen when I try to talk to them, and too many have tried to kill me for me to feel comfortable around them. Not that I have anything against them. I don't particularly like Jews, but I had many Jewish friends . . ."

Burton reddened.

Göring, after sucking on his pipe, continued, "Der Fuehrer was a great man, but he had some idiocies. One of them was his attitude toward Jews. Myself, I cared less. But the Germany of my time was anti-Jewish, and a man must go with the Zeitgeist if he wants to get any place in life. Enough of that. Even here, a man cannot get away from them."

He chattered on for a while, then asked Frigate many questions concerning the fate of his contemporaries and the history of post-war Germany.

"If you Americans had had any political sense, you would have declared war on Russia as soon as we surrendered. We would have fought with you against the Bolsheviks, and we would have crushed them."

Frigate did not reply. Göring then told several "funny," very obscene stories. He asked Burton to tell him about the strange experience he had had before being resurrected in the valley.

Burton was surprised. Had Göring learned about this from Kazz or was there an informer among the slaves?

He told in full detail everything that had happened between the time he opened his eyes to find himself in the place of floating bodies to the instant when the man in the aerial canoe pointed the metal tube at him.

"The extra-Terrestrial, Monat, has a theory that some beings—call them Whoever or X—have been observing mankind since he ceased to be an ape. For at least two million years. These superbeings have, in some manner, recorded every cell of every human being that ever lived from the moment of conception, probably, to the moment of death. This seems a staggering concept, but it is no more staggering than the resurrection of all humanity and the reshaping of this planet into one Rivervalley. The recordings may have been made when the recordees were living. Or it may be that these superbeings detected vibrations from the past, just as we on Earth saw the light of stars as they had been a thousand years before.

"Monat, however, inclines to the former theory. He does not believe in time travel even in a limited sense.

"Monat believes that the X's stored these recordings. How, he does not know. But this planet was then reshaped for us. It is obviously one great Riverworld. During our journey upRiver, we've talked to dozens whose descriptions leave no doubt that they come from widely scattered parts, from all over. One was from far up in the northern hemisphere; another, far down in the southern. All the descriptions fall together to make a picture of a world that has been reworked into one zigzagging Rivervalley.

"The people we talked to were killed or died by

138

accident here and were resurrected again in the areas we happened to be traveling through. Monat says that we resurrectees are still being recorded. And when one of us dies again, the up-to-the-minute recordings are being placed somewhere—maybe under the surface of this planet—and played into energy-matter converters. The bodies were reproduced as they were at the moment of death and then the rejuvenating devices restored the sleeping bodies. Probably in that same chamber in which I awoke. After this, the bodies, young and whole again, were recorded and then destroyed. And the recordings were played out again, this time through devices under the ground. Once more, energy-matter converters, probably using the heat of this planet's molten core as energy, reproduced us above the ground, near the grailstones. I do not know why they are not resurrected a second time in the same spot where they died. But then I don't know why all our hairs were shaven off or why men's facial hairs don't grow or why men were circumcised and women made virgins again. Or why we were resurrected. For what purpose? Whoever put us here has not shown up to tell us why."

"The thing is," Frigate said, "the thing is, we are *not* the *same* people we were on Earth. I died. Burton died. You died, Hermann Göring. Everybody died. And we *cannot* be brought back to life!"

Göring sucked on his pipe noisily, stared at Frigate, and then said, "Why not? *I* am living again? Do you deny that?"

"Yes! I do deny that—in a sense. *You* are living. But you are *not* the Hermann Göring who was born in Marienbad Sanatorium at Rosenheim in Bavaria on January 12, 1893. You are *not* the Hermann Göring whose godfather was Dr. Hermann Eppenstein, a Jew converted to Christianity. You are *not* the Göring who succeeded von Richthofen after his death and continued to lead his fliers against the Allies even after the war ended. You are *not* the Reichsmarschal of Hitler's Germany *nor* the refugee arrested by Lieutenant Jerome N. Shapiro. Eppenstein and Shapiro, hah! And you are *not* the

Hermann Göring who took his life by swallowing potassium cyanide during his trial for his crimes against humanity!"

Göring tamped his pipe with tobacco and said, mildly, "You certainly know much about me. I should be flattered, I suppose. At least, I was not forgotten."

"Generally, you were," Frigate said. "You did have a long-lived reputation as a sinister clown, a failure, and a toady."

Burton was surprised. He had not known that the fellow would stand up to someone who had power of life and death over him or who had treated him so painfully. But then perhaps Frigate hoped to be killed.

It was probable that he was banking on Göring's curiosity.

Göring said, "Explain your statement. Not about my reputation. Every man of importance expects to be reviled and misunderstood by the brainless masses. Explain why I am not the same man."

Frigate smiled slightly and said, "You are the product, the hybrid, of a recording and an energy-matter converter. You were made with all the *memories* of the dead man Hermann Göring and with every cell of his body a duplicate. You have everything he had. So you *think* you are Göring. But you are not! You are a duplication, and that is all! The original Hermann Göring is nothing but molecules that have been absorbed into the soil and the air and so into plants and back into the flesh of beasts and men and out again as excrement, *und so weiter!*

"But you, here before me, are not the original, any more than the recording on a disc or a tape is the original voice, the vibrations issuing from the mouth of a man and detected and converted by an electronic device and then replayed."

Burton understood the reference, since he had seen an Edison phonograph in Paris in 1888. He felt outraged, actually violated, at Frigate's assertions.

Göring's wide-open eyes and reddening face indicated that he, too, felt threatened down to the core of his being.

After stuttering, Göring said, "And why would these

140

beings go to all this trouble just to make duplicates?"

Frigate shrugged and said, "I don't know."

Göring heaved up from his chair and pointed the stem of his pipe at Frigate.

"You lie!" he screamed in German. "You lie, *scheisshund*!"

Frigate quivered as if he expected to be struck over the kidneys again, but he said, "I must be right. Of course, you don't have to believe what I say. I can't prove anything. And I understand exactly how you feel. I *know* that I am Peter Jairus Frigate, born 1918, died 2008 A.D. But I also must believe, because logic tells me so, that I am only, really, a being who has the *memories* of that Frigate who will never rise from the dead. In a sense, I am the son of that Frigate who can never exist again. Not flesh of his flesh, blood of his blood, but mind of his mind. I am *not* the man who was born of a woman on that lost world of Earth. I am the byblow of science and a machine. Unless . . ."

Göring said, "Yes? Unless what?"

"Unless there is some entity attached to the human body, an entity which *is* the human being. I mean, it contains all that makes the individual what he is, and when the body is destroyed, this entity still exists. So that, if the body were to be made again, this entity, storing the essence of the individual, could be attached again to the body. And it would record everything that the body recorded. And so the original individual *would* live again. He would not be just a duplicate."

Burton said, "For God's sake, Pete! Are you proposing the *soul*?"

Frigate nodded and said, "Something analagous to the soul. Something that the primitives dimly apprehended and called a soul."

Göring laughed uproariously. Burton would have laughed, but he did not care to give Göring any support, moral or intellectual.

When Göring had quit laughing, he said, "Even here, in a world which is clearly the result of science, the supernaturalists won't quit trying. Well, enough of that.

141

To more practical and immediate matters. Tell me, have you changed your mind? Are you ready to join me?"

Burton glared and said, "I would not be under the orders of a man who rapes women; moreover, I respect the Israelis. I would rather be a slave with them than free with you."

Göring scowled and said, harshly, "Very well. I thought as much. But I had hoped . . . well, I have been having trouble with the Roman. If he gets his way, you will see how merciful I have been to you slaves. You do not know him. Only my intervention has saved one of you being tortured to death every night for his amusement."

At noon, the two returned to their work in the hills. Neither got a chance to speak to Targoff or any of the slaves, since their duties happened not to bring them into contact. They did not dare make an open attempt to talk to him, because that would have meant a severe beating.

After they returned to the stockade in the evening, Burton told the others what had happened.

"More than likely Targoff will not believe my story. He'll think we're spies. Even if he's not certain, he can't afford to take chances. So there'll be trouble. It's too bad that this had to happen. The escape plan will have to be cancelled for tonight."

Nothing untoward took place—at first. The Israelis walked away from Burton and Frigate when they tried to talk to them. The stars came out, and the stockade was flooded with a light almost as bright as a full moon of Earth.

The prisoners stayed inside their barracks, but they talked in low voices with their heads together. Despite their deep tiredness, they could not sleep. The guards must have sensed the tension, even though they could not see or hear the men in the huts. They walked back and forth on the walks, stood together talking, and peered down into the enclosure by the light of the night sky and the flames of the resin torches.

"Targoff will do nothing until it rains," Burton said. He gave orders. Frigate was to stand first watch; Robert Spruce, the second; Burton, third. Burton lay down on his pile of leaves and, ignoring the murmuring of voices and the moving around of bodies, fell asleep.

It seemed that he had just closed his eyes when Spruce touched him. He rose quickly to his feet, yawned, and stretched. The others were all awake. Within a few minutes, the first of the clouds formed. In ten minutes, the stars were blotted out. Thunder grumbled way up in the mountains, and the first lightning flash forked the sky.

Lightning struck near. Burton saw by its flash that the guards were huddled under the roofs sticking out from the base of the watch houses at each corner of the stockade. They were covered with towels against the chill and the rain.

Burton crawled from his barracks to the next. Targoff was standing inside the entrance. Burton stood up and said, "Does the plan still hold?"

"You know better than that," Targoff said. A bolt of lightning showed his angry face. "You Judas!"

He stepped forward, and a dozen men followed him, Burton did not wait; he attacked. But, as he rushed forward, he heard a strange sound. He pushed to look out through the door. Another flash revealed a guard sprawled face down in the grass beneath a walk.

Targoff had put his fists down when Burton turned his back on him. He said, "What's going on, Burton?"

"Wait," the Englishman replied. He had no more idea than the Israeli about what was happening, but anything unexpected could be to his advantage.

Lightning illuminated the squat figure of Kazz on the wooden walk. He was swinging a huge stone axe against a group of guards who were in the angle formed by the meeting of the two walls. Another flash. The guards were sprawled out on the walk. Darkness. At the next blaze of light, another was down; the remaining two were running away down the walk in different directions.

Another bolt very near the wall showed that, finally, the other guards were aware of what was happening. They ran down the walk, shouting and waving their spears.

Kazz, ignoring them, slid a long bamboo ladder down into the enclosure and then he threw a bundle of spears after it. By the next flash, he could be seen advancing toward the nearest guards.

Burton snatched a spear and almost ran up the ladder. The others, including the Israeli, were behind him. The fight was bloody and brief. With the guards on the walk either stabbed or hurled to their deaths, only those in the watch houses remained. The ladder was carried to the other end of the stockade and placed against the gate. In two minutes, men had climbed to the outside, dropped down, and opened the gate. For the first time, Burton found the chance to talk to Kazz.

"I thought you had sold us out."

"No. Not me, Kazz," Kazz said reproachfully. "You know I love you, Burton-*naq*. You're my friend, my chief. I pretend to join your enemies because that's playing it smart. I surprise you don't do the same. You're no dummy."

"Certainly, you aren't," Burton said. "But I couldn't bring myself to kill those slaves."

Lightning revealed Kazz shrugging. He said, "That don't bother me. I don't know them. Besides, you hear Göring. He say they die anyway."

"It's a good thing you chose tonight to rescue us," Burton said. He did not tell Kazz why since he did not want to confuse him. Moreover, there were more important things to do.

"Tonight's a good night for this," Kazz said. "Big battle going on. Tullius and Göring get very drunk and quarrel. They fight; their men fight. While they kill each other, invaders come. Those brown men across The River . . . what you call them? . . . Onondagas, that's them. Their boats come just before rain come. They make raid to steal slaves, too. Or maybe just for the hell of it. So, I think, now's good time to start my plan, get Burton-*naq* free."

As suddenly as it had come, the rain ceased. Burton could hear shouts and screams from far off, toward The River. Drums were beating up and down The Riverbanks. He said to Targoff, "We can either try to escape, and probably do so easily, or we can attack."

"I intend to wipe out the beasts who enslaved us,"

Targoff said. "There are other stockades nearby. I've sent men to open their gates. The rest are too far away to reach quickly; they're strung out at half-mile intervals."

By then, the blockhouse in which the off-duty guards lived had been stormed. The slaves armed themselves and then started toward the noise of the conflict. Burton's group was on the right flank. They had not gone half a mile before they came upon corpses and wounded, a mixture of Onondagas and whites.

Despite the heavy rain, a fire had broken out. By its increasing light, they saw that the flames came from the longhouse. Outlined in the glare were struggling figures. The escapees advanced across the plain. Suddenly, one side broke and ran toward them with the victors, whooping and screaming jubilantly, after them.

"There's Göring," Frigate said. "His fat isn't going to help him get away, that's for sure."

He pointed, and Burton could see the German desperately pumping his legs but falling behind the others. "I don't want the Indians to have the honor of killing him," Burton said. "We owe it to Alice to get him."

Campbell's long-legged figure was ahead of them all, and it was toward him that Burton threw his spear. To the Scot, the missile must have seemed to come out of the darkness from nowhere. Too late, he tried to dodge. The flint head buried itself in the flesh between his left shoulder and chest, and he fell on his side. He tried to get up a moment afterward, but he was kicked back down by Burton.

Campbell's eyes rolled; blood trickled from his mouth. He pointed at another wound, a deep gash in his side just below the ribs. "You . . . your woman . . . Wilfreda . . . did that," he gasped. "But I killed her, the bitch . . ."

Burton wanted to ask him where Alice was, but Kazz, screaming phrases in his native tongue, brought his club down on the Scot's head. Burton picked up his spear and ran after Kazz. "Don't kill Göring!" he shouted. "Leave him to me!"

Kazz did not hear him; he was busy fighting with two Onondagas. Burton saw Alice as she ran by him. He

145

reached out and grabbed her and spun her around. She screamed and started to struggle. Burton shouted at her; suddenly, recognizing him, she collapsed into his arms and began weeping. Burton would have tried to comfort her, but he was afraid that Göring would escape him. He pushed her away and ran toward the German and threw his spear. It grazed Göring's head, and he screamed and stopped running and began to look for the weapon but Burton was on him. Both fell to the ground and rolled over and over, each trying to strangle the other.

Something struck Burton on the back of his head. Stunned, he released his grip. Göring pushed him down on the ground and dived toward the spear. Seizing it, he rose and stepped toward the prostrate Burton. Burton tried to get to his feet, but his knees seemed to be made of putty and everything was whirling. Göring suddenly staggered as Alice tackled his legs from behind, and he fell forward. Burton made another effort, found he could at least stagger, and sprawled over Göring. Again they rolled over and over with Göring squeezing Burton's throat. Then a shaft slid over Burton's shoulder, burning his skin, and its stone tip drove into Göring's throat.

Burton stood up, pulled the spear out, and plunged it into the man's fat belly. Göring tried to sit up, but he fell back and died. Alice slumped to the ground and wept.

Dawn saw the end of the battle. By then, the slaves had broken out of every stockade. The warriors of Göring and Tullius were ground between the two forces, Onondaga and slaves like husks between millstones. The Indians, who had probably raided only to loot and get more slaves and their grails, retreated. They climbed aboard their dugouts and canoes and paddled across the lake. Nobody felt like chasing them.

17

The days that followed were busy ones. A rough census
indicated that at least half of the 20,000 inhabitants of
Göring's little kingdom had been killed, severely wounded, abducted by the Onondaga, or had fled. The Roman
Tullius Hostilius had apparently escaped. The survivors
chose a provisional government. Targoff, Burton, Spruce,
Ruach, and two others formed an executive committee
with considerable, but temporary, powers. John de
Greystock had disappeared. He had been seen during the
beginning of the battle and then he had just dropped out
of sight.

Alice Hargreaves moved into Burton's hut without
either saying a word about the why or wherefore.

Later, she said, "Frigate tells me that if this entire
planet is constructed like the areas we've seen, and there's
no reason to believe it isn't, then The River must be at
least 20,000,000 miles long. It's incredible, but so is our
resurrection, everything about this world. Also, there may
be thirty-five to thirty-seven billion people living along
The River. What chance would I have of ever finding my
Earthly husband?

"Moreover, I love you. Yes, I know I didn't act as if I
loved you. But something has changed in me. Perhaps it's
all I've been through that is responsible. I don't think I
could have loved you on Earth. I might have been
fascinated, but I would also have been repelled, perhaps
frightened. I couldn't have made you a good wife there.
Here, I can. Rather, I'll make you a good mate, since
there doesn't seem to be any authority or religious
institution that could marry us. That in itself shows how

I've changed. That I could be calmly living with a man I'm not married to . . . ! Well, there you are."

"We're no longer living in the Victorian age," Burton said. "What would you call this present age . . . the Mélange era? The Mixed Age? Eventually, it will be The River Culture, The Riparian World, rather, *many* River cultures."

"Providing it lasts," Alice said. "It started suddenly; it may end just as swiftly and unexpectedly."

Certainly, Burton thought, the green River and the grassy plain and the forested hills and the unscalable mountains did not seem like Shakespeare's insubstantial vision. They were solid, real, as real as the men walking toward him now, Frigate, Monat, Kazz, and Ruach. He stepped out of the hut and greeted them.

Kazz began talking. "A long time ago, before I speak English good, I see something. I try to tell you then, but you don't understand me. I see a man who don't have this on his forehead."

He pointed at the center of his own forehead and then at that of the others.

"I know," Kazz continued, "you can't see it. Pete and Monat can't either. Nobody else can. But I see it on everybody's forehead. Except on that man I try to catch long time ago. Then, one day, I see a woman don't have it, but I don't say nothing to you. Now, I see a third person who don't have it."

"He means," Monat said, "that he is able to perceive certain symbols or characters on the forehead of each and every one of us. He can see these only in bright sunlight and at a certain angle. But everyone he's ever seen has had these symbols—except for the three he's mentioned."

"He must be able to see a little further into the spectrum than we," Frigate said. "Obviously, Whoever stamped us with the sign of the beast or whatever you want to call it, did not know about the special ability of Kazz's species. Which shows that They are not omniscient."

"Obviously," Burton said. "Nor infallible. Otherwise, I would never have awakened in that place before being

148

resurrected. So, *who* is this person who does not have these symbols on his skin?"

He spoke calmly, but his heart beat swiftly. If Kazz was right, he might have detected an agent of the beings who had brought the entire human species to life again. Would They be gods in disguise?

"Robert Spruce!" Frigate said.

"Before we jump to any conclusions," Monat said, "don't forget that the omission may have been an accident."

"We'll find out," Burton said ominously. "But *why* the symbols? Why should we be marked?"

"Probably for identification or numbering purposes," Monat said. "Who knows, except Those Who put us here."

"Let's go face Spruce," Burton said.

"We have to catch him first," Frigate replied. "Kazz made the mistake of mentioning to Spruce that he knew about the symbols. He did so at breakfast this morning. I wasn't there, but those who were said Spruce turned pale. A few minutes later, he excused himself, and he hasn't been seen since. We've sent search parties out up and down The River, across The River, and also into the hills."

"His flight is an admission of guilt," Burton said. He was angry. Was man a kind of cattle branded for some sinister purpose?

That afternoon, the drums announced that Spruce had been caught. Three hours later, he was standing before the council table in the newly built meeting hall. Behind the table sat the Council. The doors were closed, for the Councilmen felt that this was something that could be conducted more efficiently without a crowd. However, Monat, Kazz, and Frigate were also present.

"I may as well tell you now," Burton said, "that we have decided to go to any lengths to get the truth from you. It is against the principles of every one at this table to use torture. We despise and loathe those who resort to torture. But we feel that this is one issue where principles must be abandoned."

149

"Principles must never be abandoned," Spruce said evenly. "The end never justifies the means. Even if clinging to them means defeat, death, and remaining in ignorance."

"There's too much at stake," Targoff said. "I, who have been the victim of unprincipled men; Ruach, who has been tortured several times; the others, we all agree. We'll use fire and the knife on you if we must. It is necessary that we find out the truth.

"Now, tell me, are you one of Those responsible for this resurrection?"

"You will be no better than Göring and his kind if you torture me," Spruce said. His voice was beginning to break. "In fact, you will be far worse off, for you are forcing yourselves to be like him in order to gain something that may not even exist. Or, if it does, may not be worth the price."

"Tell us the truth," Targoff said. "Don't lie. We know that you must be an agent; perhaps one of Those directly responsible."

"There is a fire blazing in that stone over there," Burton said. "If you don't start talking at once, you will . . . well, the roasting you get will be the least of your pain. I am an authority on Chinese and Arabic methods of torture. I assure you that they had some very refined means for extracting the truth. And I have no qualms about putting my knowledge into practice."

Spruce, pale and sweating, said, "You may be denying yourself eternal life if you do this. It will at least set you far back on your journey, delay the final goal."

"What is that?" Burton replied.

Spruce ignored him. "We can't stand pain," he muttered. "We're too sensitive."

"Are you going to talk?" Targoff said.

"Even the idea of self-destruction is painful and to be avoided except when absolutely necessary," Spruce mumbled. "Despite the fact that I know I shall live again."

"Put him over the fire," Targoff said to the two men who held Spruce.

Monat spoke up. "Just one moment. Spruce, the science of my people was much more advanced than that of Earth's. So I am more qualified to make an educated guess. Perhaps we could spare you the pain of the fire, and the pain of betraying your purpose, if you were merely to affirm what I have to say. That way, you wouldn't be making a positive betrayal."

Spruce said, "I'm listening."

"It's my theory that you are a Terrestrial. You belong to an age chronologically far past 2008 A.D. You must be the descendant of the few who survived my death scanner. Judging by the technology and power required to reconstruct the surface of this planet into one vast Rivervalley, your time must be much later than the twenty-first century. Just guessing, the fiftieth century A.D.?"

Spruce looked at the fire, then said, "Add two thousand more years."

"If this planet is about the size of Earth, it can hold only so many people. Where are the others, the still-born, the children who died before they were five, the imbeciles and idiots, and those who lived after the twentieth century?"

"They are elsewhere," Spruce said. He glanced at the fire again, and his lips tightened.

"My own people," Monat said, "had a theory that they would eventually be able to see into their past. I won't go into the details, but it was possible that past events could be visually detected and then recorded. Time travel, of course, was sheer fantasy.

"But what if your culture was able to do what we only theorized about? What if you recorded every single human being that had ever lived? Located this planet and constructed this Rivervalley? Somewhere, maybe under the very surface of this planet, used energy-matter conversion, say from the heat of this planet's molten core, and the recordings to re-create the bodies of the dead in the tanks? Used biological techniques to rejuvenate the bodies and to restore limbs, eyes, and so on and also to correct any physical defects?"

151

"Then," Monat continued, "you made more recordings of the newly created bodies and stored them in some vast memory-tank? Later, you destroyed the bodies in the tanks? Re-created them again through means of the conductive metal which is also used to charge the grails? These could be buried beneath the ground. The resurrection then occurs without recourse to supernatural means.

"The big question is why?"

"If you had it in your power to do all this, would you not think it was your *ethical* duty?" Spruce asked.

"Yes, but I would resurrect only those worth resurrecting."

"And what if others did not accept your criteria?" Spruce said. "Do you really think you are wise enough and good enough to judge? Would you place yourself on a level with God? No, all must be given a second chance, no matter how bestial or selfish or petty or stupid. Then, it will be up to them . . ."

He fell silent, as if he had regretted his outburst and meant to say no more.

"Besides," Monat said, "you would want to make a study of humanity as it existed in the past. You would want to record all the languages that man ever spoke, his mores, his philosophies, biographies. To do this, you need agents, posing as resurrectees, to mingle with the Riverpeople and to take notes, to observe, to study. How long will this study take? One thousand years? Two? Ten? A million?

"And what about the eventual disposition of us? Are we to stay here forever?"

"You will stay here as long as it takes for you to be rehabilitated," Spruce shouted. "Then . . ."

He closed his mouth, glared, then opened it to say, "Continued contact with you makes even the toughest of us take on your characteristics. We have to go through a rehabilitation ourselves. Already, I feel unclean . . ."

"Put him over the fire," Targoff said. "We'll get the entire truth."

"No, you won't!" Spruce cried. "I should have done

this long ago! Who knows what . . ."

He fell to the ground, and his skin changed to a gray-blue color. Doctor Steinborg, a Councilman, examined him, but it was apparent to all that he was dead.

Targoff said, "Better take him away now, doctor. Dissect him. We'll wait here for your report."

"With stone knives, no chemicals, no microscopes, what kind of a report can you expect?" Steinborg said. "But I'll do my best."

The body was carried off. Burton said, "I'm glad he didn't force us to admit we were bluffing. If he had kept his mouth shut, he could have defeated us."

"Then you really weren't going to torture him?" Frigate said. "I was hoping you didn't mean your threat. If you had, I was going to walk out then and there and never see any of you again."

"Of course we didn't mean it," Ruach said. "Spruce would have been right. We'd have been no better than Göring. But we could have tried other means. Hypnotism for instance. Burton, Monat, and Steinborg were experts in that field."

"The trouble is, we still don't know if we did get the truth," Targoff said. "Actually, he may have been lying. Monat supplied some guesses, and, if these were wrong, Spruce could have led us astray by agreeing with Monat. I'd say we can't be at all sure."

They agreed on one thing. Their chances of detecting another agent through the absence of symbols on the forehead would be gone. Now that They—whoever They were—knew about the visibility of the characters to Kazz's species, They would take the proper measures to prevent detection.

Steinborg returned three hours later. "There is nothing to distinguish him from any other member of *Homo sapiens*. Except this one little device."

He held up a black shiny ball about the size of a matchhead.

"I located this on the surface of the forebrain. It was attached to some nerves by wires so thin that I could see them only at a certain angle, when they caught the light.

153

It's my opinion that Spruce killed himself by means of this device and that he did so by literally thinking himself dead. Somehow, this little ball translated a wish for death into the deed. Perhaps, it reacted to the thought by releasing a poison which I do not have facilities for analyzing." He concluded his report and passed the ball around to the others.

18

Thirty days later, Burton, Frigate, Ruach, and Kazz were returning from a trip upRiver. It was just before dawn.

The cold heavy mists that piled up to six or seven feet above The River in the latter part of the night swirled around them. They could not see in any direction further than a strong man might make a standing broad jump. But Burton, standing in the prow of the bamboo-hulled single-masted boat, knew they were close to the western shore. Near the relatively shallow depths the current ran more slowly, and they had just steered to port from the middle of The River.

If his calculations were correct, they should be close to the ruins of Göring's hall. At any moment, he expected to see a strip of denser darkness appear out of the dark waters, the banks of that land he now called home. Home, for Burton, had always been a place from which to sally forth, a resting-place, a temporary fortress in which to write a book about his last expedition, a lair in which to heal fresh hurts, a conning tower from which he looked out for new lands to explore.

Thus, only two weeks after the death of Spruce, Burton had felt the need to get to some place other than the one in which he now was. He had heard a rumor that copper had been discovered on the western shore about a hundred miles upRiver. This was a length of shore of not more than twelve miles, inhabited by fifth-century B.C. Sarmatians and thirteenth-century A.D. Frisians.

Burton did not really think the story was true—but it gave him an excuse to travel. Ignoring Alice's pleas to take her with him, he had set off.

Now, a month later and after some adventures, not all unpleasant, they were almost home. The story had not been entirely unfounded. There was copper but only in minute amounts. So the four had gotten into their boat for the easy trip downcurrent, their sail pushed by the neverceasing wind. They journeyed during the daytime and beached the boat during mealtimes wherever there were friendly people who did not mind strangers using their grailstones. At night they either slept among the friendlies or, if in hostile waters, sailed by in the darkness.

The last leg of their trip was made after the sun went down. Before getting home, they had to pass a section of the valley where slave-hungry eighteenth-century Mohawks lived on one side and equally greedy Carthaginians of the third century B.C. on the other. Having slipped through under cover of the fog, they were almost home.

Abruptly, Burton said, "There's the bank. Pete, lower the mast! Kazz, Lev, back oars! Jump to it!"

A few minutes later, they had landed and had pulled the lightweight craft completely out of the water and upon the gently sloping shore. Now that they were out of the mists, they could see the sky paling above the eastern mountains.

"Dead reckoning come alive!" Burton said. "We're ten paces beyond the grailstone near the ruins!"

He scanned the bamboo huts along the plain and the buildings evident in the long grasses and under the giant trees of the hills.

Not a single person was to be seen. The valley was asleep.

He said, "Don't you think it's strange that no one's up yet? Or that we've not been challenged by the sentinels?"

Frigate pointed toward the lookout tower to their right.

Burton swore and said, "They're asleep, by God, or deserted their post!"

But he knew as he spoke that this was no case of dereliction of duty. Though he had said nothing to the others about it, the moment he had stepped ashore, he had been sure something was very wrong. He began running across the plain toward the hut in which he and Alice lived.

Alice was sleeping on the bamboo-and-grass bed on the right side of the building. Only her head was visible, for she was curled up under a blanket of towels fastened to each other by the magnetic clasps. Burton threw the blanket back, got down on his knees by the low bed, and raised her to a sitting position. Her head lolled forward, and her arms hung limply. But she had a healthy color and breathed normally.

Burton called her name three times. She slept on. He slapped both her cheeks sharply; red splotches sprang up on them. Her eyelids fluttered, then she went back to sleep.

By then Frigate and Ruach appeared. "We've looked into some of the other huts," Frigate said. "They're all asleep. I tried to wake a couple of them, but they're out for the count. What's wrong?"

Burton said, "Who do you think has the power or the need to do this? Spruce! Spruce and his kind, Whoever They are!"

"Why?" Frigate sounded frightened.

"They were looking for me! They must have come in under the fog, somehow put this whole area to sleep!"

"A sleep-gas would do it easily enough," Ruach said. "Although people who have powers such as Theirs could have devices we've never dreamed of."

"They were looking for me!" Burton shouted.

"Which means, if true, that They may be back tonight," Frigate said. "But why would They be searching for you?"

Ruach replied for Burton. "Because he, as far as we know, was the only man to awaken in the preresurrection phase. Why he did is a mystery. But it's evident something went wrong. It may also be a mystery to Them. I'd be

156

inclined to think They've been discussing this and finally decided to come here. Maybe to kidnap Burton for observation—or some more sinister purpose."

"Possibly They wanted to erase from my memory all that I'd seen in that chamber of floating bodies," Burton said. "Such a thing should not be beyond Their science."

"But you've told that story to many," Frigate said. "They couldn't possibly track down all those people and remove the memory of your story from their minds."

"Would that be necessary? How many believe my tale? Sometimes I doubt it myself."

Ruach said, "Speculation is fruitless. What do we do now?"

Alice shrieked, "Richard!" and they turned to see her sitting up and staring at them.

For a few minutes, they could not get her to understand what had happened. Finally she said, "So that's why the fog covered the land, too! I thought it was strange, but of course I had no way of knowing what was really happening."

Burton said, "Get your grails. Put anything you want to take along in your sack. We're leaving as of now. I want to get away before the others awake."

Alice's already large eyes became even wider. "Where are we going?"

"Anywhere from here. I don't like to run away but I can't stand up and fight people like that. Not if They know where I am. I'll tell you, however, what I plan to do. I intend to find the end of The River. It must have an inlet and an outlet, and there must be a way for a man to get through to the source. If there's any way at all, I'll find it—you can bet your soul on that!

"Meanwhile, They'll be looking for me elsewhere—I hope. The fact that They didn't find me here makes me think that They have no means for instantly locating a person. They may have branded us like cattle—" he indicated the invisible symbols on his forehead—"but even cattle have mavericks. And we're cattle with brains."

He turned to the others. "You're more than welcome to come along with me. In fact, I'd be honored."

"I'll get Monat," Kazz said. "He wouldn't want to be left behind."

Burton grimaced and said, "Good old Monat! I hate to do this to him, but there's no helping it. He can't come along. He's too distinguishable. Their agents would have no trouble at all in locating anybody who looked like him. I'm sorry, but he can't."

Tears stood in Kazz's eyes, then ran down his bulging cheekbones. In a choked voice, he said, "Burton-*naq*, I can't go either. I look too different, too."

Burton felt tears wet his own eyes. He said, "We'll take that chance. After all, there must be plenty of your type around. We've seen at least thirty or more during our travels."

"No females so far, Burton-*naq*," Kazz said mournfully. Then he smiled. "Maybe we find one when we go along The River."

As quickly, he lost his grin. "No, damn it, I don't go! I can't hurt Monat too much. Him and me, others think we ugly and scary looking. So we become good friends. He's not my *naq*, but he's next to it. I stay."

He stepped up to Burton, hugged him in a grip that forced Burton's breath out in a great whoosh, released him, shook hands with the others, making them wince, then turned and shuffled off.

Ruach, holding his paralyzed hand, said, "You're off on a fool's errand, Burton. Do you realize that you could sail on this River for a thousand years and still be a million miles or more from the end? I'm staying. My people need me. Besides, Spruce made it clear that we should be striving for a spiritual perfection, not fighting Those Who gave us a chance to do so."

Burton's teeth flashed whitely in his dark face. He swung his grail as if it were a weapon.

"I didn't ask to be put here any more than I asked to be born on Earth. I don't intend to kowtow to another's dictates! I mean to find The River's end. And if I don't, I will at least have had fun and learned much on the way!"

By then, people were beginning to stumble out of their huts as they yawned and rubbed heavy eyes. Ruach paid

158

no attention to them; he watched the craft as it set sail close-hauled to the wind, cutting across and up The River. Burton was handling the rudder; he turned once and waved the grail so that the sun bounced off it in many shining spears.

Ruach thought that Burton was really happy that he had been forced to make this decision. Now he could evade the deadly responsibilities that would come with governing this little state and could do what he wanted. He could set out on the greatest of all his adventures.

"I suppose it's for the best," Ruach muttered to himself. "A man may find salvation on the road, if he wants to, just as well as he may at home. It's up to him. Meanwhile, I, like Voltaire's character—what was his name? Earthly things are beginning to slip away from me—will cultivate my own little garden."

He paused to look somewhat longingly after Burton.

"Who knows? He may some day run into Voltaire."

He sighed, then smiled.

"On the other hand, Voltaire may some day drop in on me!"

19

"I hate you, Hermann Göring!"

The voice sprang out and then flashed away as if it were a gear tooth meshed with the cog of another man's dream and rotated into and then out of his dream.

Riding the crest of the hypnopompic state, Richard Francis Burton knew he was dreaming. But he was helpless to do anything about it.

The first dream returned.

Events were fuzzy and encapsulated. A lightning streak of himself in the unmeasurable chamber of floating bodies; another flash of the nameless Custodians finding him and putting him back to sleep; then a jerky synopsis of the dream he had had just before the true Resurrection on the banks of The River.

God—a beautiful old man in the clothes of a mid-Victorian gentleman of means and breeding—was poking him in the ribs with an iron cane and telling him that *he owed for the flesh.*

"What? What flesh?" Burton said, dimly aware that he was muttering in his sleep. He could not hear his words in the dream.

"*Pay up!*" God said. His face melted, then was recast into Burton's own features.

God had not answered in the first dream five years before. He spoke now, "*Make your Resurrection worth my while, you fool! I have gone to great expense and even greater pains to give you, and all those other miserable and worthless wretches, a second chance.*"

"Second chance at what?" Burton said. He felt frightened at what God might answer. He was much relieved when God the All-Father—only now did Burton see that one eye of Jahweh-Odin was gone and out of the empty socket glared the flames of hell—did not reply. He was gone—no, not gone but metamorphosed into a high gray tower, cylindrical and soaring out of gray mists with the roar of the sea coming up through the mists.

"The Grail!" He saw again the man who had told him of the Big Grail. This man had heard it from another man, who had heard of it from a woman, who had heard it from . . . and so forth. The Big Grail was one of the legends told by the billions who lived along The River—this River that coiled like a serpent around this planet from pole to pole, issued from the unreachable and plunged into the inaccessible.

A man, or a subhuman, had managed to climb through the mountains to the North Pole. And he had seen the Big Grail, the Dark Tower, the Misty Castle just before he had stumbled. Or he was pushed. He had fallen headlong and bellowing into the cold seas beneath the mists and died. And then the man, or subhuman, had awakened again

160

along The River. Death was not forever here, although it had lost nothing of its sting.

He had told of his vision. And the story had traveled along the valley of The River faster than a boat could sail.

Thus, Richard Francis Burton, the eternal pilgrim and wanderer, had longed to storm the ramparts of the Big Grail. He would unveil the secret of resurrection and of this planet, since he was convinced that the beings Who had reshaped this world had also built that tower.

"Die, Hermann Göring! Die, and leave me in peace!" a man shouted in German.

Burton opened his eyes. He could see nothing except the pale sheen of the multitudinous stars through the open window across the room of the hut.

His vision bent to the shape of the black things inside, and he saw Peter Frigate and Loghu sleeping on their mats by the opposite wall. He turned his head to see the white, blanket-sized towel under which Alice slept. The whiteness of her face was turned toward him, and the black cloud of her hair spilled out on the ground by her mat.

That same evening, the single-masted boat on which he and the other three had been sailing down The River had put into a friendly shore. The little state of Sevieria was inhabited largely by sixteenth-century Englishmen, although its chief was an American who had lived in the late eighteenth and early nineteenth century. John Sevier, founder of the "lost state" of Franklin, which had later become Tennessee, had welcomed Burton and his party.

Sevier and his people did not believe in slavery and would not detain any guest longer than he desired. After permitting them to charge their grails and so feed themselves, Sevier had invited them to a party. It was the celebration of Resurrection Day; afterward, he had had them conducted to the guest hostelry.

Burton was always a light sleeper, and now he was an uneasy one. The others began breathing deeply or snoring long before he had succumbed to weariness. After an interminable dream, he had wakened on hearing the voice that had interlocked with his dreams.

161

Hermann Göring, Burton thought. He had killed Göring, but Göring must be alive again somewhere along The River. Was the man now groaning and shouting in the neighboring hut one who had also suffered because of Göring, either on Earth or in the Rivervalley?

Burton threw off the black towel and rose swiftly but noiselessly. He secured a kilt with magnetic tabs, fastened a belt of human skin around his waist, and made sure the human-leather scabbard held the flint poignard. Carrying an assegai, a short length of hardwood tipped with a flint point, he left the hut.

The moonless sky cast a light as bright as the full moon of Earth. It was aflame with huge many-colored stars and pale sheets of cosmic gas.

The hostelries were set back a mile and a half from The River and placed on one of the second row of hills that edged the Riverplain. There were seven of the one-room, leaf-thatch-roofed, bamboo buildings. At a distance, under the enormous branches of the irontrees or under the giant pines or oaks, were other huts. A half-mile away, on top of a high hill, was a large circular stockade, colloquially termed the "Roundhouse." The officials of Sevieria slept there.

High towers of bamboo were placed every half-mile along The River shore. Torches flamed all night long on platforms from which sentinels kept a lookout for invaders.

After scrutinizing the shadows under the trees, Burton walked a few steps to the hut from which the groans and shouts had come.

He pushed the grass curtain aside. The starlight fell through the open window on the face of the sleeper. Burton hissed in surprise. The light revealed the blondish hair and the broad features of a youth he recognized.

Burton moved slowly on bare feet. The sleeper groaned and threw one arm over his face and half-turned. Burton stopped, then resumed his stealthy progress. He placed the assegai on the ground, drew his dagger, and gently thrust the point against the hollow of the youth's throat. The arm flopped over; the eyes opened and stared into Burton's.

162

Burton clamped his hand over the man's open mouth.

"Hermann Göring! Don't move or try to yell! I'll kill you!"

Göring's light-blue eyes looked dark in the shadows, but the paleness of his terror shone out. He quivered and started to sit up, then sank back as the flint dug into his skin.

"How long have you been here?" Burton said.

"Who . . . ?" Göring said in English, then his eyes opened even wider. "Richard Burton? Am I dreaming? Is that you?"

Burton could smell the dreamgum on Göring's breath and the sweat-soaked mat on which he lay. The German was much thinner than the last time he had seen him.

Göring said, "I don't know how long I've been here. What time is it?"

"About an hour until dawn, I'd say. It's the day after Resurrection Celebration."

"Then I've been here three days. Could I have a drink of water? My throat's dry as a sarcophagus."

"No wonder. You're a living sarcophagus—if you're addicted to dreamgum."

Burton stood up, gesturing with the assegai at a fired-clay pot on a little bamboo table nearby. "You can drink if you want to. But don't try anything."

Göring rose slowly and staggered to the table. "I'm too weak to give you a fight, even if I wanted to." He drank noisily from the pot and then picked up an apple from the table. He took a bite, and then said, "What're you doing here? I thought I was rid of you."

"You answer my question first," Burton said, "and be quick about it. You pose a problem that I don't like, you know."

163

20

Göring started chewing, stopped, stared, then said, "Why should I? I don't have any authority here, and I couldn't do anything to you if I did. I'm just a guest here. Damned decent people, these; they haven't bothered me at all except to ask if I'm all right now and then. Though I don't know how long they'll let me stay without earning my keep."

"You haven't left the hut?" Burton said. "Then who charged your grail for you? How'd you get so much dreamgum?"

Göring smiled slyly. "I had a big collection from the last place I stayed; somewhere about a thousand miles up The River."

"Doubtless taken forcibly from some poor slaves," Burton said. "But if you were doing so well there, why did you leave?"

Göring began to weep. Tears ran down his face, and over his collarbones and down his chest, and his shoulders shook.

"I . . . I had to get out. I wasn't any good to the others. I was losing my hold over them—spending too much time drinking, smoking marihuana, and chewing dreamgum. They said I was too soft myself. They would have killed me or made me a slave. So I sneaked out one night . . . took the boat. I got away all right and kept going until I put into here. I traded part of my supply to Sevier for two weeks' sanctuary."

Burton stared curiously at Göring.

"You knew what would happen if you took too much

gum," he said. "Nightmares, hallucinations, delusions. Total mental and physical deterioration. You must have seen it happen to others."

"I was a morphine addict on Earth!" Göring cried. "I struggled with it, and I won out for a long time. Then, when things began to go badly for the Third Reich—and even worse for myself—when Hitler began picking on me, I started taking drugs again!"

He paused, then continued, "But here, when I woke up to a new life, in a young body, when it looked as if I had an eternity of life and youth ahead of me, when there was no stern God in Heaven or Devil in Hell to stop me, I thought I could do exactly as I pleased and get away with it. I would become even greater than the Fuehrer! That little country in which you first found me was to be only the beginning! I could see my empire stretching for thousands of miles up and down The River, on both sides of the valley. I would have been the ruler of ten times the subjects that Hitler ever dreamed of!"

He began weeping again, then paused to take another drink of water, then put a piece of the dreamgum in his mouth. He chewed, his face becoming more relaxed and blissful with each second.

Göring said, "I kept having nightmares of you plunging the spear into my belly. When I woke up, my belly would hurt as if a flint had gone into my guts. So I'd take gum to remove the hurt and the humiliation. At first, the gum helped. I was great. I was master of the world, Hitler, Napoleon, Julius Caesar, Alexander, Genghis Khan, all rolled into one. I was chief again of von Richthofen's Red Death Squadron; those were happy days, the happiest of my life in many ways. But the euphoria soon gave way to hideousness. I plunged into hell; I saw myself accusing myself and behind the accuser a million others. Not myself but the victims of that great and glorious hero, that obscene madman Hitler, whom I worshipped so. And in whose name I committed so many crimes."

"You admit you were a criminal?" Burton said. "That's a story different than the one you used to give me. Then you said you were justified in all you did, and you were betrayed by the . . ."

He stopped, realizing that he had been sidetracked from his original purpose. "That you should be haunted with the specter of a conscience is rather incredible. But perhaps that explains what has puzzled the puritans—why liquor, tobacco, marihuana, and dreamgum were offered in the grails along with food. At least, dreamgum seems to be a gift booby-trapped with danger to those who abuse it."

He stepped closer to Göring. The German's eyes were half-closed and his jaw hung open.

"You know my identity. I am traveling under a pseudonym, with good reason. You remember Spruce, one of your slaves? After you were killed, he was revealed, quite by accident, as one of those who somehow resurrected all the dead of humanity. Those we call the Ethicals, for lack of a better term. Göring, are you listening?"

Göring nodded.

"Spruce killed himself before we could get out of him all we wanted to know. Later, some of his compatriots came to our area and temporarily put everybody to sleep—probably with a gas—intending to take me away to wherever Their headquarters are. But They missed me. I was off on a trading trip up The River. When I returned, I realized They were after me, and I've been running ever since. Göring, do you hear me?"

Burton slapped him savagely on his cheek. Göring said, "Ach!" and jumped back and held the side of his face. His eyes were open, and he was grimacing.

"I heard you!" he snarled. "It just didn't seem worthwhile to answer back. Nothing seemed worthwhile, nothing except floating away, far from . . ."

"Shut up and listen!" Burton said. "The Ethicals have men everywhere looking for me. I can't afford to have you alive, do you realize that? I can't trust you. Even if you were a friend, you couldn't be trusted. You're a gummer!"

Göring giggled, stepped up to Burton and tried to put his arms around Burton's neck. Burton pushed him back so hard that he staggered up against the table and only kept from falling by clutching its edges.

"This is very amusing," Göring said. "The day I got here, a man asked me if I'd seen you. He described you in detail and gave your name. I told him I knew you well—too well, and that I hoped I'd never see you again, not unless I had you in my power, that is. He said I should notify him if I saw you again. He'd make it worth my while."

Burton wasted no time. He strode up to Göring and seized him with both hands. They were small and delicate, but Göring winced with pain.

He said, "What're you going to do, kill me again?"

"Not if you tell me the name of the man who asked you about me. Otherwise . . ."

"Go ahead and kill me!" Göring said. "So what? I'll wake up somewhere else, thousands of miles from here, far out of your reach."

Burton pointed at a bamboo box in a corner of the hut. Guessing that it held Göring's supply of gum, he said, "And you'd also wake up without that! Where else could you get so much on such short notice?"

"Damn you!" Göring shouted, and tried to tear himself loose to get to the box.

"Tell me his name!" Burton said. "Or I'll take the gum and throw it in The River!"

"Agneau. Roger Agneau. He sleeps in a hut just outside the Roundhouse."

"I'll deal with you later," Burton said, and chopped Göring on the side of the neck with the edge of his palm.

He turned, and he saw a man crouching outside the entrance to the hut. The man straightened up and was off. Burton ran out after him; in a minute both were in the tall pines and oaks of the hills. His quarry disappeared in the waist-high grass.

Burton slowed to a trot, caught sight of a patch of white—starlight on bare skin—and was after the fellow. He hoped that the Ethical would not kill himself at once, because he had a plan for extracting information if he could knock him out at once. It involved hypnosis, but he would have to catch the Ethical first. It was possible that the man had some sort of wireless imbedded in his body and was even now in communication with his compatriots—wherever They were. If so, They would come in Their flying machines, and he would be lost.

He stopped. He had lost his quarry and the only thing to do now was to rouse Alice and the others and run. Perhaps this time they should take to the mountains and hide there for a while.

But first he would go to Agneau's hut. There was little chance that Agneau would be there, but it was certainly worth the effort to make sure.

21

Burton arrived within sight of the hut just in time to glimpse the back of a man entering it. Burton circled to come up from the side where the darkness of the hills and the trees scattered along the plain gave him some concealment. Crouching, he ran until he was at the door to the hut.

He heard a loud cry some distance behind him and whirled to see Göring staggering toward him. He was crying out in German to Agneau, warning him that Burton was just outside. In one hand he held a long spear which he brandished at the Englishman.

Burton turned and hurled himself against the flimsy bamboo-slat door. His shoulder drove into it and broke it from its wooden hinges. The door flew inward and struck Agneau, who had been standing just behind it. Burton, the door, and Agneau fell to the floor with Agneau under the door.

Burton rolled off the door, got up, and jumped again with both bare feet on the wood. Agneau screamed and then became silent. Burton heaved the door to one side to find his quarry unconscious and bleeding from the nose. Good! Now if the noise didn't bring the watch and if he could deal quickly enough with Göring, he could carry out his plan.

He looked up just in time to see the starlight on the long black object hurtling at him.

He threw himself to one side, and the spear plunged into the dirt floor with a thump. Its shaft vibrated like a rattlesnake preparing to strike.

Burton stepped into the doorway, estimated Göring's distance, and charged. His assegai plunged into the belly of the German. Göring threw his hands up in the air, screamed, and fell on his side. Burton hoisted Agneau's limp body on his shoulder and carried him out of the hut.

By then there were shouts from the Roundhouse. Torches were flaring up; the sentinel on the nearest watchtower was bellowing. Göring was sitting on the ground, bent over, clutching the shaft close to the wound.

He looked gape-mouthed at Burton and said, "You did it again! You . . ."

He fell over on his face, the death rattle in his throat.

Agneau returned to a frenzied consciousness. He twisted himself out of Burton's grip and fell to the ground. Unlike Göring, he made no noise. He had as much reason to be silent as Burton—more perhaps. Burton was so surprised that he was left standing with the fellow's loin-towel clutched in his hand. Burton started to throw it down but felt something stiff and square within the lining of the towel. He transferred the cloth to his left hand, yanked the assegai from the corpse, and ran after Agneau.

The Ethical had launched one of the bamboo canoes beached along the shore. He paddled furiously out into the starlit waters, glancing frequently behind him. Burton raised the assegai behind his shoulder and hurled it. It was a short, thick-shafted weapon, designed for in-fighting and not as a javelin. But it flew straight and came down at the end of its trajectory in Agneau's back. The Ethical fell forward and at an angle and tipped the narrow craft over. The canoe turned upside down. Agneau did not reappear.

Burton swore. He had wanted to capture Agneau alive, but he was damned if he would permit the Ethical to escape. There was a ch~~ that Agneau had not contacted other Ethicals ye..

He turned back toward the guest huts. Drums were beating up and down along the shore, and people with burning torches were hastening toward the Roundhouse. Burton stopped a woman and asked if he could borrow her torch a moment. She handed it to him but spouted questions at him. He answered that he thought the Choctaws across The River were making a raid. She hurried off toward the assembly before the stockade.

Burton drove the pointed end of the torch into the soft dirt of the bank and examined the towel he had snatched from Agneau. On the inside, just above the hard square in the lining, was a seam sealed with two thin magnetic strips, easily opened. He took the object out of the lining and looked at it by the torchlight.

For a long time he squatted by the shifting light, unable to stop looking or to subdue an almost paralyzing astonishment. A photograph, in this world of no cameras, was unheard-of. But a photograph of *him* was even more incredible, as was the fact that the picture had not been taken on this world! It had to have been made on Earth, that Earth lost now in the welter of stars somewhere in the blazing sky and in God only knew how many thousands of years of time.

Impossibility piled on impossibility! But it was taken at a time and at a place when he knew for certain that no camera had fixed upon him and preserved his image. His mustachios had been removed but the retoucher had not bothered to opaque the background nor his clothing. There he was, caught miraculously from the waist up and imprisoned in a flat piece of some material. Flat! When he turned the square, he saw his profile come into view. If he held it almost at right angles to the eye, he could get a three-quarters profile-view of himself.

"In 1848," he muttered to himself. "When I was a twenty-seven-year-old subaltern in the East Indian Army.

And those are the blue mountains of Goa. This must have been taken when I was convalescing there. But, my God, how? By whom? And how would the Ethicals manage to have it in their possession now?"

Agneau had evidently carried this photo as a mnemonic in his quest for Burton. Probably every one of the hunters had one just like it, concealed in his towel. Up and down The River They were looking for him; there might be thousands, perhaps tens of thousands of Them. Who knew how many agents They had available or how desperately They wanted him or *why* They wanted him?

After replacing the photo in the towel, he turned to go back to the hut. And at that moment, his gaze turned toward the top of the mountains—those unscalable heights that bounded The Rivervalley on both sides.

He saw something flicker against a bright sheet of cosmic gas. It appeared for only the blink of an eyelid, then was gone.

A few seconds later, it came out of nothing, was revealed as a dark hemispherical object, then disappeared again.

A second flying craft showed itself briefly, reappeared at a lower elevation, and then was gone like the first.

The Ethicals would take him away, and the people of Sevieria would wonder what had made them fall asleep for an hour or so.

He did not have time to return to the hut and wake up the others. If he waited a moment longer, he would be trapped.

He turned and ran into The River and began swimming toward the other shore, a mile and a half away. But he had gone no more than forty yards when he felt the presence of some huge bulk above. He turned on his back to stare upward. There was only the soft glare of the stars above. Then, out of the air, fifty feet above him, a disk with a diameter of about sixty feet cut out a section of the sky. It disappeared almost immediately, came into sight again only twenty feet above him.

So They had some means of seeing at a distance in the

171

night and had spotted him in his flight.

"You jackals!" he shouted at them. "You'll not get me anyway!"

He upended and dived and swam straight downward. The water became colder, and his eardrums began to hurt. Although his eyes were open, he could see nothing. Suddenly, he was pushed by a wall of water, and he knew that the pressure came from displacement by a large object.

The craft had plunged down after him.

There was only one way out. They would have his dead body, but that would be all. He could escape Them again, be alive somewhere on The River to outwit Them again and strike back at Them.

He opened his mouth and breathed in deeply through both his nose and his mouth.

The water choked him. Only by a strong effort of will did he keep from closing his lips and trying to fight back against the death around him. He knew with his mind that he would live again, but the cells of his body did not know it. They were striving for life at this very moment, not in the rationalized future. And they forced from his water-choked throat a cry of despair.

22

"Yaaaaaaaah!"

The cry raised him off the grass as if he had bounced up off a trampoline. Unlike the first time he had been resurrected, he was not weak and bewildered. He knew what to expect. He would wake on the grassy banks of The River near a grailstone. But he was not prepared for these giants battling around him.

His first thought was to find a weapon. There was

nothing at hand except the grail that always appeared with a resurrectee and the pile of towels of various sizes, colors, and thicknesses. He took one step, seized the handle of the grail, and waited. If he had to, he would use the grail as a club. It was light, but it was practically indestructible and very hard.

However, the monsters around him looked as if they could take a battering all day and not feel a thing.

Most of them were at least eight feet tall, some were surely over nine; their massively muscled shoulders were over three feet broad. Their bodies were human, or nearly so, and their white skins were covered with long reddish or brownish hairs. They were not as hairy as a chimpanzee but more so than any man he had ever seen, and he had known some remarkably hirsute human beings.

But the faces gave them an unhuman and frightening aspect, especially since all were snarling with battle-rage. Below a low forehead was a bloom of bone that ran without indentation above the eyes and then continued around to form O's. Though the eyes were as large as his, they looked small compared to the broad face in which they were set. The cheekbones billowed out and then curved sharply inward. The tremendous noses gave the giants the appearance of proboscis monkeys.

At another time, Burton might have been amused by them. Not now. The roars that tore out of their more-than-gorilla-sized chests were deep as a lion's, and the huge teeth would have made a Kodiak bear think twice before attacking. Their fists, large as his head, held clubs as thick and as long as wagonpoles or stone axes. They swung their weapons at each other, and when they struck flesh, bones broke with cracks as loud as wood splitting. Sometimes, the clubs broke, too.

Burton had a moment in which to look around. The light was weak. The sun had only half-risen above the peaks across The River. The air was far colder than any he had felt on this planet except during his defeated attempts to climb to the top of the perpendicular ranges.

Then one of the victors of a combat looked around for another enemy and saw him.

173

His eyes widened. For a second, he looked as startled as Burton had when he had first opened his eyes. Perhaps he had never seen such a creature as Burton before, any more than Burton had seen one like him. If so, he did not take long to get over his surprise. He bellowed, jumped over the mangled body of his foe, and ran toward Burton, raising an axe that could have felled an elephant.

Burton also ran, his grail in one hand. If he were to lose that, he might as well die now. Without it, he would starve or have to eke out on fish and bamboo sprouts.

He almost made it. An opening appeared before him, and he sped between two titans, their arms around each other and each straining to throw over the other, and another who was backing away before the rain of blows delivered by the club of a fourth. Just as he was almost through, the two wrestlers toppled over on him.

He was going swiftly enough that he was not caught directly under them, but the flailing arm of one struck his left heel. So hard was the blow, it smashed his foot against the ground and stopped him instantly. He fell forward and began to scream. His foot must have been broken, and he had torn muscles throughout his leg.

Nevertheless, he tried to rise and to hobble on to The River. Once in it, he could swim away, if he did not faint from the agony. He took two hops on his right foot, only to be seized from behind.

He flew up into the air, whirling around, and was caught before he began his descent.

The titan was holding him with one hand at arm's length, the enormous and powerful fist clutched around Burton's chest. Burton could hardly breathe; his ribs threatened to cave in.

Despite all this, he had not dropped his grail. Now he struck it against the giant's shoulder.

Lightly, as if brushing off a fly, the giant tapped the metal container with his axe, and the grail was torn from Burton's grip.

The behemoth grinned and bent his arm to bring Burton in closer. Burton weighed one hundred and eighty pounds, but the arm did not quiver under the strain.

For a moment, Burton looked directly into the pale blue eyes sunk in the bony circles. The nose was lined with many broken veins. The lips protruded because of the bulging prognathous jaws beneath—not, as he had first thought, because the lips were so thick.

Then the titan bellowed and lifted Burton up above his head. Burton hammered the huge arm with his fists, knowing that it was in vain but unwilling to submit like a caught rabbit. Even as he did so, he noted, though not with the full attention of his mind, several things about the scene.

The sun had been just rising above the mountain peaks when he had first awakened. Although the time passed since he had jumped to his feet was only a few minutes, the sun should have cleared the peaks. It had not; it hung at exactly the same height as when he had first seen it.

Moreover, the upward slant of the valley permitted a view for at least four miles. The grailstone by him was the last one. Beyond it was only the plain and The River.

This was the end of the line—or the beginning of The River.

There was no time nor desire for him to appreciate what these meant. He merely noted them during the passage between pain, rage, and terror. Then, as the giant prepared to bring his axe around to splinter Burton's skull, the giant stiffened and shrieked. To Burton, it was like being next to a locomotive whistle. The grip loosened, and Burton fell to the ground. For a moment, he passed out from the pain in his foot.

When he regained consciousness, he had to grind his teeth to keep from yelling again. He groaned and sat up, though not without a race of fire up his leg that made the feeble daylight grow almost black. The battle was roaring all around him, but he was in a little corner of inactivity. By him lay the tree-trunk-thick corpse of the titan who had been about to kill him. The back of his skull, which looked massive enough to resist a battering ram, was caved in.

Around the elephantine corpse crawled another casualty, on all fours. Seeing him, Burton forgot his pain

175

for a moment. The horribly injured man was Hermann Göring.

Both of them had been resurrected at the same spot. There was no time to think about the implications of the coincidence. His pain began to come back. Moreover, Göring started to talk.

Not that he looked as if he had much talk left in him or much time left to do it in. Blood covered him. His right eye was gone. The corner of his mouth was ripped back to his ear. One of his hands was smashed flat. A rib was sticking through the skin. How he had managed to stay alive, let alone crawl, was beyond Burton's understanding.

"You . . . you!" Göring said hoarsely in German, and he collapsed. A fountain poured out of his mouth and over Burton's legs; his eyes glazed.

Burton wondered if he would ever know what he had intended to say. Not that it really mattered. He had more vital things to think about.

About ten yards from him, two titans were standing with their backs to him. Both were breathing hard, apparently resting for a moment before they jumped back into the fight. Then one spoke to the other.

There was no doubt about it. The giant was not just uttering cries. He was using a language.

Burton did not understand it, but he knew it was speech. He did not need the modulated, distinctly syllabic reply of the other to confirm his recognition.

So these were not some type of prehistoric ape but a species of subhuman men. They must have been unknown to the twentieth-century science of Earth, since his friend, Frigate, had described to him all the fossils known in 2008 A.D.

He lay down with his back against the fallen giant's Gothic ribs and brushed some of the long reddish sweaty hairs from his face. He fought nausea and the agony of his foot and the torn muscles of his leg. If he made too much noise, he might attract those two, and they would finish the job. But what if they did? With his wounds, in a land of such monsters, what chance did he have of surviving?

Worse than his agony of foot, almost, was the thought

that, on his first trip on what he called The Suicide Express, he had reached his goal.

He had had only an estimated one chance in ten million of arriving at this area, and he might never have made it if he had drowned himself ten thousand times. Yet he had had a fantastically good fortune. It might never occur again. And he was to lose it and very soon.

The sun was moving half-revealed along the tops of the mountains across The River. This was the place that he had speculated would exist; he had come here first shot. Now, as his eyesight failed and the pain lessened, he knew that he was dying. The sickness was born from more than the shattered bones in his foot. He must be bleeding inside.

He tried to rise once more. He would stand, if only on one foot, and shake his fist at the mocking fates and curse them. He would die with a curse on his lips.

23

The red wing of dawn was lightly touching his eyes.

He rose to his feet, knowing that his wounds would be healed and he would be whole again but not quite believing it. Near him was a grail and a pile of six neatly folded towels of various sizes, colors, and thicknesses.

Twelve feet away, another man, also naked, was rising from the short bright-green grass. Burton's skin grew cold. The blondish hair, broad face, and light-blue eyes were those of Hermann Göring.

The German looked as surprised as Burton. He spoke slowly, as if coming out of a deep sleep. "There's something very wrong here."

"Something foul indeed," Burton replied. He knew no more of the pattern of resurrection along The River than any other man. He had never seen a resurrection, but he

177

had had them described to him by those who had. At dawn, just after the sun topped the unclimbable mountains, a shimmering appeared in the air beside a grailstone. In the flicker of a bird's wing, the distortion solidified, and a naked man or woman or child appeared from nowhere on the grass by the bank. Always the indispensable grail and the towels were by the "lazarus."

Along a conceivably ten to twenty million-mile long Rivervalley in which an estimated thirty-five to thirty-six billion lived, a million could die per day. It was true that there were no diseases (other than mental) but, though statistics were lacking, a million were probably killed every twenty-four hours by the myriads of wars between the one million or so little states, by crimes of passion, by suicides, by executions of criminals and by accidents. There was a steady and numerous traffic of those undergoing the "little resurrection," as it was called.

But Burton had never heard of two dying in the same place and at the same time being resurrected together. The process of selection of area for the new life was random—or so he had always thought.

One such occurrence could conceivably take place, although the probabilities were one in twenty million. But two such, one immediately after the other, was a miracle.

Burton did not believe in miracles. Nothing happened that could not be explained by physical principles—if you knew all the facts.

He did not know them, so he would not worry about the "coincidence" at the moment. The solution to another problem was more demanding. That was, what was he to do about Göring?

The man knew him and could identify him to any Ethicals searching for him.

Burton looked quickly around him and saw a number of men and women approaching in a seemingly friendly manner. There was time for a few words with the German.

"Göring, I can kill you or myself. But I don't want to do either—at the moment, anyway. You know why you're dangerous to me. I shouldn't take a chance with you, you treacherous hyena. But there's something different about

178

you, something I can't put my fingers on. But . . ."

Göring, who was notorious for his resilience, seemed to be coming out of his shock. He grinned slyly and said, "I do have you over the barrel, don't I?"

Seeing Burton's snarl, he hastily put up one hand and said, "But I swear to you I won't reveal your identity to anyone! Or do anything to hurt you! Maybe we're not friends, but we at least know each other, and we're in a land of strangers. It's good to have one familiar face by your side. I know, I've suffered too long from loneliness, from desolation of the spirit. I thought I'd go mad. That's partly the reason I took to the dreamgum. Believe me, I won't betray you."

Burton did not believe him. He did think, however, that he could trust him for a while. Göring would want a potential ally, at least until he took the measure of the people in this area and knew what he could or could not do. Besides, Göring might have changed for the better.

No, Burton said to himself. No. There you go again. Verbal cynic though you are, you've always been too forgiving, too ready to overlook injury to yourself and to give your injurer another chance. Don't be a fool again, Burton.

Three days later, he was still uncertain about Göring.

Burton had taken the identity of Abdul ibn Harun, a nineteenth-century citizen of Cairo, Egypt. He had several reasons for adopting the guise. One was that he spoke excellent Arabic, knew the Cairo dialect of that period, and had an excuse to cover his head with a towel wrapped as a turban. He hoped this would help disguise his appearance. Göring did not say a word to anybody to contradict the camouflage. Burton was fairly sure of this because he and Göring spent most of their time together. They were quartered in the same hut until they adjusted to the local customs and went through their period of probation. Part of this was intensive military training. Burton had been one of the greatest swordsmen of the nineteenth century and also knew every inflection of fighting with weapons or with hands. After a display of his ability in a series of tests, he was welcomed as a recruit. In fact, he was promised that he would be an instructor when he learned the language well enough.

Göring got the respect of the locals almost as swiftly. Whatever his other faults, he did not lack courage. He was strong and proficient with arms, jovial, likeable when it suited his purpose, and was not far behind Burton in gaining fluency in the language. He was quick to gain and to use authority, as befitted the ex-Reichsmarschal of Hitler's Germany.

This section of the western shore was populated largely by speakers of a language totally unknown even to Burton, a master linguist both on Earth and on the Riverplanet. When he had learned enough to ask questions, he deduced that they must have lived somewhere in Central Europe during the Early Bronze Age. They had some curious customs, one of which was copulation in public. This was interesting enough to Burton, who had co-founded the Royal Anthropological Society in London in 1863 and who had seen strange things during his explorations on Earth. He did not participate, but neither was he horrified.

A custom he did adopt joyfully was that of stained whiskers. The males resented the fact that their face hair had been permanently removed by the Resurrectors, just as their prepuces had been cut off. They could do nothing about the latter outrage, but they could correct the former to a degree. They smeared their upper lips and chins with a dark liquid made from finely ground charcoal, fish glue, oak tannin, and several other ingredients. The more dedicated used the dye as a tattoo and underwent a painful and long-drawn-out pricking with a sharp bamboo needle.

Now Burton was doubly disguised, yet he had put himself at the mercy of the man who might betray him at the first opportunity. He wanted to attract an Ethical but did not want the Ethical to be certain of his identity.

Burton wanted to make sure that he could get away in time before being scooped up in the net. It was a dangerous game, like walking a tightrope over a pit of hungry wolves, but he wanted to play it. He would run only when it became absolutely necessary. The rest of the time, he would be the hunted hunting the hunter.

Yet the vision of the Dark Tower, or the Big Grail, was always on the horizon of every thought. Why play cat and mouse when he might be able to storm the very ramparts of the castle within which he presumed the Ethicals had headquarters? Or, if stormed was not the correct description, steal into the Tower, effect entrance as a mouse does into a house—or a castle. While the cats were looking elsewhere, the mouse would be sneaking into the Tower, and there the mouse might turn into a tiger.

At this thought, he laughed, getting curious stares from his two hutmates: Göring and the seventeenth-century Englishman, John Collop. His laugh was half-ridicule of himself at the tiger image. What made him think that he, one man, could do anything to hurt the Planet-Shapers, Resurrectors of billions of dead, Feeders and Maintainers of those summoned back to life? He twisted his hands and knew that within them, and within the brain that guided them, could be the downfall of the Ethicals. What this fearful thing was that he harbored within himself, he did not know. But They feared him. If he could only find out why . . .

His laugh was only partly self-ridicule. The other half of him believed that he was a tiger among men. *As a man thinks, so is he,* he muttered.

Göring said, "You have a very peculiar laugh, my friend. Somewhat feminine for such a masculine man. It's like . . . like a thrown rock skipping over a lake of ice. Or like a jackal."

"I have something of the jackal and hyena in me," Burton replied. "So my detractors maintained—and they were right. But I am more than that."

He rose from his bed and began to exercise to work the sleep-rust from his muscles. In a few minutes, he would go with the others to a grailstone by the Riverbank and charge his grail. Afterward, there would be an hour of policing the area. Then drill, followed by instruction in the spear, the club, the sling, the obsidian-edged sword, the bow and arrow, the flint axe, and in fighting with bare

181

hands and feet. An hour for rest and talk and lunch. Then an hour in a language class. A two-hour work-stint in helping build the ramparts that marked the boundaries of this little state. A half-hour rest, then the obligatory mile run to build stamina. Dinner from the grails, and the evening off except for those who had guard duty or other tasks.

Such a schedule and such activities were being duplicated in tiny states up and down The River's length. Almost everywhere, mankind was at war or preparing for it. The citizens must keep in shape and know how to fight to the best of their ability. The exercises also kept the citizens occupied. No matter how monotonous the martial life, it was better than sitting around wondering what to do for amusement. Freedom from worry about food, rent, bills, and the gnatlike chores and duties that had kept Earthmen busy and fretful was not all a blessing. There was the great battle against ennui, and the leaders of each state were occupied trying to think up ways to keep their people busy.

It should have been paradise in Rivervalley, but it was war, war, war. Other things aside, however, war was, in this place, good (according to some)! It gave savor to life and erased boredom. Man's greediness and aggressiveness had its worthwhile side.

After dinner, every man and woman was free to do what he wished, as long as he broke no local laws. He could barter the cigarettes and liquor provided by his grail or the fish he'd caught in The River for a better bow and arrows; shields; bowls and cups; tables and chairs; bamboo flutes; clay trumpets; human or fishskin drums; rare stones (which really were rare); necklaces made of the beautifully articulated and colored bones of the deep-River fish, of jade or of carved wood; obsidian mirrors; sandals and shoes; charcoal drawings; the rare and expensive bamboo paper; ink and fishbone pens; hats made from the long and tough-fibered hill-grass; bullroarers; little wagons on which to ride down the hillsides; harps made from wood with strings fashioned from the gut of the "dragonfish"; rings of oak for fingers and toes; clay statuettes; and other devices, useful or ornamental.

Later, of course, there was the love-making Burton and his hutmates were denied, for the time being. Only when they had been accepted as full citizens would they be allowed to move into separate houses and live with a woman.

John Collop was a short slight youth with long yellow hair, a narrow but pleasant face, and large blue eyes with very long, upcurving, black eyelashes. In his first conversation with Burton, he had said, after introducing himself, "I was delivered from the darkness of my mother's womb—whose else?—into the light of God of Earth in 1625. Far too quickly, I descended again into the womb of Mother Nature, confident in the hope of resurrection and not disappointed, as you see. Though I must confess that this afterlife is not that which the parsons led me to expect. But then, how should they know the truth, poor blind devils leading the blind!"

It was not long before Collop told him that he was a member of the Church of the Second Chance.

Burton's eyebrows rose. He had encountered this new religion at many places along The River. Burton, though an infidel, made it his business to investigate thoroughly every religion. Know a man's faith, and you knew at least half the man. Know his wife, and you knew the other half.

The Church had a few simple tenets, some based on fact, most on surmise and hope and wish. In this they differed from no religions born on Earth. But the Second Chancers had one advantage over any Terrestrial religion. They had no difficulty in proving that dead men could be raised—not only once but often.

"And why has mankind been given a Second Chance?" Collop said in his low, earnest voice. "Does he deserve it? No. With few exceptions, men are a mean, miserable, petty, vicious, narrow-minded, exceedingly egotistic, generally disputing, and disgusting lot. Watching them, the gods—or God—should vomit. But in this divine spew is a clot of compassion, if you will pardon me for using such imagery. Man, however base, has a silver wire of the

183

divine in him. It is no idle phrase that man was made in God's image. There is something worth saving in the worst of us, and out of this something a new man may be fashioned.

"Whoever has given us this new opportunity to save our souls knows this truth. We have been placed here in this Rivervalley—on this alien planet under alien skies—to work out our salvation. What our time limit is, I do not know nor do the leaders of my Church even speculate. Perhaps it is forever, or it may be only a hundred years or a thousand. But we must make use of whatever time we do have, my friend."

Burton said, "Weren't you sacrificed on the altar of Odin by Norse who clung to the old religion, even if this world isn't the Valhalla they were promised by their priests? Don't you think you wasted your time and breath by preaching to them? They believe in the same old gods, the only difference in their theology now being some adjustments they've made to conditions here. Just as you have clung to your old faith."

"The Norse have no explanations for their new surroundings," Collop said, "but I do. I have a reasonable explanation, one which the Norse will eventually come to accept, to believe in as fervently as I do. They killed me, but some more persuasive member of the Church will come along and talk to them before they stretch him out in the wooden lap of their wooden idol and stab him in the heart. If *he* does not talk them out of him, the *next* missionary will.

"It was true, on Earth, that the blood of martyrs is the seed of the church. It is even truer here. If you kill a man to shut his mouth, he pops up some place elsewhere along The River. And a man who has been martyred a hundred thousand miles away comes along to replace the previous martyr. The Church will win out in the end. Then men will cease these useless, hate-generating wars and begin the real business, the only worthwhile business, that of gaining salvation."

"What you say about the martyrs is true about anyone with an idea," Burton said. "A wicked man who's killed
184

also pops up to commit his evil elsewhere."

"Good will prevail; the truth always wins out," Collop said.

"I don't know how restricted your mobility was on Earth or how long your life," Burton said, "but both must have been very limited to make you so blind. I know better."

Collop said, "The Church is not founded on faith alone. It has something very factual, very substantial, on which to base its teachings. Tell me, my friend, Abdul, have you ever heard of anybody being resurrected dead?"

"A paradox!" Burton cried. "What do you mean—resurrected dead?"

"There are at least three authenticated cases and four more of which the Church has heard but has not been able to validate. These are men and women who were killed at one place on The River and translated to another. Strangely, their bodies were re-created, but they were without the spark of life. Now, why was this?"

"I can't imagine!" Burton said. "You tell me. I listen, for you speak as one with authority."

He *could* imagine, since he had heard the same story elsewhere. But he wanted to learn if Collop's story matched the others.

It was the same, even to the names of the dead lazari. The story was that these men and women had been identified by those who had known them well on Earth. They were all saintly or near-saintly people; in fact, one of them had been canonized on Earth. The theory was that they had attained that state of sanctity which made it no longer necessary to go through the "purgatory" of the Riverplanet. Their souls had gone on to . . . someplace . . . and left the excess baggage of their physical bodies behind.

Soon, so the Church said, more would reach this state. And their bodies would be left behind. Eventually, given enough time, the Rivervalley would become depopulated. All would have shed themselves of their viciousnesses and hates and would have become illuminated with the love of mankind and of God. Even the most depraved, those who seemed to be utterly lost, would be able to abandon their physical beings. All that was needed to attain this grace was love.

Burton sighed, laughed loudly, and said, "*Plus ça change, plus c'est la même chose.* Another fairy tale to give men hope. The old religions have been discredited—although some refuse to face even that fact—so new ones must be invented."

"It makes sense," Collop said. "Do you have a better explanation of why we're here?"

"Perhaps. I can make up fairy tales, too."

As a matter of fact, Burton did have an explanation. However, he could not tell it to Collop. Spruce had told Burton something of the identity, history, and purpose of his group, the Ethicals. Much of what he had said agreed with Collop's theology.

Spruce had killed himself before he had explained about the "soul." Presumably, the "soul" had to be part of the total organization of resurrection. Otherwise, when the body had attained "salvation," and no longer lived, there would be nothing to carry on the essential part of a man. Since the post-Terrestrial life could be explained in physical terms, the "soul" must also be a physical entity, not to be dismissed with the term "supernatural" as it had been on Earth.

There was much that Burton did not know. But he had had a glimpse into the workings of this Riverplanet that no other human being possessed.

With the little knowledge he did have, he planned to lever his way into more, to pry open the lid, and crawl inside the sanctum. To do so, he would attain the Dark Tower. The only way to get there swiftly was to take The Suicide Express. First, he must be discovered by an Ethical. Then he must overpower the Ethical, render him unable to kill himself, and somehow extricate more information from him.

Meanwhile, he continued to play the role of Abdul ibn Harun, translated and transplanted Egyptian physician of the nineteenth century, now a citizen of Bargawhwdzys. As such, he decided to join the Church of the Second

186

Chance. He announced to Collop his disillusionment in Mahomet and his teachings, and so became Collop's first convert in this area.

"Then you must swear not to take arms against any man nor to defend yourself physically, my dear friend," Collop said.

Burton, outraged, said that he would allow no man to strike at him and go unharmed.

" 'Tis not unnatural," Collop said gently. "Contrary to habit, yes. But a man may become something other than he has been, something better—if he has the strength of will and the desire."

Burton rapped out a violent 'no' and stalked away. Collop shook his head sadly, but he continued to be as friendly as ever. Not without a sense of humor, he sometimes addressed Burton as his "five-minute convert," not meaning the time it took to bring him into the fold but the time it took Burton to leave the fold.

At this time, Collop got his second convert, Göring. The German had had nothing but sneers and jibes for Collop. Then he began chewing dreamgum again, and the nightmares started.

For two nights he kept Collop and Burton awake with his groanings, his tossings, his screams. On the evening of the third day, he asked Collop if he would accept him into the Church. However, he had to make a confession. Collop must understand what sort of person he had been, both on Earth and on this planet.

Collop heard out the mixture of self-abasement and self-aggrandizement. Then he said, "Friend, I care not what you may have been. Only what you are and what you will be. I listened only because confession is good for the soul. I can see that you are deeply troubled, that you have suffered sorrow and grief for what you have done, yet take some pleasure in what you once were, a mighty figure among men. Much of what you told me I do not comprehend, because I know not much about your era. Nor does it matter. Only today and tomorrow need to be our concern; each day will take care of itself."

It seemed to Burton not that Collop did not care what

187

Göring had been but that he did not believe his story of Earthly glory and infamy. There were so many phonies that genuine heroes, or villains, had been depreciated. Thus, Burton had met three Jesus Christs, two Abrahams, four King Richard the Lion-Hearteds, six Attilas, a dozen Judases (only one of whom could speak Aramaic), a George Washington, two Lord Byrons, three Jesse Jameses, any number of Napoleons, a General Custer (who spoke with a heavy Yorkshire accent), a Finn MacCool (who did not know ancient Irish), a Tchaka (who spoke the wrong Zulu dialect), and a number of others who might or might not have been what they claimed to be.

Whatever a man had been on Earth, he had to reestablish himself here. This was not easy, because conditions were radically altered. The greats and the importants of Terra were constantly being humiliated in their claims and denied a chance to prove their identities.

To Collop, the humiliation was a blessing. First, humiliation, then humility, he would have said. And then comes humanity as a matter of course.

Göring had been trapped in the Great Design—as Burton termed it—because it was his nature to overindulge, especially with drugs. Knowing that the dreamgum was uprooting the dark things in his personal abyss, was spewing them up into the light, that he was being torn apart, fragmented, he still continued to chew as much as he could get. For a while, temporarily made healthful again with a new resurrection, he had been able to deny the call of the drug. But a few weeks after his arrival in this area, he had succumbed, and now the night was ripped apart with his shrieks of "Hermann Göring, I hate you!"

"If this continues," Burton said to Collop, "he will go mad. Or he will kill himself again, or force someone to kill him, so that he can get away from himself. But the suicide will be useless, and it's all to do over again. Tell me truly, now, is this not hell?"

"Purgatory, rather," Collop said. "Purgatory is hell with hope."

24

Two months passed. Burton marked the days off on a pine stick notched with a flint knife. This was the fourteenth day of the seventh month of 5 A.R., the fifth year After the Resurrection. Burton tried to keep a calendar, for he was, among many other things, a chronicler. But it was difficult. Time did not mean much on The River. The planet had a polar axis that was always at ninety degrees to the ecliptic. There was no change of seasons, and the stars seemed to jostle each other and made identification of individual luminaries or of constellations impossible. So many and so bright were they that even the noonday sun at its zenith could not entirely dim the greatest of them. Like ghosts reluctant to retreat before daylight, they hovered in the burning air.

Nevertheless, man needs time as a fish needs water. If he does not have it, he will invent it; so to Burton, it was July 14, 5 A.R.

But Collop, like many, reckoned time as having continued from the year of his Terrestrial death. To him, it was 1667 A.D. He did not believe that his sweet Jesus had become sour. Rather, this river was the River Jordan; this valley, the vale beyond the shadow of death. He admitted that the afterlife was not that which he had expected. Yet it was, in many respects, a far more glorious place. It was evidence of the all-encompassing love of God for His creation. He had given all men, altogether undeserving of such a gift, another chance. If this world was not the New Jerusalem, it was a place prepared for its building. Here the bricks, which were the love of God, and the mortar, love for man, must be fashioned in this kiln and this mill: the planet of The River of The Valley.

Burton poohpoohed the concept, but he could not help loving the little man. Collop was genuine; he was not stoking the furnace of his sweetness with leaves from a book or pages from a theology. He did not operate under forced draft. He burned with a flame that fed on his own being, and this being was love. Love even for the unloveable, the rarest and most difficult species of love.

He told Burton something of his Terrestrial life. He had been a doctor, a farmer, a liberal with unshakable faith in his religion, yet full of questions about his faith and the society of his time. He had written a plea for religious tolerance which had aroused both praise and damnation in his time. And he had been a poet, well-known for a short time, then forgotten.

> Lord, let the faithless see
> Miracles ceased, revive in me.
> The leper cleansed, blind healed,
> dead raised by Thee.

"My lines may have died, but their truth has not," he said to Burton. He waved his hand to indicate the hills, The River, the mountains, the people. "As you may see if you open your eyes and do not persist in this stubborn myth of yours that this is the handiwork of men like us."

He continued, "Or grant your premise. It still remains that these Ethicals are but doing the work of Their Creator."

"I like better those other lines of yours," Burton said.

> Dull soul aspire;
> Thou art not the Earth. Mount higher!
> Heaven gave the spark;
> to it return the fire.

Collop was pleased, not knowing that Burton was thinking of the lines in a different sense than that intended by the poet.

"Return the fire."

190

That meant somehow getting into the Dark Tower, discovering the secrets of the Ethicals, and turning Their devices against Them. He did not feel gratitude because They had given him a second life. He was outraged that They should do this without his leave. If They wanted his thanks, why did They not tell him why They had given him another chance? What reason did They have for keeping Their motives in the dark? He would find out why. The spark They had restored in him would turn into a raging fire to burn Them.

He cursed the fate that had propelled him to a place so near the source of The River, hence so close to the Tower, and in a few minutes had carried him away again, back to some place in the middle of The River, millions of miles away from his goal. Yet, if he had been there once, he could get there again. Not by taking a boat, since the journey would consume at least forty years and probably more. He could also count on being captured and enslaved a thousand times over. And if he were killed along the way, he might find himself raised again far from his goal and have to start all over again.

On the other hand, given the seemingly random selection of resurrection, he might find himself once more near The River's mouth. It was this that determined him to board The Suicide Express once more. However, even though he knew that his death would be only temporary, he found it difficult to take the necessary step. His mind told him that death was the only ticket, but his body rebelled. The cells' fierce insistence on survival overcame his will.

For a while, he rationalized that he was interested in studying the customs and languages of the prehistorics among whom he was living. Then honesty triumphed, and he knew he was only looking for excuses to put off the Grim Moment. Despite this, he did not act.

Burton, Collop, and Göring were moved out of their bachelor barracks to take up the normal life of citizens. Each took up residence in a hut, and within a week had found a woman to live with him. Collop's Church did not require celibacy. A member could take an oath of chastity

191

if he wished to. But the Church reasoned that men and women had been Resurrected in bodies that retained the full sex of the original. (Or, if lacking on Earth, supplied here.) It was evident that the Makers of Resurrection had meant for sex to be used. It was well-known, though still denied by some, that sex had other functions than reproduction. So go ahead, youths, roll in the grass.

Another result of the inexorable logic of the Church (which, by the way, decried reason as being untrustworthy) was that any form of love was allowed, as long as it was voluntary and did not involve cruelty or force. Exploitation of children was forbidden. This was a problem that, given time, would cease to exist. In a few years all children would be adults.

Collop refused to have a hutmate solely to relieve his sexual tensions. He insisted on a woman whom he loved. Burton jibed at him for this, saying that it was a prerequisite easily—therefore cheaply—fulfilled. Collop loved all humanity; hence, he should theoretically take the first woman who would say yes to him.

"As a matter of fact, my friend," Collop said, "that is exactly what happened."

"It's only a coincidence that she's beautiful, passionate, and intelligent?" Burton said.

"Though I strive to be more than human, rather, to become a complete human, I am all-too-human," Collop replied. He smiled. "Would you have me deliberately martyr myself by choosing an ugly shrew?"

"I'd think you more of a fool than I do even now," Burton said. "As for me, all I require in a woman is beauty and affection. I don't care a whit about her brains. And I prefer blondes. There's a chord within me that responds to the fingers of a golden-haired woman."

Göring took into his hut a Valkyrie, a tall, great-busted, wide-shouldered, eighteenth-century Swede. Burton wondered if she was a surrogate for Göring's first wife, the sister-in-law of the Swedish explorer Count von Rosen. Göring admitted that she not only looked like his Karin but even had a voice similar to hers. He seemed to be very happy with her and she with him.

Then, one night, during the invariable early-morning rain, Burton was ripped from a deep sleep.

He thought he had heard a scream, but all he could hear when he became fully awake was the explosion of thunder and the crack of nearby lightning. He closed his eyes, only to be jerked upright again. A woman had screamed in a nearby hut.

He jumped up, shoved aside the bamboo-slat door, and stuck his head outside. The cold rain hit him in the face. All was dark except for the mountains in the west, lit up by flashes of lightning. Then a bolt struck so close that he was deafened and dazzled. However, he did catch a glimpse of two ghostly white figures just outside Göring's hut. The German had his hands locked around the throat of his woman, who was holding onto his wrists and trying to push him away.

Burton ran out, slipped on the wet grass, and fell. Just as he arose, another flash showed the woman on her knees, bending backward, and Göring's distorted face above her. At the same time, Collop, wrapping a towel around his waist, came out of his hut. Burton got to his feet and, still silent, ran again. But Göring was gone. Burton knelt by Karla, felt her heart, and could detect no beat. Another glare of lightning showed him her face, mouth hanging open, eyes bulging.

He rose and shouted, "Göring! Where are you?"

Something struck the back of his head. He fell on his face.

Stunned, he managed to get to his hands and knees, only to be knocked flat again by another heavy blow. Half-conscious, he nevertheless rolled over on his back and raised his legs and hands to defend himself. Lightning revealed Göring standing above him with a club in one hand. His face was a madman's.

Darkness sliced off the lightning. Something white and blurred leaped upon Göring out of the darkness. The two pale bodies went down onto the grass beside Burton and rolled over and over. They screeched like tomcats, and another flash of lightning showed them clawing at each other.

193

Burton staggered to his feet and lurched toward them but was knocked down by Collop's body, hurled by Göring. Again Burton got up. Collop bounded to his feet and charged Göring. There was a loud crack, and Collop crumpled. Burton tried to run toward Göring. His legs refused to answer his demands; they took him off at an angle, away from his point of attack. Then another blast of light and noise showed Göring, as if caught in a photograph, suspended in the act of swinging the club at Burton.

Burton felt his arm go numb as it received the impact of the club. Now not only his legs but his left arm disobeyed him. Nevertheless he balled his right hand and tried to swing at Göring. There was another crack; his ribs felt as if they had become unhinged and were driven inward into his lung. His breath was knocked out of him, and once again he was on the cold wet grass.

Something fell by his side. Despite his agony, he reached out for it. The club was in his hand; Göring must have dropped it. Shuddering with each painful breath, he got to one knee. Where was the madman? Two shadows danced and blurred, merged and half-separated. The hut! His eyes were crossed. He wondered if he had a concussion of the brain, then forgot it as he saw Göring dimly in the illumination of a distant streak of lightning. Two Görings, rather. One seemed to accompany the other; the one on the left had his feet on the ground; the right one was treading on air.

Both had their hands held high up into the rain, as if they were trying to wash them. And when the two turned and came toward him, he understood that that was what they were trying to do. They were shouting in German (with a single voice), "Take the blood off my hands! Oh, God, wash it off!"

Burton stumbled toward Göring, his club held high. Burton meant to knock him out, but Göring suddenly turned and ran away. Burton followed him as best he could, down the hill, up another one, and then out onto the flat plain. The rains stopped, the thunder and lightning died, and within five minutes the clouds, as always, had cleared away. The starlight gleamed on Göring's white skin.

Like a phantom he flitted ahead of his pursuer, seemingly bent upon getting to The River. Burton kept after him, although he wondered why he was doing so. His legs had regained most of their strength, and his vision was no longer double. Presently, he found Göring. He was squatting by The River and staring intently at the star-fractured waves.

Burton said, "Are you all right now?"

Göring was startled. He began to rise, then changed his mind. Groaning, he put his head down on his knees.

"I knew what I was doing, but I didn't know why," he said dully. "Karla was telling me she was moving out in the morning, said she couldn't sleep with all the noise I made with my nightmares. And I was acting strangely. I begged her to stay; I told her I loved her very much. I'd die if she deserted me. She said she was fond of me, had been, rather, but she didn't love me. Suddenly, it seemed that if I wanted to keep her, I'd have to kill her. She ran screaming out of the hut. You know the rest."

"I intended to kill you," Burton said. "But I can see you're no more responsible than a madman. The people here won't accept that excuse, though. You know what they'll do to you; hang you upside down by your ankles and let you hang until you die."

Göring cried, "I don't understand it! What's happening to me? Those nightmares! Believe me, Burton, if I've sinned, I've paid! But I can't stop paying! My nights are hell, and soon my days will become hell, too! Then I'll have only one way to get peace! I'll kill myself! But it won't do any good! I'll wake up—then hell again!"

"Stay away from the dreamgum," Burton said. "You'll have to sweat it out. You can do it. You told me you overcame the morphine habit on Earth."

Göring stood up and faced Burton. "That's just it! I haven't touched the gum since I came to this place!"

Burton said, "What? But I'll swear . . . !"

"You assumed I was using the stuff because of the way I was acting! No, I have not had a bit of the gum! But it

195

doesn't make any difference!"

Despite his loathing of Göring, Burton felt pity. He said, "You've opened the pandora of yourself, and it looks as if you'll not be able to shut the lid. I don't know how this is going to end, but I wouldn't want to be in your mind. Not that you don't deserve this."

Göring said, in a quiet and determined voice, "I'll defeat them."

"You mean you'll conquer yourself," Burton said. He turned to go but halted for a last word. "What are you going to do?"

Göring gestured at The River. "Drown myself. I'll get a fresh start. Maybe I'll be better equipped the next place. And I certainly don't want to be trussed up like a chicken in a butcher shop window."

"Au revoir, then," Burton said. "And good luck."

"Thank you. You know, you're not a bad sort. Just one word of advice."

"What's that?"

"You'd better stay away from the dreamgum yourself. So far, you've been lucky. But one of these days, it'll take hold of you as it did me. Your devils won't be mine, but they'll be just as monstrous and terrifying to you."

"Nonsense! I've nothing to hide from myself!" Burton laughed loudly. "I've chewed enough of the stuff to know."

He walked away, but he was thinking of the warning. He had used the gum twenty-two times. Each time had made him swear never to touch the gum again.

On the way back to the hills, he looked behind him. The dim white figure of Göring was slowly sinking into the black-and-silver waters of The River. Burton saluted, since he was not one to resist the dramatic gesture. Afterward, he forgot Göring. The pain in the back of his head, temporarily subdued, came back sharper than before. His knees turned to water, and, only a few yards from his hut, he had to sit down.

He must have become unconscious then, or half-conscious since he had no memory of being dragged along on the grass. When his wits cleared, he found himself lying

196

on a bamboo bed inside a hut.

It was dark with the only illumination the starlight filtering in through the tree branches outside the square of window. He turned his head and saw the shadowy and pale-white bulk of a man squatting by him. The man was holding a thin metal object before his eyes, the gleaming end of which was pointed at Burton.

25

As soon as Burton turned his head, the man put the device down. He spoke in English. "It's taken me a long time to find you, Richard Burton."

Burton groped around on the floor for a weapon with his left hand, which was hidden from the man's view. His fingers touched nothing but dirt. He said, "Now you've found me, you damn Ethical, what do you intend doing with me?"

The man shifted slightly and he chuckled. "Nothing." He paused, then said, "I am not one of Them." He laughed again when Burton gasped. "That's not quite true. I am *with* Them, but I am not *of* Them."

He picked up the device which he had been aiming at Burton.

"This tells me that you have a fractured skull and a concussion of the brain. You must be very tough, because you should be dead, judging from the extent of the injury. But you may pull out of it, if you take it easy. Unfortunately, you don't have time to convalesce. The Others know you're in this area, give or take thirty miles. In a day or so, They'll have you pinpointed."

Burton tried to sit up and found that his bones had become soft as taffy in sunlight, and a bayonet was prying

197

open the back of his skull. Groaning, he lay back down.

"Who are you and what's your business?"

"I can't tell you my name. If—or much more likely when—They catch you, They'll thread out your memory and run it off backward to the time you woke up in the preresurrection bubble. They won't find out what made you wake before your time. But They will know about this conversation. They'll even be able to see me but only as you see me, a pale shadow with no features. They'll hear my voice too, but They won't recognize it. I'm using a transmuter.

"They will, however, be horrified. What they have slowly and reluctantly been suspecting will all of a sudden be revealed as the truth. They have a traitor in Their midst."

"I wish I knew what you were talking about," Burton said.

The man said, "I'll tell you this much. You have been told a monstrous lie about the purpose of the Resurrection. What Spruce told you, and what that Ethical creation, the Church of the Second Chance, teaches—are lies! All lies! The truth is that you human beings have been given life again only to participate in a scientific experiment. The Ethicals—a misnomer if there ever was one—have reshaped this planet into one Rivervalley, built the grailstones, and brought all of you back from the dead for one purpose. To record your history and customs. And, as a secondary matter, to observe your reactions to Resurrection and to the mixing of different peoples of different eras. That is all it is: a scientific project. And when you have served your purpose, back into the dust you go!

"This story about giving all of you another chance at eternal life and salvation because it is Their ethical duty—lies! Actually, my people do not believe that you are worth saving. They do not think you have 'souls'!"

Burton was silent for a while. The fellow was certainly sincere. Or, if not sincere, he was very emotionally involved, since he was breathing so heavily.

Finally, Burton spoke. "I can't see anybody going to all this expense and labor just to run a scientific experiment, or to make historical recordings."

"Time hangs heavy on the hands of immortals. You would be surprised what we do to make eternity interesting. Furthermore, given all time, we can take our time, and we do not let even the most staggering projects dismay us. After the last Terrestrial died, the job of setting up the Resurrection took several thousands of years, even though the final phase took only one day."

Burton said, "And you? *What* are you doing? And *why* are you doing whatever you're doing?"

"I am the only true Ethical in the whole monstrous race! I do not like toying around with you as if you were puppets, or mere objects to be observed, animals in a laboratory! After all, primitive and vicious though you be, you are sentients! You are, in a sense, as . . . as . . ."

The shadowy speaker waved a shadowy hand as if trying to grasp a word out of the darkness. He continued, "I'll have to use your term for yourselves. You're as *human* as we. Just as the subhumans who first used language were as human as you. And you are our forefathers. For all I know, I may be your direct descendant. My whole people could be descended from you."

"I doubt it," Burton said. "I had no children—that I know of, anyway."

He had many questions, and he began to ask them. But the man was paying no attention. He was holding the device to his forehead. Suddenly, he withdrew it and interrupted Burton in the middle of a sentence. "I've been . . . you don't have a word for it . . . let's say . . . listening. They've detected my . . . *wathan* . . . I think you'd call it an aura. They don't know whose *wathan*, just that it's an Ethical's. But They'll be zeroing in within the next five minutes. I have to go."

The pale figure stood up. "You have to go, too."

"Where are you taking me?" Burton said.

"I'm not. You must die; They must find only your

corpse. I can't take you with me; it's impossible. But if you die here, They'll lose you again. And we'll meet again. Then . . . !"

"Wait!" Burton said. "I don't understand. Why can't They locate me? They built the Resurrection machinery. Don't They know where my particular resurrector is?"

The man chuckled again. "No. Their only recordings of men on Earth were visual, not audible. And the location of the resurrectees in the preresurrection bubble was random, since They had planned to scatter you humans along The River in a rough chronological sequence but with a certain amount of mixing. They intended to get down to the individual basis later. Of course, They had no notion then that I would be opposing Them. Or that I would select certain of Their subjects to aid me in defeating the Plan. So They do not know where you, or the others, will next pop up.

"Now, you may be wondering why I can't set your resurrector so that you'll be translated near your goal, the headwaters. The fact is that I did set yours so that the first time you died, you'd be at the very first grailstone. But you didn't make it; so I presume the Titanthrops killed you. That was unfortunate, since I no longer dare to go near the bubble until I have an excuse. It is forbidden for any but those authorized to enter the preresurrection bubble. They are suspicious; They suspect tampering. So it is up to you, and to chance, to get back to the north polar region.

"As for the others, I never had an opportunity to set their resurrectors. They have to go by the laws of probabilities, too. Which are about twenty million to one."

"Others?" Burton said. "Others? But why did you choose us?"

"You have the right aura. So did the others. Believe me, I know what I'm doing; I chose well."

"But you intimated that you woke me up ahead of time . . . in the preresurrection bubble, for a purpose. What did it accomplish?"

"It was the only thing that would convince you that the Resurrection was not a supernatural event. And it started you sniffing on the track of the Ethicals. Am I right? Of course, I am. Here!"

He handed Burton a tiny capsule. "Swallow this. You will be dead instantly and out of Their reach—for a while. And your brain cells will be so ruptured They'll not be able to read them. Hurry! I *must* go!"

"What if I don't take it?" Burton said. "What if I allow Them to capture me now?"

"You don't have the aura for it," the man said.

Burton almost decided not to take the capsule. Why should he allow this arrogant fellow to order him around?

Then he considered that he should not bite off his nose to spite his face. As it was, he had the choice of playing along with this unknown man or of falling into the hands of the Others.

"All right," he said. "But why don't you kill me? Why make me do the job?"

The man laughed and said, "There are certain rules in this game, rules that I don't have time to explain. But you are intelligent, you'll figure out most of them for yourself. One is that we *are* Ethicals. We can give life, but we can't directly take life. It is not unthinkable for us or beyond our ability. Just very difficult."

Abruptly, the man was gone. Burton did not hesitate. He swallowed the capsule. There was a blinding flash . . .

26

And light was full in his eyes, from the just-risen sun. He had time for one quick look around, saw his grail, his pile of neatly folded towels—and Hermann Göring.

Then Burton and the German were seized by small dark men with large heads and bandy legs. These carried spears and flint-headed axes. They wore towels but only as capes secured around their thick short necks. Strips of leather, undoubtedly human skin, ran across their disproportionately large foreheads and around their heads to bind their long, coarse black hair. They looked semi-Mongolian and spoke a tongue unknown to him.

An empty grail was placed upside down over his head; his hands were tied behind him with a leather thong. Blind and helpless, stone-tipped spears digging into his back, he was urged across the plain. Somewhere near, drums thundered, and female voices wailed a chant.

He had walked three hundred paces when he was halted. The drums quit beating, and the women stopped their singsong. He could hear nothing except for the blood beating in his ears. What the hell was going on? Was he part of a religious ceremony which required that the victim be blinded? Why not? There had been many cultures on Earth which did not want the ritually slain to view those who shed his blood. The dead man's ghost might want to take revenge on his killers.

But these people must know by now that there were no such things as ghosts. Or did they regard *lazari* as just that, as ghosts that could be dispatched back to their land of origin by simply killing them again?

Göring! He, too, had been translated here. At the same grailstone. The first time could have been coincidence, although the probabilities against it were high. But three times in succession? No, it was . . .

The first blow drove the side of the grail against his head, made him half-unconscious, sent a vast ringing through him and sparks of light before his eyes, and knocked him to his knees. He never felt the second blow, and so awoke once more in another place—

27

And with him was Hermann Göring.

"You and I must be twin souls," Göring said. "We seem to be yoked together by Whoever is responsible for all this."

"The ox and the ass plow together," Burton said, leaving it to the German to decide which he was. Then the two were busy introducing themselves, or attempting to do so, to the people among whom they had arrived. These, as he later found out, were Sumerians of the Old or Classical period; that is, they had lived in Mesopotamia between 2500 and 2300 B.C. The men shaved their heads (no easy custom with flint razors), and the women were bare to the waist. They had a tendency to short squat bodies, pop-eyes, and (to Burton) ugly faces.

But if the index of beauty was not high among them, the pre-Columbian Samoans who made up 30 percent of the population were more than attractive. And, of course, there was the ubiquitous 10 percent of people from anywhere-everyplace, twentieth-centurians being the most numerous. This was understandable, since the total number of these constituted a fourth of humanity. Burton had no scientific statistical data, of course, but his travels had convinced him that the twentieth-centurians had been deliberately scattered along The River in a proportion to the other peoples even greater than was to be expected. This was another facet of the Riverworld setup which he did not understand. What did the Ethicals intend to gain by this dissemination?

There were too many questions. He needed time to think, and he could not get it if he spent himself with one trip after another on The Suicide Express. This area, unlike most of the others he would visit, offered some peace and quiet for analysis. So he would stay here a while.

And then there was Hermann Göring. Burton wanted to observe his strange form of pilgrim's progress. One of the many things that he had not been able to ask the Mysterious Stranger (Burton tended to think in capitals) was about the dreamgum. Where did it fit into the picture? Another part of the Great Experiment?

Unfortunately, Göring did not last long.

The first night, he began screaming. He burst out of his hut and ran toward The River, stopping now and then to strike out at the air or to grapple with invisible beings and to roll back and forth on the grass. Burton followed him as far as The River. Here Göring prepared to launch himself out into the water, probably to drown himself. But he froze for a moment, began shuddering, and then toppled over, stiff as a statue. His eyes were open, but they saw nothing outside him. All vision was turned inward. What horrors he was witnessing could not be determined, since he was unable to speak.

His lips writhed soundlessly, and did not stop during the ten days that he lived. Burton's efforts to feed him were useless. His jaws were locked. He shrank before Burton's eyes, the flesh evaporating, the skin falling in and the bones beneath resolving into the skeleton. One morning, he went into convulsions, then sat up and screamed. A moment later he was dead.

Curious, Burton did an autopsy on him with the flint knives and obsidian saws available. Göring's distended bladder had burst and poured urine into his body.

Burton proceeded to pull Göring's teeth out before burying him. Teeth were trade items, since they could be strung on a fishgut or a tendon to make much-desired necklaces. Göring's scalp also came off. The Sumerians had picked up the custom of taking scalps from their enemies, the seventeenth-century Shawnee across The River. They had added the civilized embellishment of sewing scalps together to make capes, skirts, and even curtains. A scalp was not worth as much as teeth in the trade mart, but it was worth something.

It was while digging a grave by a large boulder at the foot of the mountains that Burton had an illuminating flash of memory. He had stopped working to take a drink of water when he happened to look at Göring. The completely stripped head and the features, peaceful as if sleeping, opened a trapdoor in his mind.

When he had awakened in that colossal chamber and found himself floating in a row of bodies, he had seen this face. It had belonged to a body in the row next to his. Göring, like all the other sleepers, had had his head shaved. Burton had only noted him in passing during the short time before the Warders had detected him. Later, after the mass Resurrection, when he had met Göring, he had not seen the similarity between the sleeper and this man who had a full head of blondish hair.

But he knew now that this man had occupied a space close to his.

Was it possible that their two resurrectors, so physically close to each other, had become locked in phase? If so, whenever his death and Göring's took place at the same approximate time, then the two would be raised again by the same grailstone. Göring's jest that they were twin souls might not be so far off the mark.

Burton resumed digging, swearing at the same time, because he had so many questions and so few answers. If he had another chance to get his hands on an Ethical, he would drag the answers out of him, no matter what methods he had to use.

The next three months, Burton was busy adjusting himself to the strange society in this area. He found himself fascinated by the new language that was being formed out of the clash between Sumerian and Samoan. Since the former were the more numerous, their tongue dominated. But here, as elsewhere, the major language suffered a Pyrrhic victory. Result of the fusion was a pidgin, a speech with greatly reduced flexion and simplified syntax. Grammatical gender went overboard; words were syncopated; tense and aspect of verbs were cut

205

to a simple present, which was used also for the future. Adverbs of time indicated the past. Subtleties were replaced by expressions that both Sumerian and Samoan could understand, even if they seemed at first to be awkward and naive. And many Samoan words, in somewhat changed phonology, drove out Sumerian words.

This rise of pidgins was taking place everywhere up and down the Rivervalley. Burton reflected that if the Ethicals had intended to record all human tongues, They had best hurry. The old ones were dying out, transmuting rather. But for all he knew, They had already completed the job. Their recorders, so necessary for accomplishing the physical translation, might also be taking down all speech.

In the meantime, in the evenings, when he had a chance to be alone, he smoked the cigars so generously offered by the grails and tried to analyze the situation. Whom could he believe, the Ethicals or the Renegade, the Mysterious Stranger? Or were both lying?

Why did the Mysterious Stranger need him to throw a monkey wrench into Their cosmic machinery? What could Burton, a mere human being, trapped in this valley, so limited by his ignorance, do to help the Judas?

One thing was certain. If the Stranger did not need him, he would not have concerned himself with Burton. He wanted to get Burton into that Tower at the north pole.

Why?

It took Burton two weeks before he thought of the only reason that could be.

The Stranger had said that he, like the other Ethicals, would not directly take human life. But he had no scruples about doing so vicariously, as witness his giving the poison to Burton. So, if he wanted Burton in the Tower, he needed Burton to kill for him. He would turn the tiger loose among his own people, open the window to the hired assassin.

An assassin wants pay. What did the Stranger offer as pay?

Burton sucked the cigar smoke into his lungs, exhaled and then downed a shot of bourbon. Very well. The

Stranger would try to use him. But let him beware. Burton would also use the Stranger.

At the end of three months, Burton decided that he had done enough thinking. It was time to get out.

He was swimming in The River at the moment and, following the impulse, he swam to its middle. He dived down as far as he could force himself before the not-to-be-denied will of his body to survive drove him to claw upward for the dear air. He did not make it. The scavenging fishes would eat his body and his bones would fall to the mud at the bottom of the 1000-foot deep River. So much the better. He did not want his body to fall into the hands of the Ethicals. If what the Stranger had said was true, They might be able to unthread from his mind all he had seen and heard if They got to him before the brain cells were damaged.

He did not think They had succeeded. During the next seven years, as far as he knew, he escaped detection of the Ethicals. If the Renegade knew where he was, he did not let Burton know. Burton doubted that anyone did; he himself could not ascertain in what part of the Riverplanet he was, how far or how near the Tower headquarters. But he was going, going, going, always on the move. And one day he knew that he must have broken a record of some sort. Death had become second nature to him.

If his count was correct, he had made 777 trips on The Suicide Express.

28

Sometimes Burton thought of himself as a planetary grasshopper, launching himself out into the darkness of death, landing, nibbling a little at the grass, with one eye cocked for the shadow that betrayed the downswoop of the shrike—the Ethicals. In this vast meadow of humanity, he had sampled many blades, tasted briefly, and then had gone on.

Other times he thought of himself as a net scooping up specimens here and there in the huge sea of mankind. He got a few big fish and many sardines, although there was as much, if not more, to be learned from the small fish as from the large ones.

He did not like the metaphor of the net, however, because it reminded him that there was a much larger net out for him.

Whatever metaphors or similes he used, he was a man who got around a lot, to use a twentieth-century Americanism. So much so that he several times came across the legend of Burton the Gypsy, or, in one English-speaking area, Richard the Rover, and, in another, the Loping Lazarus. This worried him somewhat, since the Ethicals might get a clue to his method of evasion and be able to take measures to trap him. Or They might even guess at his basic goal and set up guards near the headwaters.

At the end of seven years, through much observation of the daystars and through many conversations, he had formed a picture of the course of The River.

It was not an amphisbaena, a snake with two heads, headwaters at the north pole and mouth at the south pole. It was a Midgard Serpent, with the tail at the north pole, the body coiled around and around the planet and the tail in the serpent's mouth. The River's source stemmed from the north polar sea, zigzagged back and forth across one hemisphere, circled the south pole and then zigzagged across the face of the other hemisphere, back and forth, ever working upward until the mouth opened into the hypothetical polar sea.

Nor was the large body of water so hypothetical. If the story of the Titanthrop, the subhuman who claimed to have seen the Misty Tower, was true, the Tower rose out of the fog-shrouded sea.

208

Burton had heard the tale only at second-hand. But he had seen the Titanthrops near the beginning of The River on his first "jump," and it seemed reasonable that one might actually have crossed the mountains and gotten close enough to get a glimpse of the polar sea. Where one man had gone, another could follow.

And how did The River flow uphill?

Its rate of speed seemed to remain constant even where it should have slowed or refused to go further. From this he postulated localized gravitational fields that urged the mighty stream onward until it had regained an area where natural gravity would take over. Somewhere, perhaps buried under The River itself, were devices that did this work. Their fields must be very restricted, since the pull of the earth did not vary on human beings in these areas to any detectable degree.

There were too many questions. He must go on until he got to the place or to the beings Who could answer them.

And seven years after his first death, he reached the desired area.

It was on his 777th "jump." He was convinced seven was a lucky number for him. Burton, despite the scoffings of his twentieth-century friends, believed steadfastly in most of the superstitions he had nourished on Earth. He often laughed at the superstitions of others, but he knew that some numbers held good fortune for him, that silver placed on his eyes would rejuvenate his body when it was tired and would help his second sight, the perception that warned him ahead of time of evil situations. True, there seemed to be no silver on this mineral-poor world, but if there were, he could use it to advantage.

All that first day, he stayed at the edge of The River. He paid little attention to those who tried to talk to him, giving them a brief smile. Unlike people in most of the areas he had seen, these were not hostile. The sun moved along the eastern peaks, seemingly just clearing their tops. The flaming ball slid across the valley, lower than he had ever seen it before, except when he had landed among the grotesquely nosed Titanthrops. The sun flooded the valley for a while with light and warmth, and then began its circling just above the western mountains. The valley became shadowed, and the air became colder than it had been any other place, except, of course, on that first jump. The sun continued to circle until it was again at the point where Burton had first seen it on opening his eyes.

Weary from his twenty-four hour vigil, but happy, he turned to look for living quarters. He knew now that he was in the arctic area, but he was not at a point just below the headwaters. This time, he was at the other end, the mouth.

As he turned, he heard a voice, familiar but unidentifiable. (He had heard so many.)

> *"Dull soul aspire;*
> *Thou art not the Earth. Mount higher!*
> *Heaven gave the spark;*
> *to it return the fire."*

"John Collop!"

"Abdul ibn Harun! And they say there are no miracles! What has happened to you since last I saw you?"

"I died the same night you did," Burton said. "And several times since. There are many evil men in this world."

" 'Tis only natural. There were many on Earth. Yet I dare say their number has been cut down, for the Church has been able to do much good work, praise God. Especially in this area. But come with me, friend. I'll introduce you to my hutmate. A lovely woman, faithful in a world that still seems to put little value on marital fidelity or, indeed, in virtue of any sort. She was born in the twentieth century A.D. and taught English most of her life. Verily, I sometimes think she loves me not so much for myself as for what I can teach her of the speech of my time."

He gave a curious nervous laugh, by which Burton knew he was joking.

They crossed the plains toward the foothills where fires

were burning on small stone platforms before each hut. Most of the men and women had fastened towels around them to form parkas which shielded them from the chill of the shadows.

"A gloomy and shivering place," Burton said. "Why would anybody want to live here?"

"Most of these people be Finns or Swedes of the late twentieth century. They are used to the midnight sun. However, you should be happy you're here. I remember your burning curiosity about the polar regions and your speculations anent. There have been others like you who have gone on down The River to seek their ultima Thule, or if you will pardon me for so terming it, the fool's gold at the end of the rainbow. But all have either failed to return or have come back, daunted by the forbidding obstacles."

"Which are what?" Burton said, grabbing Collop's arm.

"Friend, you're hurting me. Item, the grailstones cease, so that there is nothing wherewith they may recharge their grails with food. Item, the plains of the valley suddenly terminate, and The River pursues its course between the mountains themselves, through a chasm of icy shadows. Item, what lies beyond, I do not know, for no man has come back to tell me. But I fear they've met the end of all who commit the sin of hubris."

"How far away is this plunge of no return?"

"As The River winds, about 25,000 miles. You may get there with diligent sailing in a year or more. The Almighty Father alone knows how far you must then go before you arrive at the very end of The River. Belike you'd starve before then, because you'd have to take provisions on your boat after leaving the final grailstone."

"There's one way to find out," Burton said.

"Nothing will stop you then, Richard Burton?" Collop said. "You will not give up this fruitless chase after the physical when you should be hot on the track of the metaphysical?"

Burton seized Collop by the arm again. "You said *Burton?*"

211

"Yes, I did. Your friend Göring told me some time ago that that was your true name. He also told me other things about you."

"Göring is here?"

Collop nodded and said, "He has been here for about two years now. He lives a mile from here. We can see him tomorrow. You will be pleased at the change in him, I know. He has conquered the dissolution begun by the dreamgum, shaped the fragments of himself into a new, and a far better, man. In fact, he is now the leader of the Church of the Second Chance in this area.

"While you, my friend, have been questing after some irrelevant grail outside you, he has found the Holy Grail inside himself. He almost perished from madness, nearly fell back into the evil ways of his Terrestrial life. But through the grace of God and his true desire to show himself worthy of being given another opportunity at life, he . . . well, you may see for yourself tomorrow. And I pray you will profit from his example."

Collop elaborated. Göring had died almost as many times as Burton, usually by suicide. Unable to stand the nightmares and the self-loathing, he had time and again purchased a brief and useless surcease. Only to be faced with himself the next day. But on arriving at this area and seeking help from Collop, the man he had once murdered, he had won.

"I am astonished," Burton said. "And I'm happy for Göring. But I have other goals. I would like your promise that you'll tell no one my true identity. Allow me to be Abdul ibn Harun."

Collop said that he would keep silent, although he was disappointed that Burton would not be able to see Göring again and judge for himself what faith and love could do for even the seemingly hopeless and depraved. He took Burton to his hut and introduced him to his wife, a short, delicately boned brunette. She was very gracious and friendly and insisted on going with the two men while they visited the local boss, the *valkotukkainen*. (This word was regional slang for the white-haired boy or big shot.)

212

Ville Ahonen was a huge quiet-spoken man who listened patiently to Burton. Burton revealed only half of his plan, saying that he wanted to build a boat so he could travel to the end of The River. He did not mention wanting to take it further. But Ahonen had evidently met others like him.

He smiled knowingly and replied that Burton could build a craft. However, the people hereabouts were conservationists. They did not believe in despoiling the land of its trees. Oak and pine were to be left untouched, but bamboo was available. Even this material would have to be purchased with cigarettes and liquor, which would take him some time to accumulate from his grail.

Burton thanked him and left. Later, he went to bed in a hut near Collop's, but he could not get to sleep.

Shortly before the inevitable rains came, he decided to leave the hut. He would go up into the mountains, take refuge under a ledge until the rains ceased, the clouds dissipated, and the eternal (but weak) sun reasserted itself. Now that he was so near his goal, he did not want to be surprised by Them. And it seemed likely that the Ethicals would concentrate agents here. For all he knew, Collop's wife could be one of Them.

Before he had walked half a mile, rain struck him and lightning smashed nearby into the ground. By the dazzling flash, he saw something flicker into existence just ahead and about twenty feet above him.

He whirled and ran toward a grove of trees, hoping that They had not seen him and that he could hide there. If he was unobserved, then he could get up into the mountains. And when They had put everybody to sleep here, They would find him gone again . . .

29

"You gave us a long hard chase, Burton," a man said in English.

Burton opened his eyes. The transition to this place was so unexpected that he was dazed. But only for a second. He was sitting in a chair of some very soft buoyant material. The room was a perfect sphere; the walls were a very pale green and were semitransparent. He could see other spherical chambers on all sides, in front, behind, above and, when he bent over, below. Again he was confused, since the other rooms did not just impinge upon the boundaries of his sphere. They intersected. Sections of the other rooms came into his room, but then became so colorless and clear that he could barely detect them.

On the wall at the opposite end of his room was an oval of darker green. It curved to follow the wall. There was a ghostly forest portrayed in the oval. A phantom fawn trotted across the picture. From it came the odor of pine and dogwood.

Across the bubble from him sat twelve in chairs like his. Six were men; six, women. All were very good-looking. Except for two, all had black or dark brown hair and deeply tanned skins. Three had slight epicanthic folds; one man's hair was so curly it was almost kinky.

One woman had long wavy yellow hair bound into a psyche knot. A man had red hair, red as the fur of a fox. He was handsome, his features were irregular, his nose large and curved, and his eyes were dark green.

All were dressed in silvery or purple blouses with short flaring sleeves and ruffled collars, slender luminescent belts, kilts, and sandals. Both men and women had painted fingernails and toenails, lipstick, earrings, and eye makeup.

Above the head of each, almost touching the hair, spun a many-colored globe about a foot across. These whirled and flashed and changed color, running through every hue in the spectrum. From time to time, the globes thrust out long hexagonal arms of green, of blue, of black, or of gleaming white. Then the arms would collapse, only to be succeeded by other hexagons.

Burton looked down. He was clad only in a black towel secured at his waist.

"I'll forestall your first question by telling you we won't give you any information on where you are."

The speaker was the red-haired man. He grinned at Burton, showing unhumanly white teeth.

"Very well," Burton said. "What questions will you answer, Whoever you are? For instance, how did you find me?"

"My name is Loga," the red-haired man said. "We found you through a combination of detective work and luck. It was a complicated procedure, but I'll simplify it for you. We had a number of agents looking for you, a pitifully small number, considering the thirty-six billion, six million, nine thousand, six hundred and thirty-seven candidates that live along The River."

Candidates? Burton thought. Candidates for what? For eternal life? Had Spruce told the truth about the purpose behind the Resurrection?

Loga said, "We had no idea that you were escaping us by suicide. Even when you were detected in areas so widely separated that you could not possibly have gotten to them except through resurrection, we did not suspect. We thought that you had been killed and then translated. The years went by. We had no idea where you were. There were other things for us to do, so we pulled all agents from the Burton Case, as we called it, except for some stationed at both ends of The River. Somehow, you had knowledge of the polar tower. Later we found out how.

215

Your friends Göring and Collop were very helpful, although they did not know they were talking to Ethicals, of course."

"Who notified you that I was near The River's end?" Burton said.

Loga smiled and said, "There's no need for you to know. However, we would have caught you anyway. You see, every space in the restoration bubble—the place where you unaccountably awakened during the preresurrection phase—has an automatic counter. They were installed for statistical and research purposes. We like to keep records of what's going on. For instance, any candidate who has a higher than average number of deaths sooner or later is a subject for study. Usually later, since we're short-handed.

"It was not until your 777th death that we got around to looking at some of the higher frequency resurrections. Yours had the highest count. You may be congratulated on this, I suppose."

"There are others, as well?"

"They're not being pursued, if that's what you mean. And, relatively speaking, they're not many. We had no idea that it was you who had racked up this staggering number. Your space in the PR bubble was empty when we looked at it during our statistical investigation. The two technicians who had seen you when you woke up in the PR chamber identified you by your . . . photograph.

"We set the resurrector so that the next time your body was to be re-created, an alarm would notify us, and we would bring you here to this place."

"Suppose I hadn't died again?" Burton said.

"You were destined to die! You planned on trying to enter the polar sea via The River's mouth, right? That is impossible. The last hundred miles of The River go through an underground tunnel. Any boat would be torn to pieces. Like others who have dared the journey, you would have died."

Burton said, "My photograph—the one I took from Agneau. That was obviously taken on Earth when I was

216

an officer for John Company in India. How was that gotten?"

"Research, Mr. Burton," Loga said, still smiling.

Burton wanted to smash the look of superiority on his face. He did not seem to be restrained by anything; he could, seemingly, walk over to Loga and strike him. But he knew that the Ethicals were not likely to sit in the same room with him without safeguards. They would as soon have given a rabid hyena its freedom.

"Did you ever find out what made me awaken before my time?" he asked. "Or what made those others gain consciousness, too?"

Loga gave a start. Several of the men and women gasped.

Loga rallied first. He said, "We've made a thorough examination of your body. You have no idea how thorough. We have also screened every component of your . . . psychomorph, I think you could call it. Or aura, whichever word you prefer." He gestured at the sphere above his head. "We found no clues whatsoever."

Burton threw back his head and laughed loudly and long.

"So you bastards don't know everything!"

Loga smiled tightly. "No. We never will. Only One is omnipotent."

He touched his forehead, lips, heart, and genitals with the three longest fingers of his right hand. The others did the same.

"However, I'll tell you that you frightened us—if that'll make you feel any better. You still do. You see, we are fairly sure that you may be one of the men of whom we were warned."

"Warned against? By whom?"

"By a . . . sort of giant computer, a living one. And by its operator." Again, he made the curious sign with his fingers. "That's all I care to tell you—even though you won't remember a thing that occurs down here after we send you back to the Rivervalley."

Burton's mind was clouded with anger, but not so much

that he missed the "down here." Did that mean that the resurrection machinery and the hideout of the Ethicals were below the surface of the Riverworld?

Loga continued, "The data indicates you may have the potentiality to wreck our plans. Why you should or how you might, we do not know. But we respect our source of information, how highly you can't imagine."

"If you believe that," Burton said, "why don't you just put me in cold storage? Suspend me between those two bars. Leave me floating in space, turning around and around forever, like a roast on a spit, until your plans are completed?"

Loga said, "We couldn't do that! That act alone would ruin everything! How would you attain your salvation? Besides, that would mean an unforgivable violence on our part! It's unthinkable!"

"You were being violent when you forced me to run and hide from you," Burton said. "You are being violent now by holding me here against my will. And you will violate me when you destroy my memory of this little tête-à-tête with you."

Loga almost wrung his hands. If he was the Mysterious Stranger, the renegade Ethical, he was a great actor. In a grieved tone, Loga said, "That is only partly true. We had to take certain measures to protect ourselves. If the man had been anyone but you, we would have left you strictly alone. It is true we violated our own code of ethics by making you run from us and by examining you. That had to be, however. And, believe me, we are paying for this in mental agony."

"You could make up for some of it by telling me why I, why all the human beings that ever lived, have been resurrected. And how you did it."

Loga talked, with occasional interruptions from some of the others. The yellow-haired woman broke in most often, and after a while Burton deduced from her attitude and Loga's that she was either his wife or she held a high position.

218

Another man interrupted at times. When he did, there was a concentration and respect from the others that led Burton to believe he was the head of this group. Once he turned his head so that the light sparkled off one eye. Burton stared, because he had not noticed before that the left eye was a jewel.

Burton thought that it probably was a device which gave him a sense, or senses, of perception denied the others. From then on, Burton felt uncomfortable whenever the faceted and gleaming eye was turned on him. What did that many-angled prism see?

At the end of the explanation, Burton did not know much more than he had before. The Ethicals could see back into the past with a sort of chronoscope; with this they had been able to record whatever physical beings they wished to. Using these records as models, they had then performed the resurrection with energy-matter converters.

"What," Burton said, "would happen if you re-created two bodies of an individual at the same time?"

Loga smiled wryly and said that the experiment had been performed. Only one body had life.

Burton smiled like a cat that has just eaten a mouse. He said, "I think you're lying to me. Or telling me half-truths. There is a fallacy in all this. If human beings can attain such a rarefiedly high ethical state that they 'go on,' why are you Ethicals, supposedly superior beings, still here? Why haven't you, too, 'gone on'?"

The faces of all but Loga and the jewel-eyed man became rigid. Loga laughed and said, "Very shrewd. An excellent point. I can only answer that some of us *do* go on. But more is demanded of us, ethically speaking, than of you resurrectees."

"I still think you're lying," Burton said. "However there's nothing I can do about it." He grinned and said, "Not just now, anyway."

"If you persist in that attitude, you will never Go On," Loga said. "But we felt that we owed it to you to explain what we are doing—as best we could. When we catch those others who have been tampered with, we'll do the same for them."

"There's a Judas among you," Burton said, enjoying the effect of his words.

But the jewel-eyed man said, "Why don't you tell him the truth, Loga? It'll wipe off that sickening smirk and put him in his proper place."

Loga hesitated, then said, "Very well, Thanabur. Burton, you will have to be very careful from now on. You *must not* commit suicide and you must fight as hard to stay alive as you did on Earth, when you thought you had only one life. There is a limit to the number of times a man may be resurrected. After a certain amount—it varies and there's no way to predict the individual allotment—the psychomorph seems unable to reattach itself to the body. Every death weakens the *attraction* between body and psychomorph. Eventually, the psychomorph comes to the point of no return. It becomes a—well, to use an unscientific term—a 'lost soul.' It wanders bodiless through the universe; we can detect these unattached psychomorphs without instruments, unlike those of the—how shall I put it?—the 'saved,' which disappear entirely from our ken.

"So you see, you must give up this form of travel by death. This is why continued suicide by those poor unfortunates who cannot face life is, if not the unforgivable sin, the irrevocable."

The jewel-eyed man said, "The traitor, the filthy unknown who claims to be aiding you, was actually using you for his own purposes. He did not tell you that you were expending your chance for eternal life by carrying out his—and your—designs. He, or she, whoever the traitor is, is evil. Evil, evil!

"Therefore, you must be careful from now on. You may have a residue of a dozen or so deaths left to you. Or your next death may be your last!"

Burton stood up and shouted, "You don't want me to

get to the end of The River? Why? Why?"

Loga said, "Au revoir. Forgive us for this violence."

Burton did not see any of the twelve persons point an instrument at him. But consciousness sprang from him as swiftly as an arrow from the bow, and he awoke . . .

30

The first person to greet him was Peter Frigate. Frigate lost his customary reserve; he wept. Burton cried a little himself and had difficulty for a while in answering Frigate's piled-one-on-the-other questions. First, Burton had to find out what Frigate, Loghu, and Alice had done after he had disappeared. Frigate replied that the three had looked for him, then had sailed back up The River to Theleme.

"Where have you been?" Frigate said.

"From going to and fro in the earth, and from walking up and down in it," Burton said. "However, unlike Satan, I found at least several perfect and upright men, fearing God and eschewing evil. Damn few, though. Most men and women are still the selfish, ignorant, superstitious, self-blinding, hypocritical, cowardly wretches they were on Earth. And in most, the old red-eyed killer ape struggles with its keeper, society, and would break out and bloody its hands."

Frigate chattered away as the two walked toward the huge stockade a mile away, the council building which housed the administration of the state of Theleme. Burton half-listened. He was shaking and his heart was beating hard, but not because of his home-coming.

He remembered!

Contrary to what Loga had promised, he remembered

221

both his wakening in the preresurrection bubble, so many years ago, and the inquisition with the twelve Ethicals.

There was only one explanation. One of the twelve must have prevented the blocking of his memory and done so without the others knowing it.

One of the twelve was the Mysterious Stranger, the Renegade.

Which one? At present, there was no way of determining. But some day he would find out. Meanwhile, he had a friend in court, a man who might be using Burton for his own ends. And the time would come when Burton would use him.

There were the other human beings with whom the Stranger had also tampered. Perhaps he would find them; together they would assault the Tower.

Odysseus had his Athena. Usually Odysseus had had to get out of perilous situations through his own wits and courage. But every now and then, when the goddess had been able, she had given Odysseus a helping hand.

Odysseus had his Athena; Burton, his Mysterious Stranger.

Frigate said, "What do you plan on doing, Dick?"

"I'm going to build a boat and sail up The River. All the way! Want to come along?"

POSTSCRIPT

This ends Volume I of the *Riverworld* series. Volume II will tell how Samuel Clemens looked for iron in the mineral-poor valley, found it, and built his great paddle-wheeled Riverboat, the *NOT FOR HIRE*.